Basic Black-Scholes:
Option Pricing and Trading

Basic Black-Scholes:
Option Pricing and Trading

Timothy Falcon Crack
BSc (HONS 1st Class), PGDipCom, MCom, PhD (MIT), IMC

Published January 2004, April 2009 (2nd Edition).

ISBN: 0-9700552-4-2

Typeset by the author. Printed in the USA or UK.
www.BasicBlackScholes.com
timcrack@alum.mit.edu

Contents

Preface

MY EXPERIENCE IS THAT OPTION PRICING THEORY is usually presented in a clinical and theoretical fashion. Book and classroom explanations often deteriorate into an unhelpful tangle of mathematics, out of which is born the Black-Scholes formula, without regard to simple economic intuition or real-world application.

This tangled mess creates a "barrier to entry" that stops most students from mastering option pricing theory. The accompanying lack of simple economic intuition makes it impossible for an individual to know how to use the theory to trade options profitably on his or her own account. To compound this situation, the significant differences between the assumed Black-Scholes world and the real world can easily transform a profitable strategy in the Black-Scholes world into a losing strategy in the real world.

I remove the above-mentioned barrier to entry—and thus distinguish this book from its competitors—by giving clear explanations of Black-Scholes option pricing theory, by discussing direct applications of the theory to trading, and by discussing differences between the theoretical Black-Scholes world and the real world and the impact of those differences on trading.

My explanations of the theory do not go far beyond basic Black-Scholes for three reasons: First, a novice need not go far beyond Black-Scholes to make money in the options markets; second, all high-level option pricing theory is simply an extension of Black-Scholes; and third, there already exist many books that look far beyond Black-Scholes without first laying the firm foundation that I give here. In similar fashion, my trading advice does not go far beyond elementary call and put positions because more complex trades are simply combinations of these.

This book can be used as a supplement by students (undergraduate, masters, PhD) who need to better understand fundamental option pricing theory. It can also be used by anyone who has a basic understanding and wants to trade options for the first time. My trading advice is aimed at the novice, but it may also be useful to more experienced traders. It is limited to exchange-traded equity options in the US, but some of it applies to non-equity options; little of it applies to non-exchange-traded options (e.g., those granted to employees as part of a compensation package and known as "warrants" in the US).

I thank generations of undergraduate, MBA, and PhD students at MIT and Indiana University; Don Chance, Scott Chaput, Tony Hutchins, Mikhail Voropaev, and Craig Wisen for contributions; Genna Freeberg, the Chicago Board Options Exchange, Incorporated (CBOE), and Thomson Financial for supplying market data;[1] Peter Grundy, Dale Hallett, and Vivien Pullar for technical assistance; Christopher Lembke at PR Newswire; and Kate Brown and the Department of Finance and Quantitative Analysis at the University of Otago for office space, resources, and hospitality during 2003.

This book draws on my prize-winning teaching at Indiana University, and my practical trading experience in the US equity and equity options markets. Some parts of this book draw on my other book *Heard on The Street: Quantitative Questions from Wall Street Job Interviews* (see the advertisement on the last page of this book).

My first option pricing classes were from Professors John C. Cox and Chi-fu Huang at MIT, and Professor Robert C. Merton at Harvard. My instruction cannot help but influence some aspects of my presentation, but any errors are my own. If you discover any errors, or wish to give me feedback, send me an e-mail at `timcrack@alum.mit.edu`. The errata appears at `www.BasicBlackScholes.com`.

This book was written while I was a visiting scholar at the University of Otago in Dunedin, New Zealand, on sabbatical from my quantitative active equity research job at Barclays Global Investors (BGI) in London. Opinions expressed in this book are my own, and are not necessarily those of BGI nor of its parent company Barclays, PLC.

TFC/BGI/2003

I updated this book while holding the Chair in Finance at Otago University in New Zealand. I now also thank Tiago Bento, Marianne Lown, and Andreas Stirnemann.

TFC/OU/2009

---

[1]Any market data that appear within the body of the text without explicit acknowledgement are supplied by Thomson Financial, and provided as a courtesy by the Chicago Board Options Exchange, Incorporated.

Tables

Figures

Chapter 1

Introduction to Options

Options give you options. Owning an option (i.e., being "long an option") gives you the *right* to take an action. Selling an option that you do not already own (i.e., "writing an option") means, however, that you have sold your rights to a counterparty, and you therefore have an *obligation* to fulfil your counterparty's rights.

Option contracts come in two elementary types: calls and puts. The names "call" and "put" come from the actions potentially taken by the holder of the contract (the long position). Call options give the holder the right to buy, or "call," the underlying asset away from the counterparty at a pre-agreed price (the "exercise" or "strike" price). Put options give the holder the right to sell, or "put," the underlying asset to the counterparty at the strike price.

The underlying asset could be 100 shares of stock, a futures contract on 100 troy ounces of gold, 62,500 British pounds, or one of many other alternatives. The value of the underlying asset changes daily in the market, but the strike price is fixed. This means that the value of the option changes daily. For example, other things being equal, if you hold the right to buy a share of stock at a fixed price (i.e., you hold a call option) and the stock price rises, then the value of your call option rises too. Option contracts are thus one type of "derivative security" because they derive their value from the value of the underlying asset.[1]

Options may be viewed as insurance contracts. Payment for an option is, correspondingly, called the option "premium," and a seller who did not already own the option is referred to as an option "writer"—a direct analogy to the names "insurance premium" and "insurance underwriter."

The trading of option contracts on organized exchanges is not a recent innovation. Joseph de la Vega's 1688 book *Confusion de Confusiones* describes the stock exchange in Amsterdam (then the leading financial center of the world). He discusses futures contracts with monthly settlement, the clearinghouse, put and call options, and various transactions that have no current equivalent, as well as all

---

[1]Differential calculus derivatives derive their mathematical value from an underlying function. This is exactly the sort of mathematical tool needed to understand how financial derivatives derive their financial value from an underlying asset. Thus, differential calculus is popular for exploring the behavior of financial derivatives.

manner of wonderful stock price manipulation schemes. It was roughly 300 years later that the first organized exchange for formal options trading in the US opened in Chicago in April 1973. Modern options pricing theory is also relatively recent. Although pioneering theoretical work was conducted around 1900, option pricing theory has come into full bloom only since the late-1960s.

Other things being equal, a call option on a stock increases in value if the stock price increases, so why buy a call option on a stock rather than simply buying the stock itself on margin?[2] Buying a call option on a stock and buying a stock on margin are similar, in that both trades provide a "levered" position in the stock. That is, in both cases you put down less money than the face value of the stock that you control, but you reap benefits or suffer losses based on the full face value of the underlying stock. This multiplies, or "leverages," the return on your initial investment. This is where the similarities between options on stock and stock itself end.

There are significant differences in liquidity between stock and options on stock.[3] When you buy 100 shares of stock on the stock exchange, you buy them through your broker from someone who has held the stock before you. Conversely, anyone else who wants to buy stock wants to buy your stock, so you can sell yours to them—again via your broker. There is typically just that one flavor of stock available for you to trade. Options are different: There are many different maturities and strike prices available for exchange-traded options on any given stock (each particular combination is known as an "option series"). These options do not come into existence until they are traded. For example, if you go long, and a counterparty goes short, the option need not have been held by anyone before that trade.[4] Your long option position may well be the first long position to exist; and, if no one else trades it, you may be the only person who ever holds options in that particular option series. Although the organized exchanges try to improve liquidity by restricting the number of strike prices and maturities of options that are available—thereby concentrating trade in a few option series—the fact is that options on a stock are much less liquid than the stock itself. Transactions costs (or simply "T-costs") for trading options on stock can therefore easily be 10 times those for trading the underlying stocks. T-costs differ markedly and predictably between different option series on a given

---

[2]A typical margin trade in the stock market involves buying a $100 stock using $50 of your money and $50 borrowed from your broker. You must satisfy some simple requirements to be granted a "margin account." Once granted, you do not actually have to ask to borrow the money to buy the stock, you simply place the trade and the broker takes care of the details—lending you cash up to 50% of the face value of the stock if you do not have enough cash in your margin account to execute the trade. It is not always 50%—see the discussion of Regulation T (Reg T) and pattern day trading in section 10.1.2.

[3]"Liquidity" is the ability to get out of a position as quickly as possible at a price not too different from that most recently quoted. Good liquidity goes hand-in-hand with many market participants, high volume of trade, large market depth (i.e., the volume you can trade without pushing prices against you), and low transactions costs.

[4]Buying a security you do not own is called buying or "going long"; selling a security you do own is "selling"; selling a security you do not own is shorting, or "going short," or "writing" in the case of an option; and buying back a security you have already sold short is "covering." Thus, you are said to "cover a short sale" when you unwind a short position.

---

stock—see the examples in section 1.3.2 and the detailed discussion in chapter 10.

One result of the above discussion is that because you buy someone else's stock, and you can subsequently sell it on to someone else, stock is a long-term instrument, and it can potentially exist for longer than you may live. Stock ceases to exist only because of big events in the life of a company such as takeovers, mergers, liquidations, and so on. Stock options, however, are short-term instruments by design. They have maturities of between one day and three years. At the end of this time period, they "expire" and can no longer be traded. A by-product of this short lifespan is that, other things being equal (e.g., stock price, volatility, interest rates), most stock options decay in value simply with the passage of time (table 3.2 notes one exception). When trading options, short lifespan and time decay make it vital that you have not just a view, but an horizon. For example, if you think a stock price will rise 20% within three months, you might buy a speculative call option on the stock with a maturity greater than three months.

The fact that so many different combinations of strike price and maturity exist is problematic. Which option series should you choose for a given view? If you buy the wrong call option on a stock, and even if the stock price rises significantly in value before the option expires, then time decay and T-costs can easily eat away most of your initial investment leaving you worse off than if you had simply bought the stock!

In addition to having different strike prices and maturities, options can have different exercise styles. The style of an option refers to when that option is exercisable. There are three exercise styles for standardized options trading on US markets: American, European, and capped. An American-style option may be exercised at any time prior to its expiration. A European-style option may be exercised only during a specified period before the option expires (typically only on the expiration date itself). Capped options are rare enough for us to ignore. European-style options are less sophisticated than American-style ones, and are therefore easier to price.[5]

You do not need to exercise an option to exit a long position; you may simply sell it. An option seller gives up a previously owned right, and is left with neither a right nor an obligation. Contrast this with an option writer who, by selling an option he or she does not already own, is left with an obligation.

Which exercise style to use is often not your choice—unlike maturity and strike, which may be chosen from among those option series on offer. For example, ignoring flex options, all Chicago Board of Options Exchange (CBOE)[6] options on individual stocks are American style and you simply cannot get a European-style option on

---

[5] Where do the names "American-style" and "European-style" come from? I once went to a St. Patrick's Day seminar given by Nobel Prize winner Paul Samuelson at MIT (he wore bright green socks) during which he said that he had carefully chosen the names European and American back in the 1960s. As a US immigrant from Europe, he wanted to take a swipe at snobby European economists who thought themselves more sophisticated than their American counterparts, so he named the more sophisticated exercise style American and the less sophisticated one European.

[6] No one calls it the "Chicago Board of Options Exchange." They always drop the "of," and usually say simply the CBOE ("see-bee-oh-ee") or just CBOE ("see-boe").

an individual stock.[7] If you are trading Foreign Currency (FX) options on the Philadelphia Exchange (PHLX), however, then you do have to make an explicit choice between American and European styles, but most people choose American style. If you are choosing equity index options on the CBOE, then you need to be aware that different options have different exercise styles, and this affects the pricing—see chapter 10 for examples.

Traded options are either physical delivery or cash-settled. Options on individual equities are usually physical delivery, but index options are usually cash-settled because it is too difficult to deliver a basket of stocks.

1.1 Hedging, Speculation, and Arbitrage

The CBOE is the largest options exchange in the world. The dollar volume of trade on the CBOE rivals that of the trade in the underlying stocks on the New York Stock Exchange (NYSE) and the NASDAQ. Options on futures are heavily traded on the Chicago Mercantile Exchange (CME), the Chicago Board of Trade (CBOT), and other exchanges, but these are beyond the scope of this book. One reason for the success of these markets is the liquidity provided by the many market participants. These include hedgers, speculators, and arbitrageurs, as well as "locals" who provide liquidity by trading on their own account.

Hedgers want to reduce risk exposure due to changes in prices. This price risk exists in business because future price levels are uncertain. The hedger may be a farmer with unpredictable future costs, a business with unpredictable future revenues, or a trader with exposure to price risk in the underlying stock.

Speculators, conversely, willingly take on the price risk that hedgers want to avoid. Speculators may bet on a price move up or a price move down, but many other types of speculative trades exist; e.g., a "short straddle" position betting that the price does not move much in either direction (see exercise 1 on page 124).

Arbitrageurs attempt to lock in riskless profits by simultaneously entering into transactions in one or more markets. When people in the financial world use the word "arbitrage," they are typically not referring to the locking in of a sure profit without investment (what I call an "academic arbitrage"). Rather, they are referring to "risk arbitrage," often simply called "risk arb." Traders say that risk arbitrage opportunities occur when attractive speculative opportunities involving an acceptable degree of risk are available. A typical risk arbitrage strategy involves trading in two or more related instruments to take advantage of some perceived pricing discrepancy. For example, I once held long positions in three Dow Jones Industrial Average (INDU) stocks balanced roughly dollar-for-dollar with a short position in INDU-tracking stock (the Dow Jones Diamonds with ticker symbol DIA

---

[7]The exception is that the CBOE will open a new "flex option" series—where you get to choose the strike, maturity, and exercise style virtually without restriction—if you will do a trade for a minimum of 250 round lots (i.e., 25,000 shares) or a minimum notional value (i.e., strike price times number of shares covered) of USD1m.

that traded on the AMEX[8]). This was a risk arbitrage trade betting that the three individual stocks would outperform the index. It was roughly market neutral in that the profit or loss on the position was almost uncorrelated with movements in the broad market, and substantially less volatile.

Although arbitrage opportunities are rare, and most arbitrageurs are actively engaged in risk arbitrage, not academic arbitrage, this does not mean that academic arbitrage is some foolish head-in-the-clouds ivory-tower academic concept; quite the opposite is true. Arbitrageurs are typically risk arbitrageurs because genuine academic arbitrage opportunities, although frequent, are typically small and short-lived. It is the very presence of the arbitrageurs that enforces this. Indeed, many of our derivatives valuation arguments depend upon the absence of academic arbitrage opportunities.

Arbitrage relationships in the market are enforced because assets are related to each other. Put-call parity (section 3.6) is a prime example of this. Black-Scholes option pricing theory is a special case because, unlike put-call parity, it is an arbitrage relationship that allows us to price a new asset in terms of simpler assets.

1.2 Forwards, Futures, and Options

This book is not about forwards or futures, but we need to discuss them in order to understand how they differ from options. We also need a foundation for understanding the relationship between the pricing of forwards/futures and the pricing of options. Some details of forwards/futures markets are discussed here, but the corresponding details for options markets are left for detailed coverage in section 10.1.

A forward contract is a private agreement between two parties either to buy or to sell a specified quantity of an asset at a specified price, with delivery at a specified time and place. If you are long a forward, you agree to buy the underlying asset; if you are short, you agree to sell it. By convention, the agreed-upon delivery price yields a "fair" price for future delivery of the underlying asset. Thus, no cash need be exchanged when the contract is initiated.[9] Indeed, no cash exchange occurs prior to the delivery date.[10] With no cash needed up front to induce either party to enter the contract, the economic value of the contract is zero at initiation by construction. In the US, forward contracts are typically used only by institutions and wealthy individuals—it is not a retail market.[11]

Throughout the life of a forward contract, the delivery price remains contractu-

---

[8]Note that following the acquisition of the American Stock Exchange by NYSE Euronext on October 1, 2008, the old AMEX has been renamed NYSE Alternext US LLC.

[9]Your counterparty (the "intermediary") is often a bank, and they make money by using a spread; that is, the quoted price if you are buying forward is higher than the quoted price if you are selling forward.

[10]An exception is that a speculator may be asked to deposit a small margin up front.

[11]My New Zealand bank manager was happy to offer me a forward and to shade (i.e., reduce) the spread when I had USD risk to offlay, but my US bank manager claimed not to know what a forward contract was when I had GBP risk to offlay.

ally fixed. However, new forward contracts are being initiated every day by other parties, so new forward prices are reported in the financial markets every day. The forward price equals the delivery price when the contract is entered into (by definition), but the two prices are equal only by chance after this. The price you locked in at can be compared to the prices at which new contracts are negotiated to see if you now have a good deal or a bad one (i.e., positive or negative economic value, respectively).

Like a forward, a futures contract is an agreement either to buy or to sell a specified quantity of an asset at a specified price, with delivery at a specified time and place. However, forwards and futures differ in many ways. Forward contracts are almost never traded on an organized exchange, and are almost always held to maturity. Futures contracts, however, are always traded on an organized exchange and are almost never held to maturity. Futures contracts are standardized to focus liquidity in only a few possible contracts—just like an option series. Forward contracts, however, are negotiated; they are tailor-made contracts drawn up between you and your financial intermediary—more like a flex option, but with a bank as the counterparty.

Unlike option contracts, which are either rights or obligations, forward and futures contracts are always obligations. The absence of any rights (i.e., any optionality) in a forward or futures generates a linear payoff, in contrast to the nonlinear payoffs from options (see figure 3.1 on page 41).[12]

Your order to buy a futures contract is typically met by a floor trader (i.e., a local) on the exchange. Immediately after the trade clears, the clearinghouse intervenes and takes offsetting positions with both customers. The clearinghouse is thus the counterparty to all futures trades. Both you and the other customer look to the clearinghouse to fulfil the contract. If either party defaults on the contract, the clearinghouse steps in and becomes the seller or buyer of last resort. The clearinghouse assumes the counterparty credit risk (and in return receives a small fee for each contract executed). To minimize this counterparty credit risk, the clearinghouse imposes daily settlement and margins.

Before you are allowed to open an account to trade US futures contracts, you must deposit cash, US government securities, or shares with your broker. The exchange imposes minimum initial performance bond (i.e., initial margin) levels and minimum maintenance performance bond (i.e., maintenance margin) levels—your broker's requirements may be higher. The margin account may or may not earn interest. The margin account acts as collateral to minimize the risk of default by customers. If you are hedging, the initial margin is usually less than if you are speculating because the counterparty faces less credit/default risk by trading with you.

Futures contracts are marked-to-market every day. At the close of trading (or at the next day's open), the exchange establishes a settlement price. This price is used to compute gains and losses on the futures contract for that day. These gains

---

[12]In fact, futures contracts do sometimes contain optionality, especially with regard to the quality of the asset to be delivered.

or losses go into (or out of) your margin account.

For CME agricultural futures, the initial margin is about 5–10% of the value of the position. The maintenance margin is typically about 75% of the initial margin. If your margin account falls below the maintenance margin, you get a margin call, and you must deposit more money in the account to bring the balance back up to the initial margin. This contrasts with stock options, which cannot be bought on margin on the CBOE; you do, however, have to post margin if you short stock options—see section 10.1.4 for details.

To avoid your contractual obligation to take physical delivery, you should close out a long futures position on or before the position day (the first day upon which the short position can notify the clearing corporation of the intent to make delivery). The following day is the notice of intention day (when the clearing corporation matches the oldest long to the delivering short, notifies both parties, and the short invoices the long). The following day is the delivery day (when the short delivers the warehouse receipt or financial instrument to the long and the long makes payment to the short).

A forward contract and a futures contract yield the same total profit or loss (assuming that the futures margin account does not earn interest, that the forward and futures contracts have the same maturity, that the forward and futures prices are the same at initiation, and that the T-costs are the same). The difference is that for the futures contract, the gain or loss accrues as a series of daily payments spread over the life of the contract, whereas the total gain or loss on the forward is realized only at maturity.

For many years, the Securities and Exchange Commission (SEC) in the US prohibited futures contracts on individual equities. The law has now changed. A joint venture between the CBOE, the CME, and the CBOT led to the launch in 2002 of an electronic exchange "OneChicago" (`www.OneChicago.com`) trading single stock futures (SSFs) on the leading US stocks, futures on leading exchange-traded funds (ETFs) (see section 10.1.2), and some futures on sector indexes. Outside of the 1,000+ SSFs available through OneChicago, if you want a long futures-type payoff linked to an individual equity, your only choices are buying stock on margin, negotiating a forward with an investment bank, or "spread betting."

The degree of leverage with a margin trade is, however, much lower than with futures because you put down 40–50% with a margin trade, but only 5–10% with futures. You could try to negotiate an individual equity forward contract with an investment bank, but the time, effort, and fees required to do so are high unless you are a major player. In the UK, there is spread betting, which, as a form of betting, is free of capital gains and income tax for UK residents as of 2009.[13] Spread betting often involves sports results, but financial spread betting is popular, and you can place online bets on US market outcomes (including individual equities) using UK spread betting firms. Like the old bucket shops described in many of the novels by Edwin Lefevre, financial spread betting requires a small wager, with quoted prices typically drawn from the markets themselves. If, for example, you are betting on

---

[13]Take a look at spread-betting firm `www.igindex.co.uk`, for example.

the FTSE 100 three months ahead, you place an "up bet" (i.e., buy order) of so many pounds sterling per point of index value if you think the FTSE 100 will rise above a quoted "offer price" (or a "down bet" selling order if you think the index will fall below a quoted "bid price"). You can close out the bet at any time with an offsetting trade at the most recent bid or offer. It is a tax-efficient futures-like position requiring a small initial bet, and having relatively low T-costs, but it is really only targeted at UK residents. Spread betting may also avoid compliance restrictions on equity trading if you work in a financial firm, but you should talk to your compliance officer before betting. If you are an individual small investor in the US, however, and you want an individual equity position more levered than you can get from margin trading, your only choices are SSFs and stock options.

1.3 Introductory Option Examples

The following examples introduce important terms and concepts. Throughout the book, I give real-world examples with real-world dates and prices. Although these examples are necessarily drawn from the past, the lessons to be learned are current.

1.3.1 Buying a Protective Put

Suppose you own one "round lot" (i.e., 100 shares) of Boeing (BA). It is 3:00PM EST Monday, April 14, 2003 in New York, and the NYSE is open until 4:00PM EST. It is 2:00PM CST in Chicago and both equity options and LEAPS (long-term equity options) trade until 3:02PM CST. Ignoring after-hours trading, when liquidity can be quite low,[14] you have one hour until the markets close.

BA just traded at $26.95 on the NYSE, up almost 50 cents on the open. Your round lot of BA shares is now worth approximately $2,700. You are hoping this investment will help buy your son a used car for his 18th birthday—which falls conveniently on the Saturday following the third Friday in January 2005 (stock options usually expire on the Saturday following the third Friday of the month). You fear, however, that the threat of terrorism may lead to lower aircraft orders from airlines and that this will push the price of BA down before your son's birthday. You want to be sure that you will have at least $2,000 to contribute toward your son's car on this date. What you need is an option that gives you the right to sell (or "put") your stock to someone else for $20 per share on or before this future date. Buying the put when you already own the stock is a "protective put" position—an options hedge.

---

[14]For example, on Monday, May 19, 2003, 5,917,900 shares of AT&T (T) changed hands on the NYSE during regular trading hours (RTH), but only 400 changed hands in the after-hours (AH) market. For McDonald's (MCD), the analogous numbers were 3,927,000 during RTH and 200 AH, respectively. Note, however, that on Tuesday, May 20, 2003 when news came out during the day that Canadian beef had mad cow disease, the numbers for MCD were 27,221,800 during RTH (a fall of $1.20 to about $17) and 312,100 AH (a rise of $0.25), respectively, followed by a $0.35 rise during RTH the next day on volume of 24,424,800 and a $0.01 fall during AH trading on volume of 185,000. The AH market is like insurance, in the sense that you do not usually use it but it is there when you need it.

A January 2005 put option on BA with a strike price of $20 is trading on the CBOE with ticker symbol ZBOMD; this is a LEAP. You look at your online brokerage account screen: the "ask price" for ZBOMD is $2.30 and the "bid price" is $2.15. The ask price is what the market maker asks you to pay if you are buying; the bid price is what the market maker bids for your security if you are selling. The ask is often called the "offer" because the market maker offers the security to you at this price. The range $2.15–$2.30 is the "bid-ask spread." The most recent trade was at $2.35 (just outside the spread); the market maker has adjusted prices downwards since then because the stock price has gone up. The bid and ask prices are quoted in dollars per share, and each put option contract is for one round lot of shares. Thus, you can buy insurance on your 100 BA shares for a total premium of $230. This guarantees that you can sell your stock for at least $20 per share on or before the third Friday in January 2005.

When it comes time to liquidate (presumably mid-January 2005), what you do with the put depends upon what happens to the price of BA. If the price of BA is above $20 come January 2005, you sell your stock and the put contract may or may not have enough value left in it to warrant the commission involved in selling it. If the stock price is very high at expiration, then the put is virtually worthless, and you should certainly just let it expire worthless. If, however, BA is below $20 come January 2005, then you can either exercise your option to sell BA at $20 per share or you can simply sell your valuable put, and also sell your stock. Close to expiration, there is little difference in profitability between these two strategies, so there is typically no point in exercising the option.

Unlike a forward or futures hedge, the option hedge kicks in only when you need it (like insurance). Note, however, that some people consider options an "expensive" hedging strategy relative to futures because of the explicit up-front cost of the option ($230 in our case). In addition, my broker would charge me a commission of $10.99 to buy this put, bringing the total cost for my insurance to $240.99. Be sure to choose one contract, not 100 contracts when you place the order—100 contracts would cost $23,000 and cover 100 times your round lot of stock!

We chose the $20 strike put because you wanted a floor on your downside at $20. You may think $230 is too expensive (or, indeed, too cheap) for insurance. For comparative purposes, the quotes (i.e., bid and ask prices) for a range of January 2005 put options on BA are reported in table 1.1. These puts provide insurance ranging in price from $35 (for ZBOMB with a strike of only $10 per share) up to $2,340 (for ZBOMJ with a strike of $50 per share).

Epilogue. With hindsight, worries in March 2003 about the January 2005 price of BA were premature. Looking at figure 1.1 (p11) we see that by January 2005 BA had doubled to $50 per share. I can tell you that the $20-strike January 2005 put option (ZBOMD) was quoted each day that month with a bid-ask spread of $0.00–$0.05. So, you could have bought it for a nickel a share (i.e., $5 for the contract covering 100 shares), and sold it for zero. There was zero trading volume in this put during this month and the $230 insurance contract expired worthless. I

Table 1.1: January 2005 Put Option Quotes: BA, April 14, 2003

Strike	Ticker	Bid Price	Ask Price
$10	ZBOMB	$0.15	$0.35
$15	ZBOMC	$0.85	$0.95
$20	ZBOMD	$2.15	$2.30
$30	ZBOMF	$6.80	$7.00
$40	ZBOMH	$14.10	$14.40
$50	ZBOMJ	$23.00	$23.40

Note: The bid and ask prices for these puts are in dollars per share, and each contract covers 100 shares. Buying one contract thus provides downside insurance for one round lot of stock and costs 100 times the quoted ask price. (Data supplied by Thomson Financial, and provided as a courtesy by the Chicago Board Options Exchange, Incorporated.)

would have been happy with that outcome if I owned the round lot that doubled in value to $5,000. For comparison, note that the $50-strike put (ZBOMJ) was at-the-money during January 2005, and was quoted as high as $0.85–$0.95 per share during the month. ZBOMJ traded 6,826 contracts that month, but by expiration (Friday, January 21), ZBMOJ was also quoted at $0.00–$0.05 and expired worthless. Note that BA continued to climb, reaching a high of over $107 per share before a downward slide triggered in late 2007 by the global credit crisis.

1.3.2 Introduction to Transactions Costs (T-Costs)

Two patterns should jump out at you in the put prices in table 1.1: First, the higher the strike on the put, the more costly the option. This is because higher-strike options allow you to sell your stock for a higher price if you exercise them. Second, the higher the price of the option, the smaller the "relative spread" (i.e., the bid-ask spread as a proportion of the premium).

The width of the bid-ask spread compensates the market maker for the riskiness of holding inventory while trading with you, for the costs associated with processing your order, and for the risk that you may be better informed than he or she is (i.e., an "adverse selection" cost). There are many different drivers of these different costs, but you usually see lower relative spreads on a stock option when the stock is less volatile, when many market participants are trading the option, and when the price of the option is high compared to its peers—see chapter 10 for more details.

I usually assume that the true value of a security is within the spread and approximately equal to the "mid-spread" (i.e., [bid+ask]/2). The difference between the ask price and mid-spread is how much you pay the market maker when you buy. The difference between the mid-spread and the bid price is how much you pay the

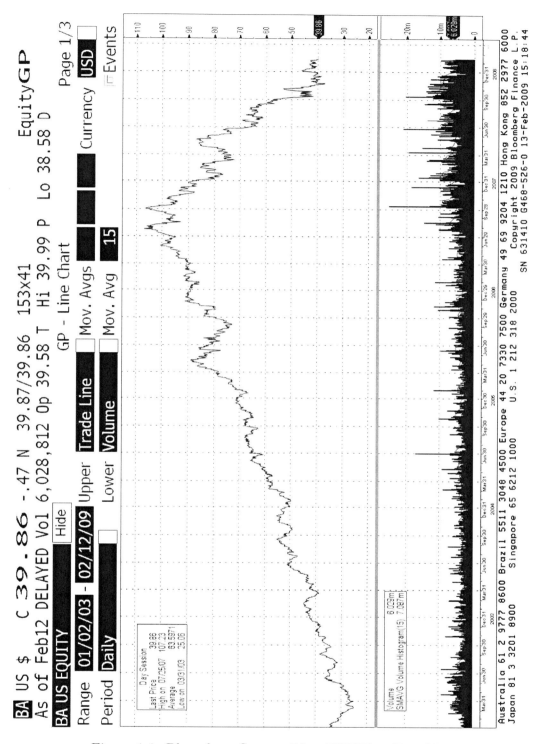

Figure 1.1: Bloomberg Screen: BA <EQUITY> GP <GO>

Note: This figures shows the stock price of Boeing (BA) from January 2003 until February 2009. Note the significant slide in price triggered in late 2007 by the global credit crisis.

Table 1.2: T-Costs of Round Trip Put Option Trade (1 Contract): BA

Strike	Buy (A)	Comm. 1 (B)	Sell (C)	Comm. 2 (D)	T-Cost (E)	$\frac{E}{A}$ (F)
$10	$35.00	$10.99	$15.00	$10.99	$41.98	119.9%
$15	$95.00	$10.99	$85.00	$10.99	$31.98	33.7%
$20	$230.00	$10.99	$215.00	$10.99	$36.98	16.1%
$30	$700.00	$10.99	$680.00	$10.99	$41.98	6.0%
$40	$1,440.00	$10.99	$1,410.00	$10.99	$51.98	3.6%
$50	$2,340.00	$10.99	$2,300.00	$10.99	$61.98	2.6%

Note: This table draws bid and ask prices from table 1.1. Column A is the ask (i.e., purchase) price for the put option contract. Column B is the commission my broker charges me to buy the option. Column C is the bid (i.e., sales) price for the put option contract. Column D is the second commission paid to sell the option. Column E is the total T-cost ($E = A - C + B + D$). Column F is the total T-cost as a percentage of the initial purchase price of the option. The percentage T-cost decreases dramatically if we buy the put option with higher strike. (Data supplied by Thomson Financial, and provided as a courtesy by the Chicago Board Options Exchange, Incorporated.)

market maker when you sell.[15] These costs, like commissions, are components of T-costs.

We can get a good feel for the relative T-costs of trading options by looking at an instantaneous "round-trip" trade: where for each option in table 1.1, we buy and then immediately sell one contract at the quoted prices.[16] Table 1.2 shows how much it costs to do this for the put options in table 1.1 using a $10.99 commission.

The first row in table 1.2 refers to the option ZBOMB described in the first row in table 1.1. Its ticker symbol "Z-BOMB" is appropriate given that the T-cost to trade in and out of it exceeds the asking price of the security![17] It makes sense to consider the purchase of only one contract when it is insurance for only one round lot of stock and, as such, comparisons within table 1.2 are fair. If we are speculating, however, it makes more sense to perform the comparison using a fixed amount of money and buying more of the cheaper contracts, thus prorating the commission (see the examples in section 1.3.3, following, and section 10.3).

---

[15]Saying that value is mid-spread makes sense if order processing costs dominate inventory holding costs and adverse selection costs. If inventory holding costs or adverse selection costs are large, then my assumption may be poor (e.g., if inventory holding costs are high, the market maker may lower the ask price below the true value of the security just to get his or her inventory down).

[16]A more realistic question to ask is what the T-cost is if you have a fixed number of dollars to invest. In this case, you can buy many more of the lower-cost contracts, and the commission gets spread over them—see the example in section 1.3.3.

[17]I am not saying that the spread is usurious. Making a market in options is a risky business, and spreads need to be wide.

1.3.3 Buying a Speculative Call

It is early morning Monday, April 21, 2003. The NYSE will open at 9:30 AM EST after a long Easter weekend. You have been watching McDonald's Corporation stock (MCD) in the recent past. MCD closed most recently at $16 on the NYSE (on the previous Thursday). MCD has risen 33% over the last six weeks from an almost 10-year low of about $12. MCD rose about 15% over the last month, matching the performance of the Dow Jones Industrial Average (INDU) of which it is a member. You know that Mondays in general tend to be bullish for underpriced stocks in the US equity markets and that after a long weekend the effect is compounded. You also know, however, that Passover does not end until Thursday the 24th, so volume will be light on the US exchanges and this could spoil the pattern. You think that MCD, like much of the market, will rise in late morning trading. You think this is the beginning of a medium-term price appreciation in MCD that may provide a 25% (i.e., $4) gain over the next three months—far outstripping the Dow (INDU).

You want to buy a call option to leverage your speculative view on MCD. MCD is on the March expiration cycle with equity options expiring in May, June, September, and December 2003.[18] There are also LEAPS that expire in January 2004 and January 2005.

If your three-month horizon is firm, the May and June expirations are too soon, and there is no point paying extra for the December expiration or the LEAPS. That leaves September. The most recent quotes (i.e., bid and ask prices) for September MCD call options are in table 1.3. Volume of trade and "open interest" are also in table 1.3. Near-the-money strike prices are available from $10 to $22.50 in $2.50 steps.

If you are correct, and your stock rises to $20 in three months, then, ignoring T-costs, each of these contracts should rise in fair value, with all but the last two being in the money (i.e., stock price above strike for a call) when you close your position in July. Which one should you buy?

Assuming you have $1,000 to spend, and taking into account the projected growth in the value of the option and both commissions and spreads, my calculations suggest that the $17.50 strike option should be most profitable with the $20 strike option a close second (details on this calculation are left for section 10.3). The $17.50 strike option does not offer the highest forecast return based on Black-Scholes values with zero T-costs (the $20 strike and $22.50 strike options are superior). Once T-

---

[18]There are January, February, and March expiration cycles. Each stock is assigned to one of these cycles. The March cycle, for example, has nominal expiration dates of March, June, September, and December. I say "nominal" because, in fact, there are always two near-month expirations (the "front month" and the "second month") and two far-month expirations; the latter two must come from that stock's expiration cycle, but the former two depend only upon which month it is now, and whether the equity option expiration date has passed for that month—usually the third Friday of the month. For example, on April 21, 2003, the (previously front-month) April options have already expired (on the previous Thursday because Friday was an exchange holiday), the May options are now the front month, the June options become the second month (stepping up from their previous position as far-month contracts), and the December options have just been introduced (as yet with zero open interest) as the second of the two far-month expirations (September and December).

Table 1.3: September 2003 Call Option Data: MCD, April 17, 2003

Strike	Ticker	Bid Price	Ask Price	Vol.	Op. Int.
$10.00	MCDIB	$6.00	$6.20	0	573
$12.50	MCDIV	$3.70	$3.90	3	1,547
$15.00	MCDIC	$1.80	$1.90	30	5,119
$17.50	MCDIW	$0.60	$0.65	99	2,115
$20.00	MCDID	$0.15	$0.25	4	524
$22.50	MCDIX	$0.00	$0.10	0	0

Note: These market data are for September 2003 MCD call options. They were available pre-trade on Monday, April 21, 2003, and therefore describe the most recent close of trade on Thursday, April 17. The bid and ask prices for these calls are in dollars per share, and each contract covers 100 shares. The volume column records how many option contracts were bought that day; it is also the number of contracts that were sold that day, because you cannot buy unless someone simultaneously sells to you. The open interest column records how many contracts are held long at the close of trade; it is also the number of contracts held short at the close of trade, because you cannot go long unless someone simultaneously goes short. Note that MCDIX has a bid price of zero; that is not unusual for the furthest out-of-the-money option if open interest is zero. (Data supplied by Thomson Financial, and provided as a courtesy by the Chicago Board Options Exchange, Incorporated.)

costs are taken into account, however, the $17.50 strike option is the most attractive (see section 10.3). The $17.50 strike option is the most expensive out-of-the-money call when the stock price is $16. Indeed, the most expensive out-of-the-money call is frequently the most profitable simple bullish trade after accounting for T-costs.

You could easily triple your money with either the $17.50 or $20 strike options if you are correct.[19] This compares favorably to the only 25% gain that you forecast for the stock. Of course, if you are wrong, and the stock price halves, you can easily lose 100% with these call options after T-costs, compared with only half that loss with the stock (see table 10.1 on page 173 for additional information).

Ignoring T-costs, buying the $22.50 strike option in table 1.3 quadruples your money if the stock price rises by 25% in three months. In practice, however, this out-of-the-money option is so lowly priced that its spread forms a large portion of T-costs, and the projected return to each of the other options in table 1.3 is significantly better after T-costs. See the analysis in section 10.3 starting on page 183, and also the epilogue on page 186.

---

[19]This leverage is why insider traders often use options for their illegal trades. The paper trail left behind is so good, however, that many get caught.

Chapter 2

Mathematics, Statistics, and Finance Prerequisites

To understand option pricing theory, we need to understand the mathematics, statistics, and finance from which it is constructed. This necessarily involves exponentials and logarithms, normality and lognormality, expected values, rates of return, and some other prerequisites.

2.1 Logarithms and Exponentials

Logarithms and exponentials appear in most option pricing formulae. Understanding logarithms and exponentials is thus essential if you are to understand basic option pricing theory. We will review each separately, then look at the inverse relationship between them.

2.1.1 Logarithms

The logarithm function may be defined as follows: if $b^l = x$, then l is the "logarithm of x to the base b." This may be written as $l = \log_b(x)$. As long as b and x are positive, then l is a unique real number. The case $b = e = 2.7182818\ldots$ (i.e., Euler's number) yields "natural" logarithms; the case $b = 10$ yields "common" logarithms.[1] The natural logarithm function is used in option pricing theory. Some authors denote the natural logarithm by $\log_e(\cdot)$, or sometimes just by $\log(\cdot)$; I use the popular notation $\ln(\cdot)$. For example, $\ln(1.025) = 0.02469261$. A graph of $\ln(x)$ appears in figure 2.1. Note from figure 2.1 that natural logarithms are defined only for positive numbers.

Logarithms are used because they have special properties. One such property is that if x is very small, $\ln(1 + x)$ is very close to x; can you see this in figure 2.1? For example, $\ln(1.0002) = 0.00019998$ is very close to 0.0002. This property is used later

---

[1]The natural logarithm is also known as the Napierian logarithm, the hyperbolic logarithm, or as "log to the base e." The common logarithm is also known as the Briggsian logarithm, or as "log to the base 10." Common logarithms are typically denoted as $\log_{10}(\cdot)$, or just by $\log(\cdot)$.

---

when different measures of returns are examined. For example, if R is a "simple" rate of return, and $X \equiv \ln(1 + R)$ is a "continuously compounded" rate of return (see section 2.4.2), then for small returns, R and X are not very different.

Another special property of logarithms is that *the log of the product equals the sum of the logs:* $\ln(X \times Y) = \ln(X) + \ln(Y)$, for all $X, Y > 0$. This is used when manipulating continuously compounded returns in chapter 8. Note also that $\ln(X \div Y) = \ln(X) - \ln(Y)$, for all $X, Y > 0$.

2.1.2   Exponentials

The exponential function may be defined as follows:

1. $\exp(x) \equiv \sum_{k=0}^{k=\infty} \frac{x^k}{k!}$, where "$\infty$" is infinity, and "$k!$" is read as "k factorial" and is calculated as $k! = k \cdot (k-1) \cdot (k-2) \cdot \ldots \cdot 2 \cdot 1$, if k is a positive integer, and $0! \equiv 1$;[2] or, equivalently,

2. $\exp(x) \equiv \lim_{n \to \infty} \left(1 + \frac{x}{n}\right)^n$.

The exponential function is typically denoted $\exp(\cdot)$; you also often see it written as $\exp(x) = e^x$. For example, $\exp(0.02) = e^{0.02} = 1.02020134$. A graph of $\exp(x)$ appears in figure 2.2. Note from figure 2.2 that the exponential function always takes positive values.

Like logs, exponentials also have special properties; one such is that *the exponential of the sum equals the product of the exponentials:* $\exp(X + Y) = \exp(X) \times \exp(Y)$, for all X, Y. This is used when manipulating stock prices in chapter 8. Note also that $\exp(X - Y) = \exp(X) \div \exp(Y)$, for all X, Y.

2.1.3   Inverse Properties

The exponential function is the inverse of the logarithm function; the logarithm function is the inverse of the exponential function. Either function "undoes" the effect of the other.[3] For example (with many decimal places to avoid rounding error),

$$\exp(0.020) = 1.02020134002676, \text{ and}$$
$$\ln(1.02020134002676) = 0.020.$$

Thus, $\ln[\exp(0.020)] = 0.020$, or, more generally, $\ln[\exp(x)] = x$ for all x. It also works the other way around, for example,

$$\ln(1.020) = 0.01980262729618, \text{ and}$$
$$\exp(0.01980262729618) = 1.020.$$

---

[2]So, for example, $3! = 6$, $4! = 24$, $5! = 120$, and $6! = 720$.

[3]Do not confuse the "inverse" with the "reciprocal." The inverse of $f(x)$ is a function $g(\cdot)$, such that $g[f(x)] = x$ and $f[g(x)] = x$. The reciprocal of the function $f(x)$ is a function h, such that $h(x) = \frac{1}{f(x)}$. For example, the inverse of $f(x) = x^2$ is $g(x) = \sqrt{x}$, but the reciprocal of $f(x) = x^2$ is $h(x) = \frac{1}{x^2}$.

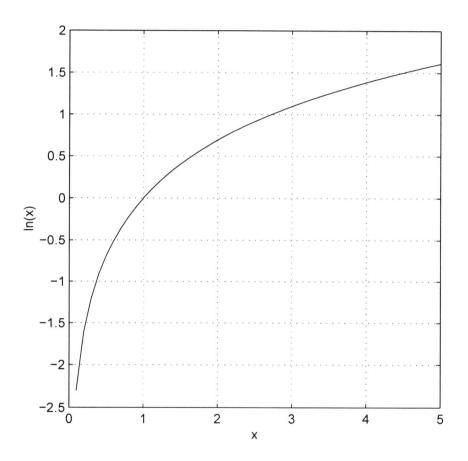

Figure 2.1: The Natural Logarithm Function

Note that $\ln(1) = 0$, and $\ln(e) = 1$, where $e = 2.7182818\ldots$ is Euler's number. Note also that $\ln(x)$ is defined only where $x > 0$.

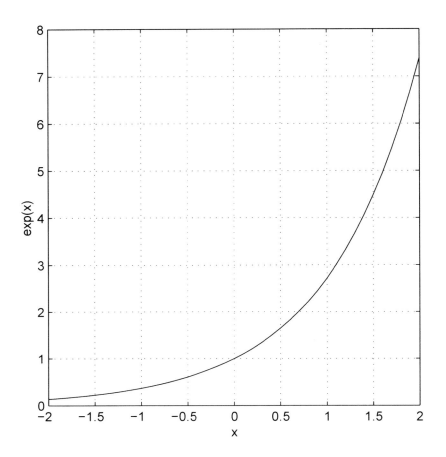

Figure 2.2: The Exponential Function.

Note that $\exp(0) = 1$, and $\exp(1) = e$, where $e = 2.7182818\ldots$ is Euler's number. Note also that $\exp(x)$ is defined for all x, and is always positive.

Thus, $\exp[\ln(1.020)] = 1.020$, or, more generally, $\exp[\ln(x)] = x$ for all $x > 0$. These inverse properties are used later on to go backward and forward between normal and lognormal distributions.

2.2 Normality and Lognormality

Normality and lognormality are essential parts of basic option pricing theory. For example, basic option pricing theory typically assumes that "continuously compounded" stock returns are normally distributed, and that stock prices are lognormally distributed (further details on these assumptions are left for section 2.4). Normality and lognormality are defined and described in terms of the logarithms and exponentials discussed in section 2.1.

2.2.1 Normal Distribution

A random variable X is distributed normal with mean ν and variance λ^2 if for any two numbers a and b satisfying $-\infty \leq a \leq b \leq \infty$ the probability that X falls between a and b is described by equations 2.1 and 2.2:

$$P(a \leq X \leq b) = \int_{x=a}^{x=b} \frac{1}{\sqrt{2\pi}\,\lambda} e^{-\frac{1}{2}\left(\frac{x-\nu}{\lambda}\right)^2} dx \qquad (2.1)$$

$$= \int_{x=a}^{x=b} f_X(x)dx, \qquad (2.2)$$

where the integrand[4] $f_X(x) \equiv \frac{1}{\sqrt{2\pi}\,\lambda} e^{-\frac{1}{2}\left(\frac{x-\nu}{\lambda}\right)^2}$ is the probability density function (or simply "pdf") of the random variable X. The pdf describes how the probability of different possible outcomes of X is distributed over those different possible outcomes.

If a random variable X is normal with mean ν and variance λ^2, I use the notation $X \sim N(\nu, \lambda^2)$, read as "X is distributed as normal, mean nu, and variance lambda squared."

A typical normal distribution is shown in figure 2.3. The normal is also known as the "Gaussian" distribution (after the mathematician Carl Friedrich Gauss, 1777–1855).[5] The normal distribution is symmetric, "bell-shaped," and described fully by its mean and variance. The distribution in figure 2.3 has mean and variance of $\nu = 0.07$ and $\lambda^2 = 0.02$, respectively.

2.2.2 Lognormal Distribution

Lognormality is defined in terms of normality. A random variable Y is lognormal if and only if $X \equiv \ln(Y)$ is normal. It follows from the inverse properties in section 2.1

---

[4]The "integrand" is that part of the integral that falls between the "$\int$" and the "dx."

[5]In fact, the Gaussian distribution is something of a misnomer. The Gaussian distribution was not discovered by Gauss, but by Abraham de Moivre. He published his discovery in 1733 (44 years before Gauss was born). Abraham de Moivre arrived at the Gaussian distribution as an approximation to the binomial distribution (Kotz et al., 1982, pp347–348).

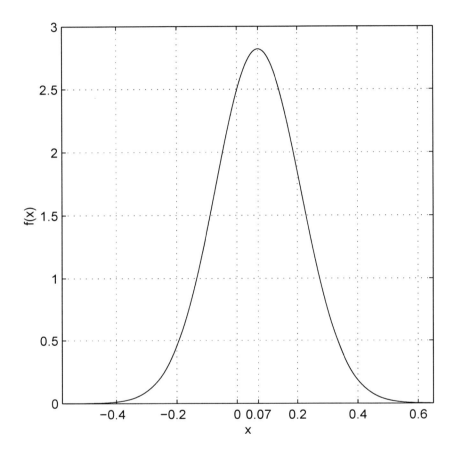

Figure 2.3: A Normal Distribution

Note: The normal probability density function $f(x)$ is plotted for the particular parameter values $\nu = 0.07$ (the mean) and $\lambda^2 = 0.02$. The functional form is given by

$$f(x) = \frac{1}{\sqrt{2\pi}\,\lambda}e^{-\frac{1}{2}\left(\frac{x-\nu}{\lambda}\right)^2}.$$

that if X is normally distributed, then $Y \equiv \exp(X)$ is necessarily lognormally distributed.

If Y is lognormal, so that $\ln(Y)$ is normal (and $\ln(Y)$ has mean ν and variance λ^2, say) then

$$P(c \leq Y \leq d) = \int_{y=c}^{y=d} \frac{1}{\sqrt{2\pi} \, \lambda y} e^{-\frac{1}{2}\left(\frac{\ln(y)-\nu}{\lambda}\right)^2} dy$$

for any $0 \leq c \leq d \leq \infty$. The pdf for the lognormal distribution can be derived directly by substituting $X = \ln(Y)$, $x = \ln(y)$, $dx = \frac{1}{y}dy$, $a = \ln(c)$, and $b = \ln(d)$ into the pdf for the normal distribution (you should try this).[6]

A typical lognormal distribution is illustrated in figure 2.4. The lognormal distribution shown is of the random variable $Y = \exp(X)$, where $X \sim N(\nu, \lambda^2)$ and $\nu = 0.07$ and $\lambda^2 = 0.02$. Although I quote $\nu = 0.07$ and $\lambda^2 = 0.02$, these are *not* the mean and variance of Y, but rather of $X = \ln(Y)$ (see tables 2.1 and 2.2 for details). The lognormal distribution is "right skewed," also known as "positively skewed." It looks as though its top has been shoved from the right while keeping its base fixed. A more skewed lognormal distribution is displayed in figure 2.5 for the random variable $Y = \exp(X)$, where $X \sim N(\nu, \lambda^2)$ and $\nu = 0.07$ and $\lambda^2 = 0.15$.

2.2.3 Inverse and Other Properties

The special properties of logarithms and exponentials flow through to both normally and lognormally distributed random variables. For example, if X_1 and X_2 are both normally distributed, and are statistically independent, then $X_1 + X_2$ is also normally distributed. Thus, *normality is closed under addition.*[7] There is a similar property for lognormally distributed random variables. If Y_1 and Y_2 are both lognormally distributed, and are statistically independent, then $Y_1 \times Y_2$ is also lognormally distributed. Thus, *lognormality is closed under multiplication.* This result can be proved using the closure properties of independent normals together with the definition of lognormality (you should try to prove it).

The relationships between logarithms and exponentials and between normality and lognormality enable you to infer the properties of one distribution from those of the other. This is useful in later chapters if, for example, you wish to infer the behavior of stock prices (assumed lognormal) from the behavior of continuously compounded returns (assumed normal), or vice versa.

The general results are displayed in tables 2.1 and 2.3 (but details for prices and returns in particular are not covered until section 8.1). The results displayed in tables 2.1 and 2.3 are not meant to be immediately obvious—you should check the algebra.

Figures 2.3 and 2.4 display the normal and lognormal probability density functions using the parameter values from the example in table 2.2. The two distributions appear quite similar except that the lognormal has been shifted to the right

---

[6]I recommend Evans et al. (1993) as an excellent reference book for most of the statistical distributions you are likely to meet.

[7]"Closed under operation $\mathcal{O}$" means that applying operation $\mathcal{O}$ to a pair of independent random variables returns a random variable of the same family of probability distributions.

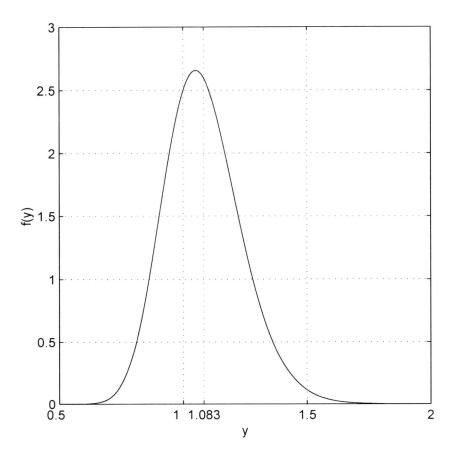

Figure 2.4: A Lognormal Distribution

Note: The lognormal probability density function $f(y)$ is plotted for the particular parameter values $\nu = 0.07$ and $\lambda^2 = 0.02$. The mean is indicated at 1.083 (see table 2.2). The functional form is given by

$$f(y) = \frac{1}{\sqrt{2\pi}\ \lambda y} e^{-\frac{1}{2}\left(\frac{\ln(y)-\nu}{\lambda}\right)^2}.$$

22

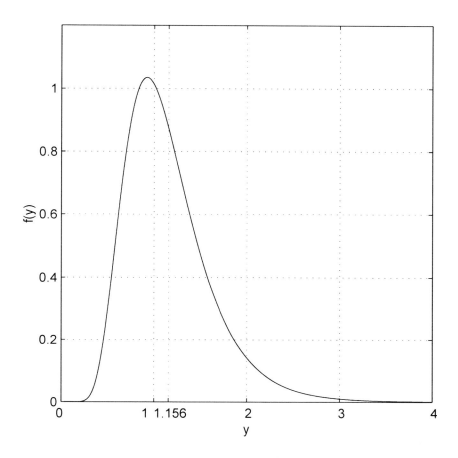

Figure 2.5: A Lognormal Distribution

Note: The lognormal probability density function $f(y)$ is plotted for the particular parameter values $\nu = 0.07$ and $\lambda^2 = 0.15$. The mean is indicated at 1.156 (see table 2.1 for the formula). The functional form is given by

$$f(y) = \frac{1}{\sqrt{2\pi}\,\lambda y} e^{-\frac{1}{2}\left(\frac{\ln(y)-\nu}{\lambda}\right)^2}.$$

Table 2.1: Translating from Normal to Lognormal: Theory

	Normal $X \sim N(\nu, \lambda^2)$	Lognormal $Y = \exp(X)$
MEAN	ν	$e^{\nu + \frac{\lambda^2}{2}}$
MEDIAN	ν	e^{ν}
MODE	ν	$e^{\nu - \lambda^2}$
VARIANCE	λ^2	$\left(e^{2\nu + \lambda^2}\right) \times \left(e^{\lambda^2} - 1\right)$
STD. DEV.	λ	$\sqrt{\left(e^{2\nu + \lambda^2}\right) \times \left(e^{\lambda^2} - 1\right)}$
LIMITS	$-\infty < X < +\infty$	$0 \le Y < +\infty$

Table 2.2: Translating from Normal to Lognormal: Example

	Normal $X \sim N(\nu, \lambda^2)$	Lognormal $Y = \exp(X)$
MEAN	0.07	1.08328707
MEDIAN	0.07	1.07250818
MODE	0.07	1.05127110
VARIANCE	0.02	0.02370649
STD. DEV.	0.14142136	0.15396913
LIMITS	$-\infty < X < +\infty$	$0 \le Y < +\infty$

by about $+1$, and a slight positive skew is visible. If you ignore the slight skew, then for small X, one plus the normally distributed X (i.e., $1 + X$) is similar to the lognormally distributed $Y \equiv \exp(X)$; that is, $Y \approx 1 + X$. However, by definition, $X \equiv \ln(Y)$, so it follows, taking logs of both sides, that for small X, we have $X \approx \ln(1 + X)$—a well-known result.

> **Exercise:** Use the formulae in table 2.3 to confirm that if you are given $s^2 = 0.02370649$ and $m = 1.08328707$ for the lognormal, then it can be deduced that $\nu = 0.07$ and $\lambda^2 = 0.02$ for the normal (i.e., the reverse of the transformations in table 2.2).

Table 2.3: Translating from Lognormal to Normal: Theory

	Lognormal Y (m, s^2)	Normal $X = \log(Y) \sim N(\nu, \lambda^2)$
MEAN	$E(Y) = m$	$\nu = E(X) = \ln\left(\dfrac{m}{\sqrt{1+\left(\frac{s}{m}\right)^2}}\right)$
VARIANCE	$Var(Y) = s^2$	$\lambda^2 = Var(X) = \ln\left[1 + \left(\frac{s}{m}\right)^2\right]$
STD. DEV.	$Std(Y) = s$	$\lambda = Std(X) = \sqrt{\ln\left[1 + \left(\frac{s}{m}\right)^2\right]}$
LIMITS	$0 \leq Y < +\infty$	$-\infty < X < +\infty$

2.2.4 Z-Score and Cumulative Standard Normal

Suppose that a particular observation x is drawn from a population that is normally distributed $X \sim N(\nu, \lambda^2)$. To get a feel for how "large" x is relative to the population, we should ask how many standard deviations our observation x is from the mean ν. This is just the distance between x and ν scaled by the standard deviation λ. We denote this as $z \equiv (x - \nu)/\lambda$. The scalar z is a particular observation of the random variable $Z \equiv (X - \nu)/\lambda$ that is itself a similarly scaled version of X. This particular scaling is referred to as a "standardization" of the original variable and the new variable Z is said to be distributed "standard normal," i.e., $Z \sim N(0, 1)$. The standardized version, z, of the original particular observation, x, is often referred to as a "Z score."

The standard normal ranges between $-\infty$ and $+\infty$, but, in practice, few observations lie beyond plus and minus 3, 99% of the observations lie between plus and minus 2.58, 95% of the observations lie between plus and minus 1.96, and 68% of the observations lie between plus and minus 1.

We may now define a new function that tells us what percentage of a distribution lies below a particular value. This is the "cumulative density function," or "cdf." Formally, in the case of $X \sim N(\nu, \lambda^2)$, the cumulative density function $F_X(x)$ (i.e., the cumulative normal) is derived from the normal probability density function $f_X(x)$ as in equations 2.3 and 2.4:

$$F_X(x) = \int_{-\infty}^{x} f_U(u)\,du \tag{2.3}$$

$$= \int_{-\infty}^{x} \frac{1}{\sqrt{2\pi}\,\lambda} e^{-\frac{1}{2}\left(\frac{u-\nu}{\lambda}\right)^2}\,du \tag{2.4}$$

Thus, $F_X(x)$ is the area under the pdf $f_X(\cdot)$ to the left of x. It follows, for example, that $F_X(-\infty) = 0$, $F_X(\text{median}) = 0.5$, and $F_X(+\infty) = 1$ (i.e., total area under the pdf equals one). Thus, the cumulative density takes values between zero and one. In the case of the *standard* normal, the cumulative density function (i.e., cdf) is often denoted by "$N(z)$" $\equiv F_Z(z)$. Thus, $N(-\infty) = 0$, $N(0) = 0.5$, and $N(+\infty) = 1$.

The cumulative standard normal has the property that $1 - N(z) = N(-z)$. This follows from the symmetry of the standard normal pdf about zero.

2.3   Expected Values

The expected value of a continuous random variable is the mean of its pdf. If X has pdf $f_X(x)$, and possible values of x range from $-a$ to $+b$, then the expected value of X (i.e., the mean of X) is denoted $E(X)$ and is given by equation 2.5:

$$E(X) = \int_{x=-a}^{x=+b} x f_X(x)dx. \tag{2.5}$$

Let me provide some simple intuition by showing clearly that equation 2.5 is directly analogous to working out the expected value of a random variable in the simpler discrete case. Suppose that X_d is a discrete random variable that takes values $\{x_1, x_2, ..., x_n\}$ with probabilities $\{p_1, p_2, ..., p_n\}$, respectively. We know that the sum of the probabilities must be one: $\sum_{i=1}^{i=n} p_i = 1$. The expected value of X_d is the weighted sum—with the p_i as weights—of the possible realizations of X, as shown in equation 2.6:

$$E(X_d) = \sum_{i=1}^{i=n} x_i \cdot p_i \tag{2.6}$$

For example, suppose X_d takes values 1, 2, and 4, with probabilities $\frac{1}{4}$, $\frac{1}{2}$, and $\frac{1}{4}$, respectively, then

$$E(X_d) = \left(1 \cdot \frac{1}{4}\right) + \left(2 \cdot \frac{1}{2}\right) + \left(4 \cdot \frac{1}{4}\right) = 2\frac{1}{4}.$$

The continuous case in equation 2.5 is analogous to equation 2.6 and to our simple example because the term $f_X(x) \cdot dx$ appearing under the integral sign in equation 2.5 is just a probability; it is the area of a small vertical slice taken under the pdf of X (with height $f_X(x)$ and width dx). The sum of all such areas (that is, the integral $\int_{x=-a}^{x=+b} f_X(x)dx$) is equal to 1 by definition of a pdf. The integral sign itself is really just an elongated "S" (S for s̲ummation). So equation 2.5 is really just a summation of possible realizations of X multiplied by their probability of occurrence and is perfectly analogous to the summation in equation 2.6.

For concreteness, note that if X is distributed normal with mean ν and variance λ^2, then X takes values between $-\infty$ and $+\infty$ and it can be shown with considerable algebra that

$$E(X) = \int_{x=-\infty}^{x=+\infty} x \cdot \frac{1}{\sqrt{2\pi}\,\lambda} e^{-\frac{1}{2}\left(\frac{x-\nu}{\lambda}\right)^2} dx = \nu.$$

All of the foregoing comments with reference to random variable X also apply if we replace X by some other distribution $Y \equiv X|A$. That is, if Y is the random variable X conditional upon having some information A, then we can work out "conditional means" as in section 2.3.1.

©2009 Timothy Falcon Crack — 26 —

2.3.1 Conditional Expected Values

Let us take an extended example to demonstrate a conditional mean in the case of a normal distribution, and also to allow a result to be derived that can be used later. Consider the case where $X \sim N(\nu, \lambda^2)$ and $Y \equiv X|X > \nu$. What is the mean of Y? That is, what is the expected value of X conditional upon the information that X is greater than its mean?[8]

Before we work it out, let us have an educated guess. Values of X greater than the mean ν are distributed from ν up to $+\infty$ but fall, on average, about one standard deviation of X higher than ν. That is, the answer should be $E(X|X > \nu) \approx \nu + \lambda$. Now we work it out formally:

$$
\begin{aligned}
E(X|X > \nu) = E(Y) &= \int_{y=-\infty}^{+\infty} y \cdot f_Y(y) dy \\
&= \int_{x=-\infty}^{x=+\infty} x \cdot f_{(X|X>\nu)}(x) dx \\
&= \int_{x=\nu}^{x=+\infty} x \cdot \frac{f_X(x)}{1/2} dx \qquad (*) \\
&= 2 \cdot \int_{x=\nu}^{x=+\infty} x \cdot f_X(x) dx \\
&= 2 \cdot \int_{x=\nu}^{x=+\infty} x \frac{1}{\sqrt{2\pi}\,\lambda} e^{-\frac{1}{2}\left(\frac{x-\nu}{\lambda}\right)^2} dx
\end{aligned}
$$

Note that at step $(*)$, above, the conditional distribution $f_{(X|X>\nu)}(x)$ is calculated to be $\frac{f_X(x)}{1/2}$ when $x > \nu$ (and zero otherwise) because the distribution's probability mass has to be re-scaled to integrate to 1. Now, let $z = \frac{x-\nu}{\lambda}$ (so that $Z \equiv (X - \nu)/\lambda$ is standard normal), then $dx = \lambda dz$, and $x = \lambda z + \nu$. Plugging these into the last equation yields

$$
\begin{aligned}
E(X|X > \nu) &= 2 \cdot \int_{x=\nu}^{x=+\infty} x \frac{1}{\sqrt{2\pi}\,\lambda} e^{-\frac{1}{2}\left(\frac{x-\nu}{\lambda}\right)^2} dx \\
&= 2 \cdot \int_{z=0}^{z=+\infty} (\lambda z + \nu) \frac{1}{\sqrt{2\pi}\,\lambda} e^{-\frac{1}{2}z^2} \lambda dz \\
&= 2 \left[\lambda \int_{z=0}^{z=+\infty} z f_Z(z) dz + \nu \int_{z=0}^{z=+\infty} f_Z(z) dz \right],
\end{aligned}
$$

where $f_Z(z) \equiv \frac{1}{\sqrt{2\pi}} e^{-\frac{1}{2}z^2}$. However, the first term is directly integrable

$$
\begin{aligned}
\int_{z=0}^{z=+\infty} z f_Z(z) dz &= \int_{z=0}^{z=+\infty} z \frac{1}{\sqrt{2\pi}} e^{-\frac{1}{2}z^2} dz \\
&= -\frac{1}{\sqrt{2\pi}} e^{-\frac{1}{2}z^2} \Big|_0^{\infty} = 0 + \frac{1}{\sqrt{2\pi}} = \frac{1}{\sqrt{2\pi}},
\end{aligned}
$$

---

[8]We care about this question or questions like it because we are often interested in strategies that pay off in cases only where the stock price or, conditional upon today's stock price, the return on the stock is above (or below) a particular level related to the strike price of an option.

and the second term satisfies $\int_{z=0}^{z=+\infty} f_Z(z) = \frac{1}{2}$, because Z is standard normal. It follows then that

$$
\begin{aligned}
E(X|X > \nu) &= 2\left[\lambda \int_{z=0}^{z=+\infty} z f_Z(z)dz + \nu \int_{z=0}^{z=+\infty} f_Z(z)\right] \\
&= 2\left[\lambda \frac{1}{\sqrt{2\pi}} + \nu \frac{1}{2}\right] \\
&= \lambda \sqrt{\frac{2}{\pi}} + \nu. \tag{2.7}
\end{aligned}
$$

Our educated guess of $E(X|X > \nu) \approx \nu + \lambda$ is quite close to the result from equation 2.7 that $E(X|X > \nu) = \nu + \left(\sqrt{2/\pi}\right)\lambda \approx \nu + 0.80 \cdot \lambda$.

There is substantial additional discussion of conditional expected values in section 8.3.6.

2.4 Rates of Return

2.4.1 Statistical/Distributional Arguments

Consider a stock with market price $P(t)$ at point in time t. For simplicity, assume that there are no dividends or other distributions, and that there are no taxes or T-costs. Suppose you observe the (unrealistically volatile) stock prices $P(1) = \$100, P(2) = \$125, P(3) = \$100$, and $P(4) = \$80$ at the end of Monday, Tuesday, Wednesday, and Thursday, respectively.

The formula $R_{t-1,t} = [P(t) - P(t-1)]/P(t-1)$ may be used to calculate the "simple return" to holding the stock from time $t-1$ to time t. These returns are $R_2 \equiv R_{1,2} = 0.25, R_3 \equiv R_{2,3} = -0.20$, and $R_4 \equiv R_{3,4} = -0.20$ in our example.[9]

Suppose you could buy the stock at $t = 1$ (close of business Monday) and sell it at $t = 4$ (close of business Thursday). The simple holding period return $R_{1,4}$, (from $t = 1$ to $t = 4$) can be calculated directly as a loss of 20%: $R_{1,4} = [P(4) - P(1)]/P(1) = (80 - 100)/100 = -0.20$.

You may also calculate $R_{1,4}$ using multiplication (i.e., compounding) of the individual daily returns. It is worth remembering that *simple returns compound using multiplication.*

$$
\begin{aligned}
(1 + R_{1,4}) &= (1 + R_2)(1 + R_3)(1 + R_4) = 1.25 \times 0.8 \times 0.8 = 0.80 \\
\Rightarrow R_{1,4} &= -0.20.
\end{aligned}
$$

Simple returns are intuitive and straightforward. Many published facts and figures quote simple returns. Normal distributions are also intuitive and appear frequently in finance and in nature. Can simple returns be assumed normal?

Although normality is the initial statistical assumption of many models, there are at least two problems with using the assumption of normality for simple returns.

---

[9]The terms "return" and "rate of return" are interchangeable. Do not confuse them with the *dollar* return on an investment.

The first problem is that limited liability implies that actual simple stock returns cannot fall below -1. The normal distribution, however, extends from $-\infty$ to $+\infty$, so the theory would not match reality. In practice this is not a major concern.[10]

The second problem is that simple returns compound using multiplication, and normality is not closed under multiplication (i.e., X, Y both normal $\Rightarrow X \cdot Y$ never normal); this is a serious concern. If the statistically independent simple returns R_1 and R_2 are normal, then so too are $1+R_1$, and $1+R_2$, but the product $(1+R_1)(1+R_2)$ is not. Thus, time aggregation (i.e., compounding) does not generate normal simple returns even when the individual returns are themselves normal simple returns. This would be impossibly clumsy and inconsistent in any theoretical work.[11]

The problems with limited liability and compounding are solved by making a different statistical assumption. If R is a simple rate of return, we assume that $X \equiv \ln(1+R)$ is distributed normal, not R. The quantity $X = \ln(1+R)$ is the continuously compounded rate of return.

In place of the traditional compounding factor $(1+R)$, we use instead the mathematically identical compounding factor e^X; in place of the traditional discounting factor $1/(1+R)$, we use instead the mathematically identical discounting factor e^{-X}; and thus in place of the traditional multi-period discounting factor $1/(1+R)^T$, we use the mathematically identical multi-period discounting factor $e^{-X \cdot T}$. Sections 2.4.2 and 2.4.3 discuss pratical interpretations of continuous compounding (with numerical examples) and applications to pricing forwards and futures, respectively.

From the properties of logarithms in section 2.1 (and the discussions in sections 2.1 and 2.2), we know that if x is small, then $\ln(1+x)$ is close to x. Thus, the simple rate of return R and the continuously compounded rate of return $X = \ln(1+R)$ are not very different for small R.

Although the logarithm transformation is slight, it eliminates the aforementioned problems with limited liability and compounding. If $X = \ln(1+R)$ is assumed normal, then, by the definition of lognormality, $(1+R)$ is lognormal and, therefore, ranges from 0 to $+\infty$. Thus, R ranges from -1 to $+\infty$, solving our limited liability problem. From the properties of logarithms in section 2.1, we see also that

$$\ln(1+R_{1,4}) = \ln[(1+R_2)(1+R_3)(1+R_4)] = \ln(1+R_2) + \ln(1+R_3) + \ln(1+R_4),$$

which is equivalent to writing[12] $X_{1,4} = X_2 + X_3 + X_4$.

---

[10]If you fit a normal distribution to the historical simple daily returns on a stock, the estimated standard deviation is almost always going to be so small relative to the mean that the lower tail of the fitted normal distribution does not breach the financial boundary of -1 except with tiny probability, i.e., $N[(-1-\hat{\mu})/\hat{\sigma}] = \epsilon$, where ϵ is tiny.

[11]I like the discussion of normality/lognormality in section VI of Case M. Sprenkle's option pricing paper (Sprenkle [1961]). I also find Sprenkle's discussion of risk neutrality in section VII of his paper to be very clear. It is historically interesting to note that Sprenkle's option pricing formula is very closely related to the Black-Scholes formula. Sprenkle did not pursue this area because he did not realize the general importance of option pricing at the time (personal communication April 3, 2008). The relationships are discussed further in Black (1989). See also Haug (2007, section 1.3.2).

[12]If you are having trouble with the subscripts, recall that $R_2 = R_{1,2}$, $R_3 = R_{2,3}$, and $R_4 = R_{3,4}$, so $(1+R_{1,4}) = (1+R_{1,2})(1+R_{2,3})(1+R_{3,4}) = (1+R_2)(1+R_3)(1+R_4)$. The notation for X is analogous.

It follows that because normality is closed under addition, time aggregation generates normal continuously compounded returns when the individual returns are also (statistically independent) normal continuously compounded returns—solving our compounding problem. It is worth remembering that *continuously compounded returns compound using addition.*

If the continuously compounded return $X_t = \ln(1 + R_t)$ is assumed normal, then $(1 + R_t)$ is lognormal. It follows that the "price relative" $\frac{P(t)}{P(t-1)}$ is also lognormal, because $\frac{P(t)}{P(t-1)} = 1 + \frac{P(t) - P(t-1)}{P(t-1)} = (1 + R_t)$. Normality, lognormality, simple returns, continuously compounded returns, and the price relative are all used extensively in Black-Scholes option pricing theory.

Story: One candidate for a futures trading position in Chicago was asked: "Would you rather be beaten up, beat someone up, or run around the block naked?" The last response did not get him the job.

Taken from "Heard on The Street: Quantitative Questions from Wall Street Job Interviews," ©2008 Timothy Falcon Crack. See advertisement on last page of this book.

2.4.2 Continuously Compounded Returns

The arguments in section 2.4.1 revolve around statistical assumptions of economic models and, although necessary, are not very intuitive. This section contains more economic intuition. Section 2.4.3, which follows, applies continuous compounding to the pricing of forwards and futures.

Continuously compounded returns are just another way of quoting rates of return. As mentioned in section 2.4.1, they are related to, and often approximately equal to, simple (i.e., effective) rates of return. All good financial hand-held calculators have e^x and ln keys for manipulating continuously compounded returns.

Suppose that you have \$1,000 to invest and that a bank offers you a CD (i.e., certificate of deposit) or term deposit with an annual percentage rate (APR) of 12% compounded m times per year for one year. The terminal value of your investment depends upon how many times per year the compounding takes place. The terminal value is calculated as $\$1,000 \times \left(1 + \frac{0.12}{m}\right)^m$, and is shown in table 2.4 for a range of values of m. The last row in the table shows what happens if you compound one billion times a second—effectively *continuous* compounding. Continuously compounded returns are APRs with extremely frequent compounding. For example, if $r = 0.12$ is a continuously compounded return, then an investment earning this rate has an annual growth factor of $(1 + \frac{r}{m})^m = (1 + \frac{0.12}{m})^m$, where m is infinitely large. However, as defined in section 2.1.2, for large m, $(1 + \frac{r}{m})^m \approx e^r$. This is the same as $(1 + EAR)$ for some simple effective annual rate EAR. Thus, $(1 + EAR) = e^r$, or equivalently, $r = \ln(1 + EAR)$. For example, $1.1275 = \exp(0.12)$ or $0.12 = \ln(1 + 0.1275)$, as in table 2.4.

Table 2.4: APRs and Continuous Compounding

Compounding Frequency at 12% (number of times compounded)	Terminal Value of $1,000.00	Effective Rate of Return
Annual (1)	$1,120.0000	12.000%
Semiannual (2)	$1,123.6000	12.360%
Quarterly (4)	$1,125.5088	12.551%
Monthly (12)	$1,126.8250	12.683%
Daily (365)	$1,127.4746	12.747%
Hourly (8760)	$1,127.4959	12.750%
Every Minute (525,600)	$1,127.4965	12.750%
Every Second (31,536,000)	$1,127.4969	12.750%
Every Nanosecond (3.15E16)	$1,127.4969	12.750%

Note: The terminal value and the effective annual rate of return increase with the compounding frequency; however, they are limited. An APR of 12%, even when compounded continuously, produces an effective yield of only 12.75%.

Key Summary: Continuously compounded returns are used in derivatives pricing. They are APRs with extremely frequent compounding. For example, if $r = 0.05$ is a continuously compounded rate of return, then an investment earning this rate has an annual growth factor of $(1 + \frac{r}{m})^m = (1 + \frac{0.05}{m})^m$, where m is infinitely large. However, for large m, $(1 + \frac{r}{m})^m \approx e^r$ (which is much easier to calculate). We compound at continuously compounded rate r over time period $(T - t)$ using multiplicative growth factor $e^{r(T-t)}$; we discount at continuously compounded rate r over time period $(T - t)$ using multiplicative discount factor $e^{-r(T-t)}$.

Exercise: Check that $(1 + \frac{0.05}{m})^m$ and $e^{0.05 \times 1}$ are 99.999% the same for $m = 365$, and deduce that daily compounding (which most banks offer) is thus very close to continuous compounding.

2.4.3 Pricing Forwards/Futures with Continuous Dividends

In this section we use the continuously compounded return concept to deduce a fair price for forward delivery of a theoretical security paying continuous dividends.

To value forwards and futures, we need the following assumptions (for at least a sizable subset of market participants): there are no T-costs and no restrictions on short sales; there is no counterparty credit risk; market participants are price takers who prefer more wealth to less wealth; all net profits from trading are subject to the same tax rate; riskless borrowing and lending can be done at the same rate; and prices have adjusted so that there are no arbitrage opportunities.

We use the following notation: T is the delivery date (expressed in years); t is today (so $T - t$ is the number of years to maturity); S is the price of the underlying asset; F is the forward price today; r is a continuously compounded riskless interest

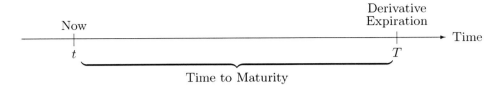

Figure 2.6: Derivative Security Timeline

Note: Our options, futures, and forwards are assumed to live from time t to time T. Both T and t are measured in years, so a six-month option has $T - t = 0.50$.

rate per annum available today until time T.[13] Recall that the delivery price, the forward price and the value of the forward contract are different concepts. Forward prices are quoted in the financial press every day as the delivery price at the initiation of new contracts. The forward price is a fair delivery price, so the initial value of the new contracts is zero. As the forward price varies in the marketplace, contractually-fixed delivery prices look attractive or unattractive and this gives existing contracts positive or negative value, respectively.

Consider a theoretical stock that provides a constant dividend yield. It may be thought of as "leaking" dividends continuously where the rate of leakage is a constant percentage of the stock price. For example, if your stock leaks a continuous dividend of 10% per annum, and this morning's stock price was $100, then at the end of today you would expect to have received dividends of very slightly larger than $100 \times \frac{1}{365} \times 10\%$.

If you continually reinvest dividends as they leak out of the company, then the number of units of stock you hold increases at a rate equal to the dividend yield on the stock (let this be q per annum, say). Starting with one unit of stock and holding it for $(T - t)$ years, you therefore end up with $1 \times e^{q(T-t)} = e^{q(T-t)}$ units of stock (alternatively, if you start with $e^{-q(T-t)}$ units of stock, you end up with 1 unit of stock after $T - t$ years). This assertion is most clearly seen if we take a two-paragraph detour and consider FX investments as an analogy to stocks that pay continuous dividends.

Suppose I live in the US, but receive a gift of GBP1,000 from a British relative. Suppose I place those GBP1,000 into a UK bank account that pays a continuously compounded interest rate of 5% per annum.[14] The bank account pays interest in GBP. At the end of one year, the balance is GBP$1,000 \times e^{0.05 \cdot 1} \approx$ GBP$1,051.27$. That is, GBP1,000 has grown to GBP$1,000 \times e^{r(T-t)}$, where r is the British interest rate and $(T - t)$ is the investment period.

In a big-picture sense, one British pound may be considered to be a share cer-

---

[13]A riskless bond that pays $1 in T years is thus worth $\$\frac{1}{e^{r(T-t)}}$, or equivalently, $\$e^{-r(T-t)}$, today.

[14]This is not as crazy as it sounds. Some US banks have offered continuous compounding (e.g., Savers Bank in Massachusetts [www.saversbank.com]). It costs the bank little compared to daily compounding (see table 2.4 and the exercise on page 31) and attracts customers.

tificate in a US-listed company called "Britain, Inc." When Britain does well (lower unemployment, higher productivity, etc.), the USD price of the pound rises; when Britain does poorly (higher unemployment, lower productivity, etc.), the USD price of the pound falls—just like a stock rising and falling when a company does well or poorly.[15] A pound held in a UK bank pays dividends in units of more pounds. This is perfectly analogous to holding a share of stock in a corporation that runs a dividend reinvestment program (DRIP).[16] From the pound example, it follows that if you hold 1,000 shares of stock in a theoretical company that pays continuous dividends at rate r per annum, and if you use their dividend reinvestment program to buy more stock, then after $(T - t)$ years you have $1,000 \times e^{r(T-t)}$ shares of stock. Change this to one share of stock and continuous dividend yield q, and we have the assertion we are trying to prove.

To arrive at a fair price for future delivery of a security, we introduce a "cash-and-carry strategy." This strategy duplicates (or "synthesizes") the payoff to a forward contract. A cash-and-carry strategy requires that you borrow enough money now to fund the purchase of the underlying security in the *cash* or "spot" market.[17] You then *carry* the underlying security through to the maturity of the forward, at which time you deliver it in exchange for a payment used to pay off the borrowing—thereby creating a synthetic forward. The costs associated with executing this strategy are referred to as "the cost of carry."

A synthetic forward and an actual forward both perform the same economic function: they have no out-of-pocket cash flow at time zero, they deliver an asset at time T, and at time T a payment is made to the deliverer (which is used to repay the loan in the case of the synthetic forward). If they perform the same function and have an identically timed single cash flow, then these cash flows must be identical, or else an arbitrage opportunity exists. If we go long one and short the other, we can deduce the cash flows.

Consider a cash-and-carry strategy combined with a short forward: you borrow enough money at time zero to buy enough stock so that with reinvestment of dividends you have one unit of stock to deliver at time T. Then you deliver the stock in exchange for the forward (delivery) price F, and you repay your borrowing. What are the cash flows?

With a known continuous dividend yield q, you borrow enough money to buy

---

[15]This is a powerful analogy. Britain, Inc. is a conglomerate of thousands of corporations, small firms, and so on, with millions of employees. Its extraordinary diversification explains why the volatility of returns to investing in the pound is much lower than the volatility of returns to investing in almost any individual British or US company. The same is true of most major currencies; and this relatively low volatility explains why, other things being equal, options on currencies are cheaper than options on stock.

[16]DRIPs are run by many companies in the US (Fisher [2001]). You can buy stock directly from the company, typically without a commission and sometimes even at a discount from market price, and sign up to have all dividends paid to you in the form of additional shares of stock (even partial shares of stock when the dividend is not sufficient for a full share). There are some restrictions on selling securities in these DRIPs, but they do not affect long-term investors.

[17]The cash market is where the actual asset (as opposed to a derivative contract on the asset) is bought or sold for immediate delivery, typically with payment one or two business days hence.

$e^{-q(T-t)}$ units of stock at time zero (at a price of S per share, this costs $Se^{-q(T-t)}$). At time $T-t$, you repay the borrowing at a cost of $Se^{-q(T-t)} \times e^{r(T-t)} = Se^{(r-q)(T-t)}$ and collect the forward price F as per the contract. With no initial outlay, you have locked in a riskless cash flow at time T of $F - Se^{(r-q)(T-t)}$. No-arbitrage arguments mean that this quantity cannot be positive, and it cannot be negative; so, it must be zero. Thus, $F = Se^{(r-q)(T-t)}$ is a fair price for future delivery of the security with known continuous dividend yield q.[18]

With $F = Se^{(r-q)(T-t)}$, the higher the interest rate r on our borrowing, the more expensive it is for us to carry the security through time (on borrowed funds). The higher the dividend yield q, however, the fewer shares we need to buy up front (because dividend reinvestment causes our initial number of stocks to grow). Thus, interest rates increase our cost of carry, and the dividend yield decreases it.[19] If we express the cost of carry as a continuously compounded rate and label it "c," then in our case, $c = r - q$, and $F = Se^{c(T-t)}$. With no dividends, the fair price for forward[20] delivery is simply $F = Se^{r(T-t)}$.

Individual stocks do not pay continuous dividends, but portfolios do (approximately). We see this again when we apply our theory to options on stock market indices in section 8.5.1.

If S is the JPY price of the USD, then $F = Se^{c(T-t)}$ is a fair price for future delivery of the dollar, where $c = r - \rho$, and r and ρ are the continuously compounded Japanese and US riskless rates, respectively.

Note: if S is in units of FX/USD, then $F = Se^{(r_{FX} - r_{US})(T-t)}$ is also in units of FX/USD, and the ordering of the countries whose interest rates appear in the exponent is the same as the ordering of the countries whose currencies appear in the units fraction FX/USD. This is a simple example of "dimensional analysis."

2.5 Other Prerequisites

2.5.1 Equilibrium versus No-Arbitrage

Finance theories derived using "equilibrium arguments" require that the theorist describes supply of the asset to be priced, describes demand of the asset to be priced, assumes that the market is in equilibrium (i.e., that supply equals demand),

---

[18]If the dividend yield is known but varying, the equation is still correct, but with $\bar{q}$ in place of q, where $\bar{q}$ is the average q over the life of the contract.

[19]More generally, the cost of carry includes the following (with signed influence): interest rates (+), storage costs (+), dividends (−), convenience yield (−). "Convenience yield" is the benefit derived from owning a consumption good. A consumption good is one not held primarily for investment purposes (e.g., the grain in the grain silo at the cereal factory, or the oil in the tank at the gas station). Even if the spot price of a consumption good is high relative to the forward price, the holder of the consumption good would not sell it in the spot market and replace it with a long forward—because of the convenience yield. This means that one-half of the no-arbitrage argument collapses and we can have an upper bound only on the forward price of a consumption good: $F \le Se^{c(T-t)}$.

[20]Note that if r is non-stochastic, no-arbitrage arguments imply that the forward price equals the futures price (Cox and Rubinstein [1985, p62]).

and then uses the equality of supply and demand to deduce a fair price for the asset at hand in equilibrium. The Capital Asset Pricing Model (CAPM) is one such example of this—though it is usually expressed in terms of expected rates of return on assets in equilibrium rather than equilibrium prices per se.

"No-arbitrage arguments" are different; they rely upon the absence of arbitrage opportunities to deduce fair prices of assets. For example, in section 2.4.3, we use no-arbitrage arguments to deduce the fair price for future delivery of a forward contract on a security.

Although equilibrium arguments and no-arbitrage arguments are different, they are related. If a market is in equilibrium, then no arbitrage opportunities can exist. That is, equilibrium implies no arbitrage, and any equilibrium model must not admit arbitrage opportunities. The converse is not true. That is, no arbitrage does not imply equilibrium.

The Black-Scholes option pricing model is unusual because it can be derived using either equilibrium arguments or no-arbitrage arguments.

2.5.2 Percent

Sometimes, the obvious needs to be stated explicitly. So, note that "cent" means 100, as in "century" or "centurion," and that "per," in mathematics, means division. It follows that

$$
\begin{aligned}
8\% &= 8 \text{ percent} = 8 \text{ per cent} \\
&= 8 \text{ per } 100 = 8 \div 100 \\
&= \frac{8}{100} = 0.08,
\end{aligned}
$$

and thus that "8%," "eight percent," and "0.08" are perfectly interchangeable representations of exactly the same number.

One percentage point is broken down into 100 smaller units, called "basis points" or "bps" for short, and pronounced "bips" or "beeps." For example, if a mutual fund outperforms the index by $\frac{1}{2}\%$, it has 50 bps of outperformance.

2.5.3 Binomial Coefficients

The binomial coefficient $\binom{K}{k} \equiv \frac{K!}{k!(K-k)!}$ is a ratio of factorials (see the definition of the factorial $k!$ in section 2.1.2). So, for example, $\binom{3}{2} = \frac{3!}{2!1!} = \frac{3 \cdot 2 \cdot 1}{(2 \cdot 1) \cdot 1} = 3$. The binomial coefficient $\binom{3}{2}$ is often read as "three choose two," because $\binom{K}{k}$ counts the number of ways to choose k items from a group of K without regard to order. For example, in the case $K = 3$, and $k = 2$, there are $\binom{3}{2} = 3$ ways to choose two items without regard to order from the group of three items labelled (a, b, c). These three choices are (a, b), (a, c), and (b, c), respectively. The phrase "without regard to order" means that (a, b) and (b, a) are considered to be the same.

Binomial coefficients are seen most frequently in statistics as the coefficient of a probability term when using binomial distributions. Under some limiting conditions,

Table 2.5: Newswire Announcement of a Dividend

```
JUNE 11, 2003 1:30 PM - BEDMINSTER, N.J., Jun 11, 2003
/PRNewswire via COMTEX/ -- AT&T's Board of Directors today
declared a regular dividend of $0.1875 (18.75 cents) per
share, payable August 1, 2003, to AT&T common shareowners
of record on June 30, 2003. Stock price:  open:  19.30,
low 19.29, high 20.52, close 20.50, vol 8,601.600, up $1.20
(6.22%).
```

Note: This table shows a standard newswire announcement of a cash dividend. The declaration date is June 11, 2003; the payment date is August 1, 2003; the record date is Monday, June 30, 2003; the ex-dividend date may be inferred to be four business days before the record date: Tuesday, June 24, 2003. The stock price jumped considerably on the news. (Reproduced with the permission of PR Newswire and AT&T.)

binomial distributions can approximate normal distributions. Normal distributions are used heavily in Black-Scholes option pricing, and binomial coefficients appear naturally in option pricing when binomial distributions are used to approximate normals—see section 8.3.3.

2.5.4 Ex-Dividend Process

As at February 2009,[21] 45.5% of NYSE stocks pay dividends. The numbers are 15.2% for the NYSE Alternext (the old AMEX), 27.3% for the NASDAQ, and only 7.2% for the OTC bulletin board. The average across the NYSE, NYSE Alternext, and NASDAQ combined is 34.8%. These numbers were roughly 50% higher for the NYSE in the 1960s, 1970s, and 1980s, but dividend payment decreased in the 1990s (often replaced by buybacks; see Lynch [2000, p19]). Dividend payment then steadily increased following the Jobs and Growth Tax Relief Reconciliation Act of 2003 (which temporarily reduced the tax rates on dividend income in the US), only to decrease slightly to the reported numbers during the 2007/2008/2009 global credit crisis.

A standard dividend announcement for a US company appears in table 2.5. Whether or not you can claim the most recently declared dividend depends upon when you bought the stock relative to the ex-dividend process described in figure 2.7.

---

[21]I got these numbers by querying dividend yields by exchange using a screening tool at my broker's Web site.

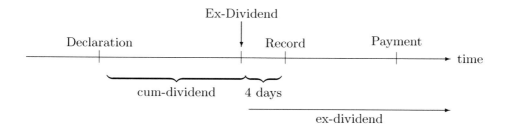

Figure 2.7: US Ex-Dividend Timeline

Note: The board of directors declares the dividend (and it becomes a legal liability of the company) on the "declaration date." The stock then trades "cum-dividend" ("cum" means "with" in Latin); if you buy the stock you will get the dividend. The ex-dividend day is the first day the stock does not trade with the right to the dividend ("ex" means "without" in Latin). The "date of record" is the date upon which official holders of the stock are acknowledged as being rightfully entitled to the recently-declared dividends. If you buy the stock on or after the ex-dividend date, then you are not the holder of record on the date of record. The stock price usually opens lower on the ex-dividend day by some tax-related fraction of the dividend. There are typically four days between the ex-dividend day and the date of record for US individual stocks.

Op Quiz: An equity option contract on the CBOE usually covers one "round lot" of stock. What is a round lot of stock?

Answer: A round lot is 100 shares of stock. Note that sometimes, after a corporate action, the CBOE adjusts the nature of the underlying, and the option contract covers whatever is the new equivalent of what was a round lot, e.g., shares in a merged entity after a merger. A round lot of options is also 100 contracts (usually covering 10,000 shares). The definition of a round lot may differ by security (e.g., five bonds) or by country (e.g., 1,000 shares in New Zealand), or by liquidity (e.g., 10 shares in a thinly traded stock). Contrast this with an "odd lot," which is a parcel of securities smaller than a round lot.

Chapter 3

Option Pricing Foundations

Speculative traders make money in options markets by using options as tools to exploit views about economic factors. For example, you may have a view about the level of an individual stock price, the level of a broad market index, or the volatility of returns in an individual stock. To get from having a view about an economic factor to knowing which option to trade, you need to understand which factors affect option prices, in which direction they affect them, and in what manner (i.e., weakly, strongly, linearly, nonlinearly, etc.).

In this chapter, we identify the factors that affect option prices and the direction of the relationships involved. We then place bounds on the relationships between these underlying factors and the option values. Black-Scholes option pricing must place the price of an option within these bounds, or else there are arbitrage opportunities. These bounds help fuel our economic intuition for the manner in which changes in these factors lead to changes in option prices. This chapter also explores fundamental parity relationships between options.

3.1 Factors Affecting Option Prices

The factors generally regarded as affecting option prices appear in table 3.1. Recall

Table 3.1: Factors Affecting Option Prices

Factors Affecting Option Prices	Notation
Price of Underlying Asset	S
Strike (i.e., Exercise) Price of Option	X
Time to Expiration (i.e., Time to Maturity) of Option	$T - t$
Variance of Returns on Underlying Asset[a]	σ^2
Riskless Interest Rate[b]	r
Present Value of Dividends from t to T	D

[a]This is variance of continuously compounded returns.
[b]This is a continuously compounded interest rate.

that we are using the timeline in figure 2.6 on page 32, that $T - t$ is measured in years, and that r is a rate of return. So, for example, $T - t = 0.50$ for a six-month option, and $r = 0.05$ for a 5% rate of return.

Some factors that affect option prices are not mentioned in table 3.1. There are direct factors like the CFO resigning for accounting fraud, or an envied invention by a competitor, or fears of war. We shall assume that these direct factors influence the option value through one of the factors in table 3.1—lower stock price, higher perceived volatility, etc. There are also indirect factors that are less likely to affect the fair value of the option, but may affect the price you pay. These include low liquidity during pre-holiday periods that results in wider bid-ask spreads, or lack of depth that means your order moves prices against you (i.e., it has "price impact"), and so on. We discuss these factors in chapter 10.

3.2 Payoffs and Payoff Diagrams

Most of our analysis focuses on "plain vanilla" options; i.e., standard calls or puts that are either American style or European style. Anything else is an "exotic option."

The value of a standard call option at maturity is the payoff to the option; this payoff is written as the maximum of two quantities in equation 3.1. For fixed X, the formula in the equation is a function of terminal stock price $S(T)$. If you plot value on the vertical and terminal stock price on the horizontal, you get the kinked payoff diagrams famous in option pricing and illustrated in figure 3.1. Bachelier was the first to publish the kinked payoff diagram to a call (Bachelier [1900, p30]).[1]

$$V_{\text{call}}(T) = \max[S(T) - X, 0] \qquad (3.1)$$

The first quantity in equation 3.1 is $[S(T) - X]$. This is what you get if you exercise at time T and gain the stock by giving up the strike price (hence the implicit "+" in front of the stock price and the explicit "−" in front of the strike). The second quantity in equation 3.1 is zero. Zero is what you get if you let the option expire unexercised at time T. The value of the standard call at maturity is thus the maximum you can gain from choosing between exercising or not exercising the option.

The same arguments lead to the value of the standard put option at maturity as shown in equation 3.2, and plotted in figure 3.1.

$$V_{\text{put}}(T) = \max[X - S(T), 0] \qquad (3.2)$$

An option position decays in value toward its final payoff as expiration approaches, so current value (at time t) is typically a smoothed-out version of final value (at time T). Do not confuse "decay" with "decrease." The decay effect helps you if the current value of your option position is less than the final value would

---

[1]See also Zimmerman and Hafner (2007) for a discussion of the Bronzin option pricing work of 1908.

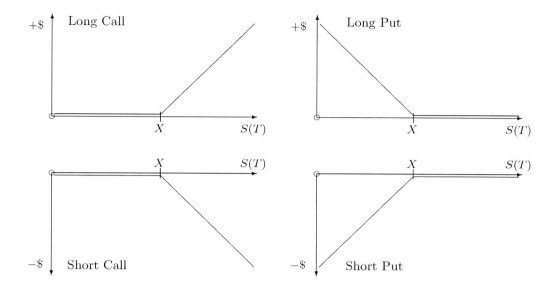

Figure 3.1: Plain Vanilla Options: Terminal Payoffs

Note: These payoff diagrams show the final (i.e., time-T) dollar value of long and short calls and puts (European-style or American-style) as a function of the final value of the underlying; they ignore any initial cash flow and assume the position is held to maturity. These simple payoff diagrams are composed of straight lines connected via kinks. The kinks are caused by the "max" function in equations 3.1 and 3.2, which in turn results from the choices embedded within the option contract. The terminal payoffs to the short positions are nowhere positive—in exchange for the up-front cash flow generated by shorting the option; the converse is true for the long positions. Zero payoffs are drawn as very slightly different from zero, so that they can be seen.

be, given the current level of the underlying (as in the case of a deep in-the-money European-style put—see figure 3.3 on page 59—or a deep in-the-money European-style call on a stock with a high dividend yield—see discussion on page 109).

If an option position includes short American-style options, then the payoff diagram may be misleading. If you are assigned an exercise on the short option, you never reach expiration. Similarly, if an option position includes options of different maturity, then final payoff is an odd concept; and in this case, the plot is not necessarily composed of straight lines with kinks.

I do not like payoff diagrams because they cause considerable confusion. Plotting value at maturity (or value at maturity adjusted by current price) does not tell you what is going on now. Payoff diagrams are useful to the extent that they describe the shape of your payoff as a function of the underlying, and to the extent that you understand that current value (time t) is a smoothed-out version of the final value (time T). They are useful also in that understanding how the plot of value at time t transforms to the plot of value at time T implicitly requires that you understand theta (discussed in section 7.6), but otherwise, I have no use for them.

> **Key Points:** *Equations 3.1 and 3.2 give the option value at maturity as the greater of exercise value and zero. Prior to maturity, the option value is discounted expected payoff. That is, the option value at time $t < T$ is the discounted expected value of equations 3.1 and 3.2. The "intrinsic value" of an option at time t is what it would be worth if someone waved a magic wand and forced the option to expire today. That is, if exercise value is positive, so too is intrinsic value; but if exercise value is negative, intrinsic value is zero. Intrinsic value is $\max[S(t) - X, 0]$ for a call, and $\max[X - S(t), 0]$ for a put.[a] If intrinsic value is positive, the option is "in-the-money"; exercising it today would give you a positive payoff—ignoring T-costs. If $S(t) < X$ for a call or $X < S(t)$ for a put, then intrinsic value is zero, and the option is "out-of-the-money," or "underwater." Even if at time $t < T$ an option is out-of-the-money, the option can still have positive value because the market recognizes that there is a chance that the option will have exercise value at maturity. If "$S(t) \approx X$," the option is "near the money"; and if "$S(t) = X$," the option is "at-the-money." In the latter case, intrinsic value must be zero. Any value in the option over and above intrinsic value is referred to as "time value" or "extrinsic value."[b] The option value prior to maturity is thus the sum of intrinsic value and time value. Equations 3.1 and 3.2 state that time value is zero at expiration; if it is out-of-the-money at time T, then it will never be otherwise. Negative time value is discussed on page 44.*
>
> ---
> [a]Some authors define intrinsic value as $S(t) - X$ for a call. This allows negative intrinsic value, which I think is contrary to the intrinsic nature of options.
>
> [b]"Extrinsic value" is a phrase you are likely to hear only from traders on the floor of an organized exchange.

3.3 Directionally Correct

We need to identify, with as few assumptions as possible, the directional relationships between changes in the factors in table 3.1 and changes in the values of American and European calls and puts. We assume no T-costs, all trading profits are taxed at the same rate, borrowing and lending are available at the riskless interest rate, there is full use of short sale proceeds, and market participants seek out and destroy arbitrage opportunities. We denote European option values as "$c(\cdot)$," and "$p(\cdot)$," and American option values as "$C(\cdot)$," and "$P(\cdot)$." The directional effects are listed in table 3.2.

Note first in table 3.2 that it says *ceteris paribus* in the title; this means "other things being equal." So, for example, in the second to last row we are asking what is the effect on option value of an interest rate rise, holding all other factors fixed. You may think that is a strange question to ask because if interest rates rise, then stock prices are likely to fall, and the effect on option price of a stock price fall is

Table 3.2: Effect of an Increase in the Factor on Equity Option Value

Effect of an Increase in the Factor *ceteris paribus*				
Factor	C	P	c	p
S	↑	↓	↑	↓
X	↓	↑	↓	↑
$T - t$ (low S)	↑	↑	↑[a]	↓[a,b]
$T - t$ (high S)	↑	↑	↑[a]	↑[a]
σ^2	↑	↑	↑	↑
r	↑	↓	↑	↓
D	↓	↑	↓	↑

[a]This assumes $D = 0$.
[b]This requires $r > 0$.

Note: The arrows show the change in value of the indicated option given an increase in the factor defined in table 3.1. Uppercase letters denote American-style options; lowercase letters denote European-style options. For X, the natural comparison is across option series, because X does not change for a given option.

likely to far outweigh the effect on option price caused solely by interest rates rising. Similarly, news of a dividend increase often pushes stock prices up, which in turn increases the value of a call (contrary to the first "↓" in the last row). This is true, but asking these questions holding all else equal allows us to understand individual effects. Combining our knowledge of these individual effects, and understanding how they interact, gives us a full understanding. We now step through each row in table 3.2 to explain the orientation of the arrows.[2]

Stock Price and Strike Price. The first two rows of arrows in table 3.2 seem quite straightforward. For example, the more valuable is the stock, the more valuable is the right to acquire it for a fixed price; and conversely the less valuable is the right to give it up for a fixed price. Thus, higher stock price is good for a long call, and bad for a long put. The opposite applies for strike price: The more you have to give up to acquire the stock, the less valuable is the right to do so, and conversely for a put.

Time to Maturity. Longer time to maturity is unambiguously good for plain vanilla American-style options. For example, everything you can do with a one-month American-style call option you can also do with a two-month American-style call, and you get an extra month of option life in which to do it! The same is true of

---

[2]These results apply only to plain vanilla options. If you have an exotic option, it may have quite different properties. For example, if you hold a "knock-out option" and the underlying is close to the barrier, then higher volatility is almost certainly bad for you.

European-style call options when $D = 0$. In fact, a call having a longer life is much like having higher volatility, because there are more possible outcomes.

The argument for the European-style put differs. If the put option is far out-of-the-money (i.e., stock price is very high), then longer life is good, because it increases the probability that the put option holder will see a positive payoff. If the European put option is deep in-the-money (i.e., stock price is very low), then because there is a lower limit of zero on the stock price, life might not get much better than this for the holder of a European put. Extending the life of the option could lead to many possible outcomes where the stock price is higher and the put payoff is lower. Consider, for example, the case where you hold a put option with a $10 strike price, and the stock has dropped from $12 when you bought the put to only a nickel ($0.05) now. If you could exercise the put now, you would get $9.95. Life does not get much better than this. The last thing you want is for someone to wave a magic wand and extend the life of the option. A European put option this deep in-the-money is valued simply as the present value (PV) of exercise $p(t) = PV[X - S(T)] = Xe^{-r(T-t)} - S(t)$. This is below the exercise value $X - S(t)$. As time passes, and if nothing else changes, the put option value "decays" upward in value to $X - S$. That is, a deep in-the-money European put with value below intrinsic value has negative time value because total value is the sum of intrinsic value and time value.

In theory, a deep in-the-money European put is the only case where you can see a plain vanilla option on a non dividend-paying stock trading below its intrinsic value; we discuss shortly the case of European-style calls trading below intrinsic value in the presence of dividends. In practice, options on individual equities are all American style, and indices have non-zero dividend yields, so there is nowhere to look to see this. In the US in 2003, interest rates were low enough that long-dated deep in-the-money European-style index puts did not trade at a noticeable discount to exercise value. Let us look at some examples and learn some other lessons in the process.

The CBOE has at least two popular European-style index option contracts. They are the SPX contracts on the S&P500 (i.e., on the SPX), and the XEO contracts on the S&P100 (i.e., on the OEX).[3] On May 6, 2003, the December 2004 700 strike XEO put (a LEAP with ticker "XLD XA-E") closed with a quoted bid and ask of 224.80 and 226.80, respectively.[4] The index closed at 472.71, up 3.42 on the day. Using this index value, the option had an intrinsic value of 227.29. On the face of it, the ask of 226.80 looks like a roughly 0.50 discount from exercise value. This may simply be because the put is deep in-the-money and European style. The XEO options close at 3:15PM CST in Chicago, and the NYSE closes at 4:00PM EST in New York. Given the different time zones, these closes are only 15 minutes apart. It is not at all clear, however, that these quotes (pulled from the CBOE Web site) are

---

[3]That is, the underlyings are the SPX and OEX, respectively, but the option base ticker symbols are SPX and XEO, respectively. The older OEX contract on the OEX is the original American-styled one. The newer XEO contracts are European-style ones introduced in mid-2001.

[4]I noticed that almost all the long-dated XEO options had a spread of two points on this day. The quotes must have been generated by an autoquote machine.

from the same 15-minute window of trade on the CBOE. The volume in this XEO option was zero on May 6, and it is possible that the quotes were stale and referred to an earlier point in the day when the index was as high as 475.66.

By 2009, US interest rates had fallen even further (which should raise put prices and decrease the discount from intrinsic value). Deep in-the-money puts should not trade above intrinsic value, so we would expect to see the same or smaller discount when compared with 2003. Sure enough, on February 5, 2009, an \$800-strike December 18, 2010 European-style put option on the XEO (681 days to maturity) was quoted at \$398.80–\$402.10 when the index was at 398.49. The intrinsic value was \$401.51, within the spread.

Note that long-dated deep in-the-money European calls can trade at a discount from intrinsic value if the dividend yield is high enough. For example, on February 5, 2009, a 250-strike December 17, 2011 European-style call option on the SPX was quoted at \$564–\$570 when the index was at 845.85. With interest rates at only 1.3%, and a dividend yield of 3.6%, the value of this call had been pushed down below the intrinsic value of \$595.85. It would take a rise in interest rates, or a drop in dividend yield to push this option's premium above intrinsic value.

Several lessons follow from these examples. First, when pulling quotes, unless done in real time, there is no guarantee that they are coincident. Second, an option need not trade to have a quoted bid and ask. You can have zero volume, but the market maker (or the market maker's autoquote machine) keeps moving the quotes during the day. Third, if you are paper trading, you may wish to do so with prices pulled live, not after the close of trade.[5] Fourth, RTH for index options can differ from those for equity options. Fifth, deep in-the-money European-style puts can trade at a discount to exercise value, but that discount is small when interest rates are low. Sixth, deep in-the-money European-style calls can trade at a discount to exercise value when there are dividends during the life of the call, but that discount is small when dividends are small or when interest rates are large.

Volatility. Higher volatility means a larger spread of possible stock prices at time T. Consider the simple case of a non dividend-paying stock that will be worth either \$90 or \$110 two months from now, each price with a probability of one-half. A call option with a strike of \$100 expiring at time T will thus be worth either zero or \$10 at time T, each price with a probability of one-half. The call option's present value is roughly[6] $(\frac{1}{2} \times \$10) + (\frac{1}{2} \times \$0) = \$5$. Now, suppose instead that returns to investing in the stock are more volatile, and the stock will take values of \$80 and \$120, each with probability of one-half; then a similar calculation yields an option value of \$10. Thus, a greater spread of possible outcomes for the underlying stock is unambiguously good for the holder of a plain vanilla call or put option

---

[5] "Paper trading" is when you keep a log of buys and sells that you would have executed, but you do not actually trade. It is a good way to dip your toes in the water without getting your feet wet.

[6] There is little harm in this simple example at this stage, but note that a formal risk-neutral binomial option pricing valuation can give answers quite different to naive intuition; e.g., see the actual job interview question on page 95 at the end of chapter 6.

because it increases the expected gain from in-the-money payoffs but does not affect out-of-the-money payoffs.

Interest Rates. Higher interest rates decrease the present value of the strike price. Other things being equal, this increases the value of a call because the strike price you potentially give up has lower present value; conversely for a put.[7]

Dividends. Consider two stocks identical in all respects, except that one promises to pay an identically timed but higher dividend than the other at some time between time t and time T. Suppose that there are identically specified European call options written on these two stocks and that they expire at time T. Dividends go to the owner of the stock, not the owner of the call option. Higher dividends mean more cash leaking out of the firm, and this is bad for the future residual value of the firm that the European call option holder has claim to. Thus, the European call on the higher-dividend stock is the less valuable of the pair of options.

How does the ability to exercise early and capture a dividend alter the above argument when we consider an American call? We shall see in section 3.4 that the only time the holder of an American call considers early exercise is just prior to the stock going ex-dividend, and at that time the option has only its exercise value: $S - X$. It follows that there are three distinct cases when applying the identical stock/different dividend argument to American-style calls. First, if the dividends on both stocks are so low that early exercise is optimal in neither case, then the European-style call argument applies. Second, if early exercise is optimal for the call option on the high-dividend stock, but not for the call on the low-dividend stock, then implicitly the call on the low-dividend stock has "time value" over and above the exercise value just prior to the ex-dividend day. Thus, it is more valuable than the call on the high-dividend stock—which is worth only $S - X$ just prior to the ex-dividend day. Third, if early exercise is optimal for options on both stocks, then both options have the same value, $S - X$, just prior to ex-dividend, and thus the options must have the same value at time t.

In summary, higher dividends are unambiguously bad for a European call option, but once they are so high that early exercise is optimal for an American call, then making them even higher no longer reduces the value of the American call.[8] See also the deeper discussion of dividends and early exercise in section 9.1.2.

You may have noticed that when stocks announce higher dividends, this is often treated as good news by shareholders who, upon this announcement, bid up the price of the stock. As already mentioned, this effect is ignored above because of the *ceteris paribus* nature of the argument. Besides, it is not the dividend announcement, per se, that shareholders are reacting to in this case; it is the implicit assurance from

---

[7]See Chance (1994) for insightful elaboration on this and related topics.

[8]Suppose there is exactly one dividend paid on the stock between time t and time T, and that the stock goes ex-dividend immediately after time t_1. Then, if early exercise is optimal, the call value is simply $C(t) = PV[S(t_1) - X] = S(t) - Xe^{r(t_1 - t)}$, which does not depend upon the size of the dividend. Thus, higher dividends no longer reduce call value.

the company that it is doing so well that it can afford to pay and sustain higher dividends.

Ignoring the effect on current stock price of an unexpected increase in future dividends during the life of your call option, call option price, be it American or European, will drop on the news—unless it is an American-style call and anticipated dividends were already so high as to make early exercise optimal (in which case there is no effect). If the announcement of higher dividends is fully anticipated, then there is no change in the value of the option because these dividends are already part of D in table 3.1.[9]

Op Quiz: It is the middle of the trading day on Tuesday, April 29, 2003. Weyerhaeuser Co. (WY) has just traded at $50 per share on the NYSE. October 2003 American-style call and put options on WY with strike price $50 are trading on the CBOE. **Question 1:** Which is more valuable: a round lot of WY or the October call option that gives you the right to buy a round lot of WY stock at $50 per share? **Question 2:** Which is more valuable: 100 times the strike price (i.e., a total of $5,000) or the October put that gives you the right to sell a round lot of WY stock at $50 per share? **Question 3:** Still looking at the $50 strike options, would your answers be different tomorrow if significant news arrives overnight and WY opens at a price dramatically higher or lower than today (say, $80 per share or $30 per share)?

Answer 1: The $50 stock is worth more than the right to buy one share for $50 (the call traded at only $4.20 per share on April 29). **Answer 2:** The $50 strike is worth more than the right to sell one share for $50 (the put traded at only $4 per share on April 29). **Answer 3:** Your answers do not change with stock price—unless stock price drops to zero, at which point the choices are equally valuable.

Looking ahead, tables 3.3 and 3.4 note that $S \geq C$ (R3a), and $X \geq P$ (R13a), respectively.

If the dividend to be paid is "abnormal," e.g., a dividend per share above 10 percent of the stock price, then the options exchange adjusts the option contract so that it covers more shares of stock (or shares of stock plus cash equivalent to the dividend) in an attempt to indemnify the option holder.

The dividend-related argument for put options is easier than for calls. Higher dividends are not an incentive for early exercise of a put (see section 3.5). Thus, we need only consider the European case, in which higher dividends are unambiguously good for a put.

---

[9]Dividend payments on individual US stocks are predictable. Companies manage dividend payments just as they manage earnings, so that there are few surprises. A naive model that uses the timing and quantity of last year's quarterly dividend to forecast this year's is quite accurate. Lintner (1956) is an excellent dividend policy article.

3.4 Call Options: Restrictions

In addition to the directional results of section 3.3, we present in this section and in section 3.5 some important economic restrictions on call and put option values. These restrictions and directional results give us a rough feel for where option prices must lie, and how they must respond to changing factors. Black-Scholes option pricing serves exactly the same purpose: the Black-Scholes formula locates an option price, and the functional form of the formula tells how that price responds to changing factors that are inputs to the formula. Indeed, we shall see that, where appropriate, the Black-Scholes formula satisfies each of the restrictions in this section and section 3.5, and that it complies with the directional results in section 3.3.[10]

These simple restrictions also allow us to explore the early exercise decision. Let me state the obvious by noting that "early exercise" is a decision that applies only to American-style options. It is never discussed in the context of European-style options because they cannot be exercised prior to maturity. Thus, early exercise is not an issue in Black-Scholes pricing, but it creates important caveats for any trade you do that contains short American-style options—see chapter 10 for details.

Let "$C(S, T, X)$" denote the time-t value of an American call recognizing explicitly the dependence of C on S, T, and X. Ten restrictions on call values are presented: R1–R7 in table 3.3 and an additional three, R8–R10. If you find the notation in the table daunting, then go directly to the discussion in section 3.4.1, and correlate the discussion there with the notation in table 3.3.

Table 3.3: Restrictions on European and American Call Values

	Restrictions on Call Values
R1	$C(0, T, X) = 0$
R2	$C(S, T, X) \geq \max(0, S - X)$
R3	$S \geq_a C(S, T, X) \geq_b c(S, T, X) \geq_c \max(0, S - Xe^{-r(T-t)} - D) \geq_d 0$
R4	$[D = 0, r > 0] \Rightarrow [C(S, T, X) = c(S, T, X)]$
R5	$[X_1 < X_2] \Rightarrow [(X_2 - X_1) \geq C(S, T, X_1) - C(S, T, X_2)]$
R6	$[X_1 < X_2 < X_3] \Rightarrow [C(X_2) \leq \lambda \cdot C(X_1) + (1 - \lambda) \cdot C(X_3)]; \lambda = \frac{X_3 - X_2}{X_3 - X_1}$
R7	$[S_1 < S_2 < S_3] \Rightarrow [C(S_2) \leq \lambda \cdot C(S_1) + (1 - \lambda) \cdot C(S_3)]; \lambda = \frac{S_3 - S_2}{S_3 - S_1}$

Note: "$C(S, T, X)$" and "$c(S, T, X)$" denote the time-t value of American-style and European-style call options recognizing explicitly their dependence on stock price, expiration date, and strike price. These restrictions are discussed in section 3.4.1.

[10]Note that, strictly speaking, Black-Scholes option pricing applies only to European-style call and put options on stocks that do not pay dividends. Thus, only some of the directional results of section 3.3 and some of the restrictions in sections 3.4 and 3.5 apply. In each of these cases, the Black-Scholes formula is compliant.

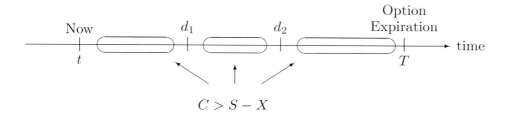

Figure 3.2: American Call Option Life with Dividends (Restriction R8)

Note: This underlying stock pays two dividends, d_1 and d_2, during the option's life (see section 2.5.4 for more details on the ex-dividend process). Away from the ex-dividend and expiration dates, the American call option takes value strictly greater than the exercise value of the option. Sale of the option dominates exercise during these periods. If there are no dividends, then the three "bubbles" become one long bubble, $C > S - X$ everywhere, and early exercise is never optimal.

- R8. If $r > 0$, call value (C, or c) must be strictly greater than $(S - X)$ at any time other than the expiration date or just before an ex-dividend date (see figure 3.2). Thus, early exercise of an American call option is never optimal unless it is just prior to an ex-dividend date (and in this case call value equals $S - X$). Ignoring T-costs, $C = S - X$ implies that you are indifferent between exercise and sale of the call;[11] otherwise, sale is preferable to exercise. In practice, it usually does not pay to exercise a listed call early, and if it does pay, the optimal time is almost always just before the last ex-dividend date during the life of the option (Cox and Rubinstein [1985, p144]; Hull [2000, pp259-261]). If there are no dividends, then $C > S - X$ at all times prior to maturity and early exercise is never optimal (Restriction R4). You do not need a non dividend-paying stock for this to hold; it is true for an option on a dividend-paying stock as long as the stock pays no dividends during the life of the option.

- R9. With $r > 0$, if the present value of the dividends to be paid during the remaining life of a call option will, at every point in time, be exceeded by the present value of the interest that can be earned on the strike during the remaining life of the call option, then it will not be optimal to exercise the call before expiration (Cox and Rubinstein [1985, p140]).

- R10. If it is optimal to exercise a call, then it is also optimal to exercise any otherwise identical call with a lower strike price, or a shorter time to maturity (Cox and Rubinstein [1985, p140]).

---

[11]...and it is a good thing they have designated market makers on the CBOE because who else will buy it if it is about to drop in value.

American calls differ from American puts in that they have unlimited upside potential. This means that there is always a benefit to waiting to exercise a call. Only if a dividend is about to be "lost" might this cost outweigh the benefit of waiting—see the summary in table 3.5 on page 54.

3.4.1 Demonstration and Discussion of Call Restrictions

When reading this section, refer to restrictions R1–R10 in section 3.4. Most of these restrictions can be demonstrated by both an informal economic intuition argument and a formal no-arbitrage argument; I choose whichever seems most appropriate.

- R1 says simply that the American call's right to buy a worthless asset is worthless. Implicit within this is that zero is an "absorbing barrier" for asset value. That is, once asset value hits zero, it never escapes from that level; i.e., the stock price cannot bounce back and reach the strike price before maturity.

- R2 gives an American call price a lower boundary of the greater of zero (because of limited liability of the call) or exercise value (because of threat of exercise).

- R3b says an American call is always worth at least what a European call is worth (because the American call is more versatile).

- R3a and R3b say a call is never worth more than the underlying (otherwise short sell the call, buy the stock, pocket the difference, and deliver the stock if it is called from you).[12]

- R3c gives a lower boundary for a European call: the greater of zero (limited liability of the call) or stock price less PV of strike less PV of dividends. If not, then buy the call, short sell the stock, lend the PV of the strike, and invest the PV of the dividends; liquidate the dividends portion of your investment as needed to pay out the dividend obligation on the short stock, and at expiration you have a positive amount whether the option is in or out-of-the-money. Note that R3d is true by definition when one argument of the max function is zero.

- R4 says that with no dividends, and with positive interest rates, the American call is worth the same as the European call (R3b already says it is not worth less). This follows from R8: away from any dividends, and prior to maturity, you must have $C > S - X$, so you would rather sell the American-style call option than exercise it early. It follows that without any dividends, the American right to exercise early is worthless, and American and European calls must have the same value.

- If R5 does not hold, enter a vertical spread (buy a call struck at $X2$, sell a call struck at $X1$, invest $X2 - X1$, pocket the difference, and you are covered if the short call is exercised). A tighter bound holds if the options are European: $e^{-r(T-t)}(X_2 - X_1) \geq [c(X_1) - c(X_2)]$.

---

[12]Note that restriction 3a implicitly depends upon the non-negativity of the price of the underlying. So, this is a sensible restriction for a GBM, but makes no sense for an ABM. See page 112.

- R6 and R7 say simply that call prices are convex in strike and in current stock price. These are here for completeness, and are not as important to us as the other restrictions. R6 can be proved via counterexample and no-arbitrage arguments, and this is best understood with a picture. For completeness, note that R7 is not enforced by no arbitrage, and could, for example, be violated under some pathological dividend policies; however, it is an empirical fact (Cox and Rubinstein [1985, pp156–157]).

- R8 says that $C > S - X$ away from ex-dividend dates (see figure 3.2). If not, then either $C = S - X$, or $C < S - X$. In the first case, if $C = S - X$, then $S = C + X$, so you can short sell the stock and use the proceeds to buy the call and invest the remainder, X, in a deposit account earning interest. If your broker calls the stock back, then exercise the call using the face value of the deposit account and pocket the interest earned; otherwise, do so when the next ex-dividend date arrives and pocket the interest. In the second case, if $C < S - X$, this is contrary to R2.

- R9 and R10 seem sufficiently reasonable, so I do not provide a formal demonstration.

You might think these restrictions are undermined because the arguments used to establish them are unrealistic. For example, you cannot borrow and lend at the same riskless rate in the US, the typical investor does not get full use of short sale proceeds, and many market participants cannot trade without incurring commissions and bid-ask spread costs. There are, however, two important real-world points to make here. The first point is that many trading costs (excluding spreads) are relatively low, even for the average investor, and especially in large volume when those costs are prorated. The second point is that market prices are determined "at the margin"; that is, the marginal trader (i.e., the next person to trade) is the one who moves prices. The marginal trader is often an institutional trader and institutional traders often have low, no, or even negative costs to trade and can negotiate full use of short sale proceeds.[13] So, while the individual investor might sit back and do nothing about a small but blatant violation of restrictions R1–R10, the institutional trader with sophisticated computerized trading systems can pounce on it before you can snap your fingers.[14] The net result is that, in practice, it is unusual to find genuine violations of R1–R10 other than very small ones that last no more than a few seconds.

[13] How can institutional traders have a negative marginal cost of trade? They can do so by buying a seat on the exchange and acting as a market maker so that they can collect, rather than pay, half the spread when they want to trade.

[14] I spoke to a former student working for a Chicago trading firm. He said that he stood on the floor in one pit wearing a headset. A colleague stood in another pit also wearing a headset and trading a related but different-sized contract. Another colleague monitored both pits remotely. When a price discrepancy appeared, the remote colleague instructed one to buy and one to sell in appropriate quantity. I asked my former student how long they had to get the arb trade off before a competitor would beat them to it; he snapped his fingers in reply.

Table 3.4: Restrictions on European and American Put Values

	Restrictions on Put Values
R11	$P(0, T, X) = X$
R12	$P(S, T, X) \geq \max(0, X - S)$
R13	$X \geq_a P(S, T, X) \geq_b p(S, T, X) \geq_c \max(0, D + Xe^{-r(T-t)} - S) \geq_d 0$
R14	$[r > 0] \Rightarrow [P(S, T, X) > p(S, T, X)]$
R15	$[X_1 < X_2] \Rightarrow [(X_2 - X_1) \geq P(S, T, X_2) - P(S, T, X_1)]$
R16	$[X_1 < X_2 < X_3] \Rightarrow [P(X_2) \leq \lambda \cdot P(X_1) + (1 - \lambda) \cdot P(X_3)]; \ \lambda = \frac{X_3 - X_2}{X_3 - X_1}$
R17	$[S_1 < S_2 < S_3] \Rightarrow [P(S_2) \leq \lambda \cdot P(S_1) + (1 - \lambda) \cdot P(S_3)]; \ \lambda = \frac{S_3 - S_2}{S_3 - S_1}$

Note: "$P(S, T, X)$" and "$p(S, T, X)$" denote the time-t value of American-style and European-style put options, recognizing explicitly their dependence on stock price, expiration date, and strike price. These restrictions are discussed in section 3.5.1.

3.5 Put Options: Restrictions

Let "$P(S, T, X)$" denote the time-t value of an American put, recognizing explicitly the dependence of P on S, T, and X. Nine restrictions on put values are presented: R11–R17 in table 3.4 and an additional two, R18–R19, following. These restrictions are demonstrated and discussed in section 3.5.1.

- R18. With $r > 0$, if there is some future time τ prior to maturity of a put option, and if during the period ending at time τ the present value of the dividends to be paid over this period will at all times exceed the concurrent present value of the interest that can be earned on the strike price during the same period, then the put should not be exercised before time τ (Cox and Rubinstein [1985, p147]).

- R19. If it is optimal to exercise a put, then it also optimal to exercise any otherwise identical put with a higher strike price, or a shorter time to maturity (Cox and Rubinstein [1985, p147]).

We cannot say, as we did for a call, that early exercise of an American put should be considered at only a few specific times. In fact, such a conclusion is not true at all. Suppose investor P is long an American put and long the stock. Suppose investor C is long an American call and has the strike in a bank account earning interest. Investor C has one factor that encourages early exercise (receiving the dividend) and two that discourage it (losing the interest that could be earned on the strike and losing the opportunity to change his or her mind later about exercising). Since exercise of a call just prior to the ex-dividend date is sufficient to receive the dividend, there is no reason to consider incurring losses at any other time. If investor P exercises early, he or she gains the interest that can be earned on the strike, but forgoes the opportunity to change his or her mind about exercising and loses the dividends that would have been earned had he or she waited. The factor encouraging early exercise of the American put is in effect at all times, not on just a few dates as with the call. Thus, early exercise of an American put may in general be optimal at any time. This difficult result is why an exact analytical pricing formula for an American put is an unsolved problem.

3.5.1 Demonstration and Discussion of Put Restrictions

- R11 says the right to sell a worthless asset is worth the strike you get (you would exercise immediately because the stock will never be worth less).

- R12 gives an American put price a lower boundary: the greater of zero (limited liability of the put) or exercise value (threat of exercise).

- R14 says that if interest rates are positive, an American put is always more than a European put (because it is more versatile).

- R13a and R13b say a put is never worth more than the strike (otherwise, sell the put, invest X of the proceeds and pocket the rest; you are covered if the stock is put to you at X).

- R13c gives a lower boundary for a European put: the greater of zero (limited liability of the put) or PV of strike less stock price plus PV of dividends. If not, borrow the PV of the dividends plus the PV of the strike, buy the put, buy the stock, and pocket the remainder. Use the stock dividends to repay the borrowed PV of dividends, and wait until maturity. If the stock is worth more than the strike at maturity, sell the stock, pay back the borrowing, and pocket the difference. Otherwise exercise the put and pay back the borrowing; either way you are covered. Note that R13d is true by definition when one argument of the max function is zero.

- If R15 does not hold, enter a vertical spread (buy put stuck at $X1$, sell put struck at $X2$, invest $X2 - X1$, pocket the difference, and you are covered if the short put is exercised).

- R16 and R17 say simply that put prices are convex in strike and in current stock price (R16 can be proved via counterexample and no-arbitrage arguments)—best understood with a picture. For completeness, note that R17 is not enforced by no arbitrage, and could be violated under some pathological dividend policies, however, it is an empirical fact (Cox and Rubinstein [1985, pp156–157]).

Table 3.5: Early Exercise Decision: Summary

	American Call + Strike	American Put + Stock
Costs of Early Exercise	Lose Interest on Strike "Regrets" if $S \downarrow$	Lose Dividends "Regrets" if $S \uparrow$
Benefits of Early Exercise	Dividend Capture (Occasional Benefit)	Earn Interest on Strike (Always Available)
When to Exercise Early	Big Dividend Due Close to Maturity Just Prior to Ex-Div Date	Small Dividends Remaining Far from Maturity Deep In-The-Money

Note: The correct comparison (see put-call parity discussion in section 3.6) is between someone holding an American-style call plus the strike price versus someone holding an American-style put plus the stock. I assume here that you flip from holding one position to holding what you get when you exercise; so, for example, if you exercise the call, you hold onto the stock so received. The benefit to early exercise always exists for the American-style put; that is why exact analytical American-style put pricing is an as yet unsolved problem, and approximate analytical techniques or numerical techniques must be used. If you exercise an American call and give up the strike in exchange for the stock, you may have "regrets" if the stock subsequently falls. These regrets, and those for the analogous American put case, are quantified explicitly in section 3.6.5 via put-call parity.

3.6 Put-Call Parity

When the CBOE opened in April 1973, call option contracts were listed on 16 stocks, but puts did not appear until 1977 (source: www.cboe.com).[15] Why did the CBOE introduce calls but not puts? It was partly to focus trade in as few contracts as possible, thereby providing liquidity, but it was also because it is possible to manufacture a put via "put-call parity" by using a call, the stock, and some borrowing or lending.

European-style put-call parity is an equality for same-strike options of the same maturity (Stoll [1969]); it is given in equation 3.3:

$$S + p - D = c + Xe^{-r(T-t)} \tag{3.3}$$

Recall that D in the equation is the present value of dividends to be paid during the life of the option. Thus, if no dividends are due during the life of the option, D drops out and the equation becomes $S + p = c + Xe^{-r(T-t)}$. I read this version as *Having the stock together with the right to sell the stock is equivalent to having the right to buy the stock together with enough money to exercise that right.*

---

[15]Before 1973, and for some time afterward, the members of the Put and Call Brokers and Dealers Association traded calls and puts off the exchange floor in an illiquid "over-the-counter" market. I think options traded informally on the precursor to the NYSE as far back as 200 years ago, but it is difficult to confirm this.

Equation 3.3 can be proved as follows: At time t, buy the stock and the European put and borrow the present value of the dividends (repaying this borrowing as the dividends are received). The cost is $S(t) + p(t) - D$. The payoff at time T is $S(T) + \max[0, X - S(T)]$. If instead you buy the European call and invest the present value of the strike, the cost is $c(t) + Xe^{-r(T-t)}$, and the payoff at time T is $\max[0, S(T) - X] + X$. These payoffs are identical.[16] With identical payoffs, a no-arbitrage argument asserts that the initial costs must also be the same. That is, equation 3.3 must hold.

European-style put-call parity is a no-arbitrage relationship. Like many such relationships, it is not a theory of pricing *per se*, but a theory of *relative* pricing. It does not tell us how to price any asset in terms of less complicated assets' prices. In this respect, put-call parity differs from Black-Scholes pricing which, although also a no-arbitrage relationship, gives an option price in terms of less complicated economic statistics. Put-call parity does, however, have many uses as discussed in sections 3.6.1–3.6.6, following.

> **Exercise:** Look ahead to equations 8.17 and 8.18 (p120) and confirm that the Black-Scholes put and call formulae satisfy European put-call parity (i.e., equation 3.3).

3.6.1 Synthetic Instruments and Arbitrage

European-style put-call parity shows us how to construct one instrument from others. For example, rearranging equation 3.3 to read $p = -S + c + Xe^{-r(T-t)} + D$, we see that a long put can be constructed by shorting the stock and using the proceeds to buy a call, while investing the balance in riskless bonds with value equal to the present value of the strike plus the present value of the dividends. The latter is liquidated as the short stock's dividends come due. Unwinding the position at time T produces exactly the same payoff as owning a put.

It follows that you may use put-call parity to design arbitrage strategies that take advantage of deviations from put-call parity. This is not for the novice: If you see an apparent deviation from put-call parity, then either your quotes are stale, or someone else just beat you to the trade, or there is a big corporate action in progress that you do not know about. A novice will not profit from such a strategy.

3.6.2 Leverage and Insurance

Assume our stock pays no dividends during the life of the options. Then equation 3.3 becomes $S + p = c + Xe^{-r(T-t)}$. If we rearrange this to make c the focus, it reads $c = S + p - Xe^{-r(T-t)}$. Thus, you can construct a call by buying the stock, buying a put, and borrowing the present value of the strike price. Buying a stock together with borrowing equates to buying a stock on margin (i.e., a levered stock position).

---

[16] Use the rule $\max(a, b) + c = \max(a + c, b + c)$ to demonstrate this to yourself if it is not already clear.

Buying a put provides downside protection if you own the stock (as per the protective put example in section 1.3.1). We can thus rearrange European-style put call parity in the absence of dividends to arrive at equation 3.4:

$$c = \underbrace{[S - Xe^{-r(T-t)}]}_{\text{levered stock}} + \underbrace{p}_{\text{insurance}} \qquad (3.4)$$

At the risk of repetition, the first component, $[S - Xe^{-r(T-t)}]$, represents stock ownership partially funded by a theoretical borrowing equal to the present value of the strike. For example, if $S = X = \$100$, $r = 0.03$, and $T - t = 0.5$ (a six-month at-the-money option on a $100 stock), then $[S - Xe^{-r(T-t)}] = \$100 - \$100e^{-0.03 \times 0.50} \approx \$1.49$. If $\sigma = 0.30$, then the Black-Scholes value of the put is approximately \$7.53; and the call, as the sum of these parts, is worth a total of \$9.02. The insurance portion of equation 3.4 is affected by volatility; the levered stock position is not.

> **Key Point:** Equation 3.4 describes three key characteristics of options. First, leverage. Second, a floor on your downside. Third, implicitly, because insurance policies are always for a fixed term and usually for one year or less, a limited lifespan. Another key characteristic of options is that T-costs are high relative to those in stocks—see section 10.1.4.

If the stock price is so low that $[S - Xe^{-r(T-t)}]$ is negative ($S = \$98.50$ is sufficiently low using the numbers given immediately above), then the borrowing fully funds the stock purchase and also funds a portion of the price of the put (the remaining unfunded portion being the price of the call). In this case, the put price is of greater magnitude but opposite sign to $[S - Xe^{-r(T-t)}]$, and the excess of put price over $|S - Xe^{-r(T-t)}|$ is the value of the call. If $[S - Xe^{-r(T-t)}] = 0$, then the borrowing exactly funds purchase of the stock, and the put and call prices are identical.

Look at equation 3.4. For a fixed strike, X, and for S high enough that $c > 0$, the higher the stock price, the higher is $[S - Xe^{-r(T-t)}]$, the lower is p, and the higher is c. Therefore, S grows more quickly in absolute dollar terms than p falls when S rises. Conversely, for a fixed strike, X, and for S high enough that $c > 0$, the lower the stock price, the lower is $[S - Xe^{-r(T-t)}]$ (turning quickly negative), the higher is the value of the insurance p, and the lower is c. Therefore, S falls more quickly than p rises for high and falling S (again, all in absolute dollar terms). Other things being equal (except changing S), higher S means a less levered call; lower S means a more levered call. The opposite is true for a put.

The payoff function to a call option is the familiar kinked payoff diagram that is flat for low stock prices then rises, as in figure 3.1 on page 41. The reason the payoff diagram is flat for low stock prices is that, as demonstrated in equation 3.4, a call owner holds insurance that provides downside protection in the form of a protective put. That is, when the stock price falls, the put takes on sufficient value to offset the drop in the value of the levered stock position; but, as mentioned in the previous paragraph, the rise in the value of the put is less than or equal to the drop in the value of the levered stock position. So, the call falls in value, down to, but not below, zero.

Op Quiz: Suppose that you are absolutely certain that a particular stock's price is going to rise significantly over the next two months. How do you profit from this using options?

Answer: The naive answer is to buy a call. However, buying a call is the same as a levered investment in the stock plus the downside protection of a put (equation 3.4):

$$c = \underbrace{[S - Xe^{-r(T-t)}]}_{\text{levered stock}} + \underbrace{p}_{\text{insurance}}$$

If you are absolutely certain, why pay for the insurance? Either buy stock with borrowed money, or buy calls and sell puts.

3.6.3   Plotting Put-Call Parity

The present (i.e., time-t) and terminal (i.e., time-T) values of a European call option are plotted as a function of S in the upper panel of figure 3.3 on page 59, assuming that $D = 0$. The present value of the call option increases as stock price increases and approaches an asymptote that is parallel to, but slightly higher than, the in-the-money terminal value of the option.[17] The terminal value of the option is the same as the intrinsic value, so the excess of present value over terminal value is the time value.

Put-call parity can be seen on figures 3.4 and 3.5 (pages 60 and 61) if we look at it from a Cartesian geometry standpoint. The plot of c against S has c on the "y-axis" and S on the "x-axis." The terminal value of the option runs along the line $c = 0$ from $S = 0$ to $S = X$, and then rises along the line $c = S - X$ (i.e., $c = 1 \times S + [-X]$; a line of slope 1 and intercept $-X$ in the S-c plane).

The present value of the option is a smooth curve rising from $c = 0$ when $S = 0$ (this is restriction R1) up to meet an asymptote which is the line with equation $c = S - e^{-r(T-t)}X$ (i.e., $c = 1 \times S + [-Xe^{-r(T-t)}]$; a line of slope 1 and intercept $-Xe^{-r(T-t)}$ in the S-c plane). The present value of the option is thus bounded below by $c = 0$ for $S \leq X$ and bounded below by $c = S - e^{-r(T-t)}X$ for $S \geq X$. This is simply a restatement of restriction R3c: $c(S, T, X) \geq \max(0, S - Xe^{-r(T-t)} - D)$, with $D = 0$. The difference between the call value and the asymptote $c = S - e^{-r(T-t)}X$ is given by $c - S + e^{-r(T-t)}X$. Put-call parity, however, tells us that this difference is the value of the put.

In summary, then, the call value is asymptotic to the line $c = S - e^{-r(T-t)}X$. The call value is above this asymptote by a distance equal to the value of the same-strike put with the same maturity. The line $c = S - X$ is below this asymptote by a distance equal to $[X - Xe^{-r(T-t)}]$; i.e., the benefit of delaying call exercise (see section 3.6.5

---

[17]A curve is "asymptotic" to a line known as an asymptote if the curve gets closer and closer to the line as you move along the graph. For example, $y = \frac{1}{x}$, for $x > 0$ is asymptotic to the line $y = 0$ as $x \to \infty$ and asymptotic to the line $x = 0$ as $y \to \infty$.

for further details). These statements are true over the full range of S. So, when $S = 0$, for example, then c is above $S - e^{-r(T-t)}X = -e^{-r(T-t)}X = -PV(X)$ by a distance equal to $p = e^{-r(T-t)}X - S = e^{-r(T-t)}X = PV(X)$. Indeed, this can be seen clearly in figure 3.5.

Let me emphasize that the algebraic manipulations in this section are not only an academic exercise. It is important that you understand how the value of an option is broken down into these component parts, how the parts relate to put-call parity, and how these parts both take and lose value with changes in S and other variables.

Op Quiz: What happens to the plots of option value in figure 3.3 if r, σ, $(T - t)$, or D rises? What if they fall?

Answer: See table 3.2 (p43) for simple directional results. For example, higher volatility, σ, raises the plot of call value. The effect is most pronounced for near-the-money options—where higher volatility lifts the plot and convexity (i.e., curvature) decreases. Away-from-the-money call options, however, change little with changing volatility. I encourage you to download the spreadsheet Greeks tool mentioned in section 10.3 to explore these results.

3.6.4 American-Style Put-Call Parity

American put-call parity is a pair of inequalities for same-strike options of the same maturity as shown in equations 3.5 and 3.6:

$$P + S - D \leq C + X \tag{3.5}$$

$$\text{and} \quad C + Xe^{-r(T-t)} \leq P + S \tag{3.6}$$

If equation 3.5 does not hold, then $P + S - D > C + X$; so, $P + S > D + C + X$. Therefore, to generate an arbitrage profit you should short the put and the stock and use the more than adequate proceeds to buy the call, invest the strike, and invest the present value, D, of the dividends. Now, pocket the excess and hold, using the dividend-sized investment to pay off the dividends on the short stock as they come due. If the short put is exercised and you are assigned the stock,[18] then deliver the stock to your broker to cover the short stock, give the strike to the put holder, sell off the call and then liquidate the remaining dividend-sized investment, putting arbitrage-earned money in your pocket.[19]

If equation 3.6 does not hold, then $C + Xe^{-r(T-t)} > P + S$. So, sell the call, borrow the PV of the strike, buy the put and the stock, and pocket the excess. If you are assigned an exercise on the call before maturity, then deliver the stock and

---

[18]If you are short an option and someone who is long exercises, then you may be "assigned the exercise." That is, you are forced to buy the stock at the strike if it is a put, and forced to sell the stock at the strike if it is a call.

[19]This proof assumes that your broker cannot ask you to cover your short stock, or at least if you are asked to cover, you can roll over.

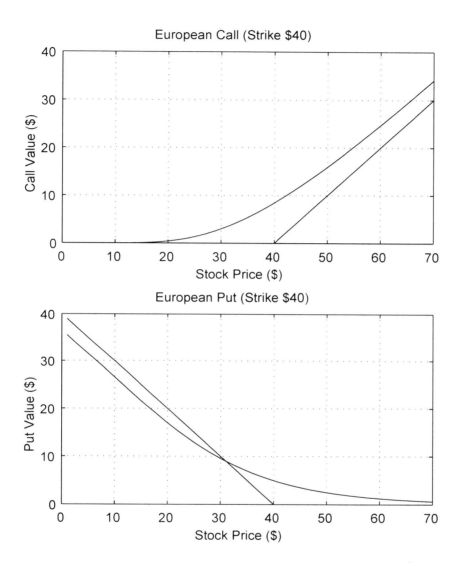

Figure 3.3: European Call and Put Values versus Underlying—No Dividends

Note: The figure shows Black-Scholes call and put prices prior to maturity (smooth curve) and at maturity (kinked curve) as a function of stock price, other things being equal, assuming $r = 0.12$, $X = 40$, $T - t = 0.75$, $D = 0$, and $\sigma = 0.50$. The deep in-the-money European put has value below exercise value. The comparable American put is worth at least the exercise value. The case of the call is explored further in figures 3.4 and 3.5.

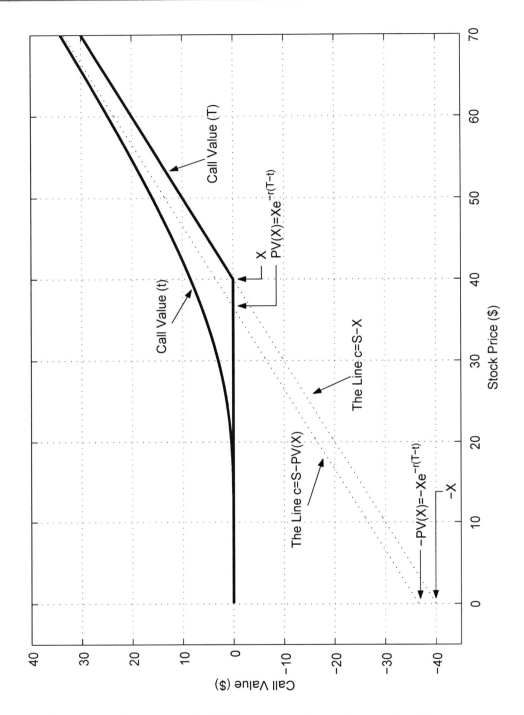

Figure 3.4: European Call Value versus Underlying—No Dividends

Note: We can see that the call value is asymptotic to the line $c = S - PV(X)$ as S gets large. For comparison, you should download the spreadsheet Greeks tool (see p183 for details), and see how this asymptotic behavior changes as you increase the dividend yield on the stock.

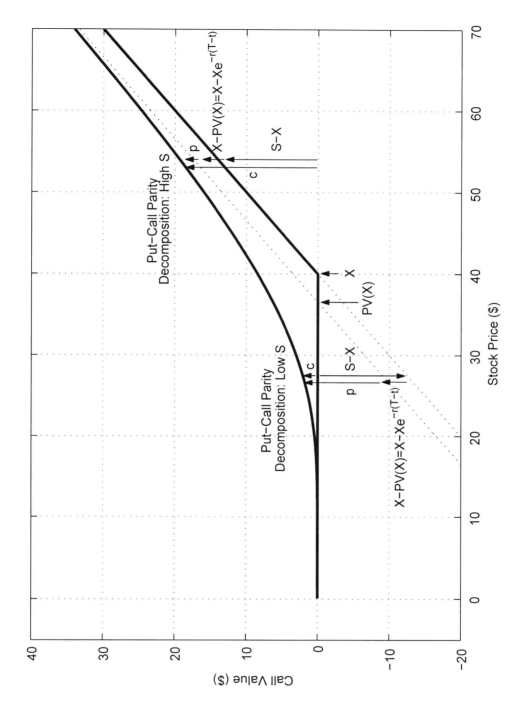

Figure 3.5: European Put-Call Parity Decomposition: Call, $D = 0$

Note: The exercise on page 65 asks you to draw an analogous figure to this, and also to figure 3.4, for a put. You should be able to infer all you need from the information in this figure.

receive the strike, which is more than enough to pay off the borrowing. You still have the put, which you can also sell. You pocketed the initial excess, the excess of strike over borrowing, and the put proceeds—an arbitrage. If you are assigned an exercise at maturity, then unwind in exactly the same way; but the strike covers the debt exactly with no excess, and this is still an arbitrage.

We cannot derive an equality for American put-call parity because one-half of the arbitrage argument breaks down. For example, if C is very high relative to P in equation 3.5 (strict inequality), you cannot generate an arbitrage by shorting the call, borrowing the strike, borrowing the present value of the dividends, and using the proceeds to buy the put and the stock. The reason is that if you are assigned an exercise on the short call, although you have the stock to deliver, the receipt of the strike combined with liquidation of the put will not necessarily cover your borrowing. A similar argument applies to equation 3.6. Suppose the equation holds with strict inequality and you short the put and stock, using the proceeds to buy a call plus invest the present value of the strike. If you are assigned an exercise on the short put, then the receipt of the stock can be used to cover your short stock, but the present value of the strike together with the liquidation value of the call will not necessarily suffice to pay the strike—and that is even ignoring that you need to meet dividends on the short stock in the interim.

This breakdown in one-half of the arbitrage argument is analogous to the trading breakdown discussed in chapter 10 (see p174) when a short position is removed from your portfolio against your wishes, but differs from the breakdown in the arbitrage argument we saw when trying to derive the forward price for a consumption commodity (see footnote 19 on page 34).[20]

3.6.5 Put-Call Parity "Regrets" Decompositions

I want to quantify explicitly the word "regrets" used in the early exercise summary in table 3.5 on page 54. As mentioned in the caption for that table, I assume you hold onto the position that you acquire when you exercise.

Suppose you hold an American-style call option on a stock that does not pay dividends during the life of the option. Then $C = c$ by restriction R4, we can exploit the European-style put-call parity breakdown of call value given in section 3.6.2, and we can both add and subtract X as shown in equation 3.7.

$$
\begin{aligned}
[D = 0, r > 0] \Rightarrow C &= c = [S - PV(X)] + p \\
&= [S - X] + [X - PV(X)] + p
\end{aligned}
\tag{3.7}
$$

I now take the decomposition in equation 3.7 and label it explicitly in equation 3.8,

---

[20]The consumption commodity argument breaks down because high cash prices do not induce people to sell consumption commodities held in inventory for purposes of production. The American-style put-call parity arbitrage argument breaks down, however, because you cannot rely upon an argument that requires you to hold a short American-style option for any length of time.

not forgetting that it assumes $D = 0$, and $r > 0$:

$$C = \underbrace{[S - X]}_{\text{exercise}} + \underbrace{\underbrace{[X - Xe^{-r(T-t)}]}_{\text{delaying call exercise}} + \underbrace{p}_{\text{insurance}}}_{\text{time value or extrinsic value (if } S > X)} \tag{3.8}$$

We see in equation 3.8 that the value of an American call (ignoring dividends) can be broken down into three components. The first, labelled "exercise," is what you get if you pull the trigger and exercise right now (and it is negative if the option is out-of-the-money). To understand the second term, labelled "delaying call exercise," note that if you exercise at time t, rather than at maturity, you have an outflow of X now instead of an outflow of X at time T. That is, you give up something of value X rather than giving up something of present value $Xe^{-r(T-t)}$. The cost of doing this is $[Xe^{-r(T-t)} - X]$. The benefit of not doing it, and of delaying call exercise, is the exact opposite, $[X - Xe^{-r(T-t)}]$, as in equation 3.8. The final term, p, is the same protective put insurance term we saw in section 3.6.2.

The second and third terms in equation 3.8 are non-negative, and usually positive. If the option is in-the-money, and you exercise early, you get only the first term, and you throw away the time value, or extrinsic value, described in the second and third terms. That is, you lose the interest you would have gained on the strike by delaying call exercise, and you lose your downside protection (these are the two costs to early exercise of a call listed in table 3.5 on page 54). If the stock subsequently falls, then you have regrets because your naked stock position no longer has downside protection. That is, the financial value of those regrets is simply the value of the put that protects your levered stock position from bearish moves.

In the case where there are dividends and $r > 0$, equation 3.8 still applies away from ex-dividend dates. Just prior to ex-dividend dates, however, either it is optimal to exercise the option, in which case $C = S - X$, or it is not, in which case equation 3.8 still applies. If $C = S - X$, then it must be because the dividend is so large that the underlying will drop so far in value that you want to capture the dividend. In the empirically usual case that this is the last dividend to be paid on the stock during the life of the option, then the next dividend is worth D. If the benefits of exercise (or sale of the option for $S - X$) outweigh the costs, it must be that $D \geq P$ (otherwise, $P - D > 0$, and equation 3.5 would then imply that $C \geq S - X + (P - D) > S - X$). So, the dividend to be captured is worth more than the American-style put, which in turn is worth strictly more than the European-style put (restriction R14 from table 3.4). That is, $D \geq P > p$. If we still think of the European-style put as the quantification of any regrets we have about the stock subsequently falling, then the dividend D is strictly larger than these, and we have an incentive to exercise the call (or to sell it for $S - X$).

The "regrets" argument is complicated for an American put. Using restriction R14 in table 3.4 and European put-call parity, we have equation 3.9:

$$P \geq p = c + Xe^{-r(T-t)} - S + D \tag{3.9}$$

Rearranging terms and adding and subtracting X yields equation 3.10:

$$P \geq (X - S) + \left[Xe^{-r(T-t)} - X \right] + c + D \qquad (3.10)$$

We now label the terms explicitly in equation 3.11:

$$P \geq \underbrace{(X - S)}_{\text{exercise}} + \underbrace{c}_{\text{upside}} + \underbrace{D}_{\text{dividends}} - \underbrace{\left[X - Xe^{-r(T-t)} \right]}_{\text{interest on strike} \geq 0} \qquad (3.11)$$

Note that I reversed the second term $[Xe^{-r(T-t)} - X]$ so that it would represent the interest that could be earned on the strike over the life of the option. Equation 3.11 differs from the analogous equation 3.7 for calls because the latter is an equality.

If exercise of an American-style put is optimal, you have $P = X - S$ (in which case, you are indifferent between exercise and sale). This means that $c + D - [X - Xe^{-r(T-t)}]$ must be zero or sufficiently negative to drag the put price down below the exercise value. Indeed, we can see from equation 3.11, that $c + D - [X - Xe^{-r(T-t)}] \leq 0$, else $P > X - S$, and early exercise would not be optimal.

Thus, early exercise implies $c + D \leq [X - Xe^{-r(T-t)}]$.[21] A sufficient condition for c to be small is that the put be deep in-the-money. If dividends D are also small, then the sum of c and D may be offset by the interest able to be earned on the strike—especially if expiration is distant, which makes $[X - Xe^{-r(T-t)}]$ large. These are exactly the costs and benefits discussed for early exercise of a put in table 3.5 on page 54; but what about the "regrets" mentioned in this table?

Table 3.5 discusses exercise decisions for someone holding the American put plus the stock: a protective put position. We may rearrange equation 3.11 to read

$$\underbrace{P + S}_{\text{protective put}} \geq \underbrace{X}_{\text{strike}} + \underbrace{c}_{\text{upside}} + \underbrace{D}_{\text{dividends}} - \underbrace{\left[X - Xe^{-r(T-t)} \right]}_{\text{interest on strike} \geq 0}. \qquad (3.12)$$

If the dividends are small, and the put is deep in-the-money (so c is small), and you are far from expiration (so $[X - Xe^{-r(T-t)}]$ is large), then you may have an incentive to give up both put and stock—via exercise—but you may have subsequent regrets if the stock price rises. This is because you have abandoned your market-linked position with upside potential (represented by stock on the LHS of equation 3.12 or the call on the RHS of equation 3.12) in favor of a fixed income position represented by receipt of the strike X and interest on the strike $[X - Xe^{-r(T-t)}]$. You have also abandoned the dividends. "Regrets" in this case are represented by the upside potential embodied within the call option that forms part of the lower bound on the RHS of equation 3.12.

As mentioned previously, if you hold a deep in-the-money American put, life does not get much better than this for a put holder. There is not much upside left for you, and there is a fair chance of you being worse off if you wait. Unlike the American call, the incentive to exercise early (or equivalently, to sell) can come at

---

[21]Note the direction of the implication here. Optimal early exercise of the American put implies $c + D \leq [X - Xe^{-r(T-t)}]$. This inequality is thus necessary, but not sufficient.

any time during the life of the American put option.

> **Exercise:** Draw figures analogous to figures 3.4 and 3.5 for the case of the European put.

3.6.6 Put-Call Parity Intrinsic Value Decomposition

Equation 3.8 can be rewritten to account for the difference between exercise value and intrinsic value of a call when $S < X$. I have replaced C by c with the understanding that if $D = 0$ and $r > 0$, then equations 3.13 and 3.14 also hold for the American-style call.

$$
c = \underbrace{\underbrace{[S - X]}_{\text{exercise}} + \underbrace{[X - Xe^{-r(T-t)}]}_{\text{delaying call exercise}} + \underbrace{p}_{\text{insurance}}}_{\text{time value or extrinsic value (if } S > X)}
$$

$$
= \underbrace{\underbrace{\max(0, S - X) - \max(0, X - S)}_{\text{equal to } S - X} + \underbrace{[X - Xe^{-r(T-t)}]}_{\text{delaying call exercise}} + \underbrace{p}_{\text{insurance}}}_{\text{time value or extrinsic value (if } S > X)}
$$

$$
= \underbrace{\max(0, S - X)}_{\text{intrinsic value of call}} + \underbrace{\underbrace{[X - Xe^{-r(T-t)}]}_{\text{delaying call exercise}} + \underbrace{[p - \max(0, X - S)]}_{\text{time value of put}}}_{\text{time value or extrinsic value of call}} \qquad (3.13)
$$

It follows immediately from equation 3.13 that the time value of a call may be written in terms of the time value of a put plus the quantity $[X - Xe^{-r(T-t)}]$ that does not change with changing S, as shown in equation 3.14. Thus, the portion of the option price that varies with volatility and stock price, holding all else constant, is the same for both a put and a call. This can, of course, be deduced directly from put-call parity, equation 3.3 (p54).

$$
\underbrace{c - \max(0, S - X)}_{\text{time value of call}} = \underbrace{\underbrace{[X - Xe^{-r(T-t)}]}_{\text{delaying call exercise}} + \underbrace{[p - \max(0, X - S)]}_{\text{time value of put}}}_{\text{time value or extrinsic value of call}}. \qquad (3.14)
$$

It is worth noting in equations 3.13 and 3.14 that although the time value of the call is non-negative (remember that $D = 0$), the time value of the put can be negative for a low enough stock price. This can be seen in the lower panel of figure 3.3 on page 59 for S below roughly \$30. The non-negativity of the time value of the call (remember $D = 0$) implies that $p - \max(0, X - S) \geq Xe^{-r(T-t)} - X$. Indeed, when $S = 0$, the time value of the call is zero, and the two terms on the RHS of equation 3.14 are of the same magnitude but opposite sign: $p - \max(0, X - S) = Xe^{-r(T-t)} - X < 0$. In this case, the time value of the put is the negative of the time value of a deep in-the-money call; that is, the negative of the interest that is earned by waiting to exercise a call. For the put, this is the interest that is lost by not being able to exercise the put. The time value of a similarly specified but American-style put would be zero in the same circumstance (restriction R11 in table 3.4 on page 52).

Chapter 4

Risk-Neutral Option Pricing

Option pricing includes two main approaches: analytical pricing and numerical pricing. In each case, you start with a model (i.e., a simplified mathematical description) of the behavior of asset prices. Analytical pricing uses mathematics (often in great quantity) to derive an exact option pricing formula based on the model of asset prices (e.g., the Black-Scholes formula). In cases where no exact formula can be derived, approximate option pricing formulae may exist (e.g., for American-style put options and for arithmetic average rate Asian options). Analytical pricing is what "rocket scientists" do. Exact analytical solutions are quite rare. For example, I present some closed-form exact analytical results in sections 9.2.2–9.2.4 that I have not seen elsewhere.

Numerical pricing differs from analytical pricing. It uses a computer and many repetitions of a simple procedure to arrive at an estimated option price. No exact pricing formula is used. Little math is needed for the simple techniques discussed in this book, but complicated numerical methods are widely used by institutional traders. We explore numerical techniques to the extent that they improve understanding of Black-Scholes option pricing in chapters 5 and 6 and in section 7.5.

Risk-neutral option pricing theory is the engine that drives almost all analytical and numerical option pricing theory; this chapter discusses the essentials. Note, however, that several different approaches to option pricing exist, and Black and Scholes (1973) contains two derivations, neither of which uses risk-neutral pricing (see section 4.4.1).

4.1 The Simple Answer: Traditional Methods Fail

Traditional finance values both real and financial assets by forecasting future cash flows and discounting these at a rate of return that reflects relevant risk. This discounted cash flow (DCF) analysis includes the Gordon-Shapiro dividend discount model for stocks (Gordon and Shapiro [1956]); bond pricing; and capital budgeting NPV analysis for new projects. The DCF discount rates are often calculated using the CAPM.

Do the traditional methods work for options? That is, can we forecast the expected payoff to an option and then discount this at a CAPM-generated rate? The simple answer is "no"; the complex answer is discussed in section 4.5.

When you buy a call option on a stock, you take a position in the stock, but you pay less than the stock price. This leverage makes the option riskier than the stock: the option has a higher standard deviation of returns than the stock, and the option's β is of larger magnitude[1] than the stock's β.

The degree of leverage in the option depends upon the level of the stock price relative to the strike price. For example, a call option that is deep in-the-money is stock-like (stock $\uparrow$ \$1 $\Rightarrow$ call $\uparrow$ \$1). A call that is deep out-of-the-money is much riskier (called a "lottery ticket" or a "cab" by some traders[2]). The relationships between beta for a stock and beta for call options on that stock are shown in equation 4.1.[3]

$$|\beta_S| \leq \left|\beta_{C(\text{in-the-money})}\right| \leq \left|\beta_{C(\text{out-of-the-money})}\right| \tag{4.1}$$

The degree of leverage of an option (and therefore its β) changes every time the stock price changes. It even changes over time if the stock price is constant because of time decay. A continuously and unpredictably changing β means that the required rate of return on the option is also changing continuously and unpredictably. The CAPM-required rate of return is valid for an horizon of no more than an instant. The simple CAPM-required return on the option over the many time steps from time t to time T is not known. The traditional method fails; we cannot use standard DCF to value the option because we do not know the discount rate (it is a path-dependent random variable).

4.2 Replication

We want to value an option. Let us assume that you can set up a trading strategy that exactly replicates the payoffs to a European stock option.[4] Suppose that this replicating strategy requires that you manage a portfolio of the underlying stock and a riskless bond (long the bond is riskless lending, short the bond is riskless borrowing).

---

[1] I say "magnitude," because a calls's β is negative if the stock's beta is negative.

[2] "Cab" is short for cabinet trade. This is one where a deep out-of-the-money option is liquidated at the lowest possible price. It might be one tick, a half-tick, or even zero. (A floor trader jokingly told me that it is called a cab because if you are reduced to buying these options, then you may soon be driving a cab at night to augment your income.)

[3] The explicit relationship is $\beta_c = \frac{S\Delta\beta_S}{c}$ for a European call, where Δ is the delta of the call option. The scaling factor $\frac{S\Delta}{c}$ is called the "elasticity" of the call option.

[4] The technical requirement for this to be possible is described nicely in Jarrow and Rudd (1983). Essentially, it requires that for very small time horizons the value of the derivative and the value of the underlying be perfectly linearly correlated and T-costs are zero. A diffusion or a pure-jump process satisfies this, but if the underlying stock price follows a jump-diffusion process (regardless of whether the jump size is deterministic, stochastic, diversifiable, or non-diversifiable), then a replicating portfolio cannot be formed, and the no-arbitrage pricing method fails (Cox and Rubinstein [1985, chapter 7]; Merton [1976]). In the jump-diffusion case where the size of the jump is random but diversifiable (i.e., non-systematic), then an equilibrium option pricing model can be derived and the Black-Scholes hedge works "on average." See section 9.4.1 starting on page 166.

Assume also that this replicating strategy is "self-financing." That is, whenever the strategy directs you to sell some stock and buy some bonds, then the proceeds from the sale of stock are exactly what is needed to buy bonds. Conversely, if the strategy directs you to sell bonds and buy some stock, the bond sale proceeds are exactly what is needed to buy the stock. Thus, the strategy finances itself, with no additional funds required from you after initiation. A strategy that directs you to change the proportions of holdings in the stock and bond through time is called a "dynamic strategy."

A dynamic, self-financing, replicating strategy has an initial setup cost, but no maintenance costs. To find the initial setup cost, you need to know how many shares of stock the strategy directs you to be long or short initially, what dollar borrowing or lending is required initially, and what the stock price is.

If the strategy is known to all market participants, and if the stock price is visible to all, then everyone knows and agrees upon the initial setup cost of the replicating strategy. No-arbitrage implies that the setup cost of a dynamic, self-financing, replicating portfolio must equal the initial cost of the option.

If everyone knows and agrees upon the initial setup cost of the replicating strategy, then—by no-arbitrage—no two people can disagree on the cost of an option. Even if one person is bullish, and the other is bearish, they agree on the cost of the option because they agree on the start-up cost of the replicating portfolio and that arbitrage opportunities cannot exist. The value of the option is therefore not a function of market view.

Likewise, even if one person is risk seeking, and one person is risk averse, they agree on the cost of the option because they agree on the start-up cost of the replicating portfolio and that arbitrage opportunities cannot exist. The value of the option is therefore not a function of risk preferences.

If the value of the option is not a function of risk preferences, then we may assume whatever we want about risk preferences of people in the economy. Let us assume that everyone in the economy is risk-neutral. This is a wildly inaccurate description of market participants, but option values are immune to the assumption, and it simplifies our valuation problem tremendously.

In a risk-neutral world, market participants are indifferent towards risk and care only about expected return. In equilibrium, the expected return on every traded asset in such a world (including options) must be the riskless rate r. If any asset offers more (less), people buy (sell) until the price adjusts and the expected return equals r.

If everyone requires the same rate of return on every asset all the time in this hypothetical economy, then we *can* use DCF after all to value options—with discounting at r. However, this is not standard DCF. We must be internally consistent. If we use risk-neutral pricing, then we must model the price process of any asset in the hypothetical risk-neutral world as having drift rate r. It is this process that determines the value of the derivative in the risk-neutral world.

When modelling price processes in the risk-neutral world, we take the initial prices of assets to be the same as those in the real world, and we adjust the drift

Table 4.1: DCF: Traditional versus Risk-Neutral

Real World DCF (Traditional)		Risk-Neutral World DCF (Options)	
1.	Forecast Expected CF in Real World.	1.	Forecast Expected CF in R-N World.
2.	Find β of Returns to Asset.		
3.	Discount CF at Risk-Adjusted Rate (via CAPM).	2.	Discount CF at r.

Note: A comparison of the basic techniques for discounted cash flow (DCF) analysis using both traditional and risk-neutral approaches.

rates of the prices to equal r. What we are doing is redistributing the real-world probabilities we attach to possible time-T stock price outcomes (but not altering the outcomes) so that the mean of the final stock price distribution yields drift rate r in the risk-neutral world. That is, equation 4.2 holds, and the expected price of the asset in the risk-neutral world is the forward price:

$$E^*[S(T)|S(t)] = S(t)e^{r(T-t)}, \tag{4.2}$$

where E^* denotes expectation in a risk-neutral world. These implicit "risk-neutral probabilities" appear explicitly in both (numerical) binomial option pricing and (analytical) Black-Scholes option pricing, both of which can rely upon risk-neutral pricing methods.

Thus, our alternative to the traditional real-world expected cash flow coupled with a risk-adjusted discount rate (not feasible for options), is a risk-neutral world expected cash flow (assuming drift r) coupled with a riskless discount rate. This is summarized in table 4.1.

4.3 *The* Formula

Let $\bar{r}$ be the average continuously compounded riskless interest rate from time t to time T. Let V denote the value of the derivative, then

$$V(t) = E_t^*[e^{-\bar{r}(T-t)}V(T)],$$

where E^* denotes expectation in a risk-neutral world, and E_t denotes expectation taken conditional upon time t information. The quantity $V(T)$ is the value at time T of the derivative. For example, if T is the expiration date of a European put, then $V(T) = \max[0, X - S(T)]$. A call would have $V(T) = \max[0, S(T) - X]$.

If the riskless rate is known and constant, then the option value is given by equation 4.3:

$$V(t) = e^{-r(T-t)}E_t^*[V(T)] \tag{4.3}$$

If the randomness driving $V(T)$ can be described as a function of the continuous pdf of $S(T)$, then risk-neutral valuation may be attempted using a great deal of integral calculus. In this case, the "E" becomes an integral with respect to the randomness driving $S(T)$. Solutions may exist (e.g., Black-Scholes as derived in section 8.2), but need not. Fortunately, risk-neutral valuation lends itself naturally to numerical procedures.

For a discussion of where risk-neutral pricing fails, see section 9.4.1, and the summary in table 9.3 on page 170. For more advanced risk-neutral pricing (including martingale methods), see section 4.4, following.

4.4 Risk-Neutral Pricing Review

This review emphasizes the bare bones of risk-neutral pricing and sets the stage for presenting three option pricing methods.

- The technical requirement for dynamic replication to be possible is described in footnote 4 (p68).

- If dynamic replication is possible, then by no-arbitrage the value of the derivative equals the start-up cost of a replicating portfolio.

- If the replication recipe is known (perhaps via an equilibrium CAPM pricing approach as in the original Black and Scholes [1973] paper), then no two market participants can disagree on the correct arbitrage-free price of the derivative. Thus, regardless of what we assume about the preferences of market participants, the pricing of the derivative is the same.

- We ease our calculations substantially by proceeding *as if* the agents in the economy are risk-neutral. That is, the risk is there, and they see the risk, but they ignore it completely. (I recall John Cox emphasizing in class at MIT that we are not assuming that anyone is really risk-neutral! It is simply that option prices are immune to assumptions about risk preferences, and this proves to be a very helpful assumption.)

- In a risk-neutral economy, people care only about expected return; so, in equilibrium, all traded assets must offer the same expected return (else investors would still be shorting low-yield securities to invest in high-yield ones, and we would not yet be in equilibrium). The existence of a government-backed, fixed-rate, riskless asset means that the riskless rate is the equilibrium-required return on all securities in this economy.

- If risk is not priced by market participants, then traded security prices (including derivatives) are simply discounted expected payoffs where discounting uses the riskless rate, and all traded security prices have riskless drift (less any dividend yield, of course, so that total expected yield is the riskless rate). Although securities are expected to return a riskless yield, they are still risky, and the realized yield is uncertain. If risk were priced, then discount rates would need to be risk adjusted, perhaps via the CAPM (Arnold and Crack [2003], Arnold, Crack, and Schwartz [2008]).

- Let $B(t) \equiv e^{rt}$ denote the price of a riskless money market instrument (i.e., you invest \$1 at time 0, and it grows at riskless rate r). Then $B(t)$ drifts upward at the riskless rate with no uncertainty. The money market account serves as a benchmark for performance in both the real and risk-neutral worlds. It seems natural to express other asset prices in terms of units of this asset.[5] So, instead of looking at stock price $S(t)$, we look at $\frac{S(t)}{B(t)}$ (i.e., stock price using the bond as numeraire).

- With $B(t)$ drifting upward at the riskless rate, and $S(t)$ expected to drift upward at the same rate in equilibrium in the risk-neutral world, it follows that $\frac{S(t)}{B(t)}$ is expected to have no drift.[6] Another way to say this is that for any $\Delta t > 0$, equation 4.4 holds:

$$E^* \left[\frac{S(t + \Delta t)}{B(t + \Delta t)} \,\middle|\, \frac{S(t)}{B(t)} \right] = \frac{S(t)}{B(t)}, \qquad (4.4)$$

where E^* denotes expectation in the risk-neutral world.[7]

- Let $S^\dagger(t) \equiv \frac{S(t)}{B(t)}$, then equation 4.4 says that for any $\Delta t > 0$,

$$E^* \left[S^\dagger(t + \Delta t) \,\middle|\, S^\dagger(t) \right] = S^\dagger(t).$$

That is, the best guess of where $S^\dagger$ will be in the future (in the risk-neutral world) is where it is today. A random variable with this property is called a "martingale." This is similar to a simple version of the efficient markets hypothesis (EMH) with no drift or predictability.[8]

- When we assume that traded securities have required returns equal to the riskless rate in the risk-neutral world, we are really just redistributing the probabilities we associate with possible final security price outcomes.[9] However, some things stay the same. For example, if a stock price outcome occurs with probability zero in the real world, then it still occurs with probability zero in the risk-neutral world (thus, the range of possible outcomes does not change, only

---

[5]This is referred to as a change of "numeraire." A numeraire is a base unit of measurement. This is similar to changing units of measurement from USD to GBP, say, except that here we choose a USD-denominated money market account instead of GBP. Section 8.3.4 describes what happens if you use the stock as numeraire. Hull (2000, section 19.5) discusses other choices of numeraire.

[6]The same is true if you replace $S(t)$ with $V(t)$ for any traded security with price $V(t)$.

[7]Look ahead to equation 8.26 in section 8.3.3 for contrasting results using the stock as numeraire.

[8]The EMH states, essentially, that news should be rapidly and unbiasedly reflected in stock market prices. As such, traders should not be able to consistently beat the market based on public information. This does not preclude predictability, just consistent abnormal profits (Lo and MacKinlay [1988]). I do not, of course, subscribe to the EMH. Most academic studies of price reaction to some event look at many stocks and conclude that the *average* price reaction is accurate. That may be, but the average includes stocks that underreact and overreact significantly, and there is money to be made by identifying them.

[9]Note the word "traded" here. A futures price, for example, is not the price of a traded asset, so its drift need not be r.

---

their probability of occurrence; and the transformation of probabilities moves the expected return on IBM, say, from 12% per annum to whatever the T-bill yield happens to be). Similarly, if a stock price outcome occurs with probability one in the real world, then it still occurs with probability one in the risk-neutral world.

- In probability theory, the mathematical function that allocates probability weight to outcomes in the sample space is called a "measure." Two probability measures that reassign probabilities to outcomes without changing the range of possible outcomes (as above) are called "equivalent measures."[10]

- Thus, in the risk-neutral world, we reallocate probabilities in an equivalent manner (i.e., same range of possible outcomes), and the price of any traded asset when "de-trended" by the money market account follows a martingale. The probability measure (i.e., allocation of probabilities to outcomes) in the risk-neutral world is thus called an "equivalent martingale measure." You see this expression in the more advanced derivatives literature. Section 8.3.4 describes a different equivalent martingale measure derived using a different numeraire.

I now present summaries of three derivative pricing methods. The first is Merton's hedging argument (section 4.4.1). Merton's method predates risk-neutral option pricing, but belongs here for clarity because it is often incorrectly labelled as a risk-neutral technique. The second and third methods follow from our risk-neutral pricing discussion. They are the original Cox and Ross technique (section 4.4.2) and the more advanced Harrison and Kreps argument (section 4.4.3).

4.4.1 First Method (Merton [1973])

Merton (1973) makes no risk-neutral assumptions or arguments whatsoever. His hedging argument is not a risk-neutral technique; I present it here to contrast it with the risk-neutral techniques following. Merton's hedging argument was first published with Merton's consent by Black and Scholes (1973) and is explored more fully in Merton (1973). Black and Scholes originally derived the option pricing formula using an instantaneous CAPM argument (also presented in their 1973 paper), but Merton's approach is now more widely known.[11] Merton's hedging argument predates the Cox and Ross discovery of risk-neutral techniques (section 4.4.2) by three years and is not to be confused with the Harrison and Kreps approach that also uses partial differential equations (PDEs) (section 4.4.3).

---

[10]The relationship between the two measures is captured by the Radon-Nikodym derivative. See Baxter and Rennie (1996, p65) for simple intuition, and Musiela and Rutkowski (1992, pp114, 121) for the advanced mathematics.

[11]Robert Merton and Myron Scholes were awarded the 1997 Nobel Prize in economics for their option pricing work. Fischer Black passed away in 1995. Had he lived, he would have shared in the prize of one million US dollars. I spoke with Fischer Black on several different occasions between 1991 and 1994 (at MIT, at Harvard, and at Goldman, Sachs). I did not know him—I was just one of the many people he spoke with one-to-one.

©2009 Timothy Falcon Crack   73

> **Note on PDEs:** PDEs can be daunting to those without higher mathematics training. In section 7.6, I look at PDEs as economic entities with simple interpretations that relate to hedged options positions. If you are not interested in hedging options positions, then you can skip any sections that explore PDEs without loss of continuity.

Assume the stock price $S(t)$ fully reflects all relevant prior and current information, and that the market reacts quickly to the arrival of new information. Consider a small time increment dt during which S changes to $S + dS$. A simple model for describing the return $\frac{dS}{S}$ is one that breaks the return into a predictable component that you would expect in the absence of new information, and a random, or "stochastic," component driven by news.

The predictable component is μdt, where μ is the average annual rate of growth of the stock price, and dt is the time increment measured as a portion of a year. The random component is σdw, where σ is a measure of annual standard deviation of returns, and "dw" is a random number drawn from a normal distribution with mean zero and variance dt. Combining these we get equation 4.5:

$$\frac{dS}{S} = \mu dt + \sigma dw, \qquad (4.5)$$

or, more correctly, equation 4.6:

$$dS = \mu S dt + \sigma S dw. \qquad (4.6)$$

Equation 4.5 is a model of the arrival of information. It describes a "random walk" in the stock price known as a geometric Brownian motion (GBM). We call "dw" a "Wiener process" after Norbert Wiener from MIT (see Harrison [1985] for more details).

Assume also that there is a riskless security with price B at time t. We may describe its return as $\frac{dB}{B} = rdt$ because it contains no random component, or, more correctly, $dB = rBdt$.

Now introduce a simple option with value V, where V is assumed to be a function of the current value of the stock and time: $V = V(S,t)$. The option value may also be a function of a contractually stated exercise price X, an expiry time T, volatility σ, and r. The option might be American style or European style; it might be a put or a call; or it might be much more complicated.

If you have a reasonably well-behaved function $V(S,t)$, then Itô's Lemma asserts (via Taylor's Theorem) that equation 4.7 holds.[12]

$$dV = \frac{\partial V}{\partial S}dS + \frac{\partial V}{\partial t}dt + \frac{1}{2}\frac{\partial^2 V}{\partial S^2}(dS)^2 \qquad (4.7)$$

With $dS = \mu S dt + \sigma S dw$, and $(dw)^2 = dt$, and all higher-order terms zero, equation 4.7 yields equation 4.8:

$$dV = \sigma S\frac{\partial V}{\partial S}dw + \left(\mu S\frac{\partial V}{\partial S} + \frac{\partial V}{\partial t} + \frac{1}{2}\sigma^2 S^2\frac{\partial^2 V}{\partial S^2}\right)dt \qquad (4.8)$$

---

[12]For more on Itô's Lemma, see Hull (2000) or Merton (1992).

Now, build a portfolio where you buy one option and sell Δ units of the stock. If $\Delta > 0$, it is a short stock position; if $\Delta < 0$ it is a long stock position. Let Π denote the value of this portfolio, then $\Pi = V - S\Delta$, and over a time interval dt the change in the value of this portfolio is given by equation 4.9:

$$d\Pi = dV - dS \cdot \Delta, \tag{4.9}$$

where Δ is held fixed over the time interval dt. Now plug equations 4.6 and 4.8 into equation 4.9 and collect terms:

$$d\Pi = \sigma S \left(\frac{\partial V}{\partial S} - \Delta \right) dw + \left(\mu S \frac{\partial V}{\partial S} + \frac{\partial V}{\partial t} + \frac{1}{2}\sigma^2 S^2 \frac{\partial^2 V}{\partial S^2} - \mu S \Delta \right) dt$$

If we eliminate the stochastic component by choosing a portfolio with $\Delta = \frac{\partial V}{\partial S}$, then the changes in portfolio value must be deterministic:

$$d\Pi = \left(\frac{\partial V}{\partial t} + \frac{1}{2}\sigma^2 S^2 \frac{\partial^2 V}{\partial S^2} \right) dt \tag{4.10}$$

With no random component, the portfolio must offer the riskless rate of return, or there would be arbitrage opportunities available. Thus, it follows that $d\Pi = r\Pi dt$.

Now plug $\Pi = V - \Delta S$ plus the choice of Δ into $d\Pi = r\Pi dt$ and equate with $d\Pi$ in equation 4.10. This yields the celebrated Black-Scholes PDE:

$$\frac{\partial V}{\partial t} + \frac{1}{2}\sigma^2 S^2 \frac{\partial^2 V}{\partial S^2} + rS\frac{\partial V}{\partial S} - rV = 0 \tag{4.11}$$

Any derivative security whose price depends only upon the current value of S and on t, and which is paid for up front, must satisfy the Black-Scholes equation or some variation of it that incorporates dividends or time-dependent parameters.

Exercise: Use Merton's hedge argument to prove that the PDE for a derivative on a stock following an arithmetic Brownian motion (ABM):

$$dS = \mu dt + \sigma_A dw$$

is given by

$$\frac{\partial V}{\partial t} + \frac{1}{2}\sigma_A^2 \frac{\partial^2 V}{\partial S^2} + rS\frac{\partial V}{\partial S} - rV = 0.$$

Hint: The derivation appears in section 9.2.1 with discussion.

4.4.2   Second Method (Cox and Ross [1976])

Let V be the derivative price we seek, then the martingale property applied to de-trended V (i.e., $V^\dagger = V/B = Ve^{-rt}$) implies

$$
\begin{aligned}
V^\dagger(t) &= E^* \left[V^\dagger(T) \,\middle|\, V^\dagger(t) \right] \\
\Rightarrow V(t)e^{-rt} &= E^* \left[V(T)e^{-rT} \,\middle|\, V(t) \right] \\
\Rightarrow V(t) &= e^{-r(T-t)} E^* \left[V(T) \,|\, V(t) \right].
\end{aligned}
$$

That is, the derivative value today is the discounted expected payoff, where expectations are taken in a world in which investors behave as if they are risk neutral, and discounting is done at the riskless rate.

I like the risk-neutral world, discounted expected payoff approach because it does not require familiarity with PDEs, and it correlates directly with the Monte Carlo methods described in chapter 5. Indeed, I derive the Black-Scholes formula in section 8.2 using precisely this approach.

4.4.3 Third Method (Harrison and Kreps [1979])

Let V be the derivative price we seek, then the martingale property applied to detrended V (i.e., $V^\dagger = V/B = Ve^{-rt}$) implies that $dV^\dagger$ has no time trend; that is, no drift. We can apply Itô's Lemma to $V^\dagger$ to calculate

$$dV^\dagger = [\text{time trend}]dt + \sum_i [\text{diffusion coefficients}]_i dw_i,$$

where dw_i is the ith Brownian motion driving the underlyings. If V is a function of $S(t)$ and t only, and $dS(t) = rSdt + \sigma Sdw$ then

$$
\begin{aligned}
dV^\dagger(S(t), t) &= d[V(S(t), t)e^{-rt}] \\
&\overset{\text{Itô}}{=} \left(\frac{\partial V}{\partial S}dS + \frac{\partial V}{\partial t}dt + \frac{1}{2}\frac{\partial^2 V}{\partial S^2}(dS)^2 \right) e^{-rt} \\
&\qquad\qquad\qquad\qquad -rVe^{-rt}dt \\
&= \left(\frac{1}{2}\frac{\partial^2 V}{\partial S^2}\sigma^2 S^2 + \frac{\partial V}{\partial S}rS + \frac{\partial V}{\partial t} - rV \right) e^{-rt}dt \\
&\qquad\qquad\qquad\qquad + \frac{\partial V}{\partial S}\sigma Se^{-rt}dw,
\end{aligned}
$$

where we used $(dw \cdot dw) = dt$, and $(dt \cdot dw) = 0$ (Merton [1992, pp122–123]). However, $V^\dagger = Ve^{-rt}$ is a martingale in the risk-neutral world by construction, so it must be that there is no drift term. Thus, we deduce that

$$\frac{1}{2}\frac{\partial^2 V}{\partial S^2}\sigma^2 S^2 + \frac{\partial V}{\partial S}rS + \frac{\partial V}{\partial t} - rV = 0.$$

If we know the boundary conditions, we may now solve this (Black-Scholes) PDE to find the option value $V(S(t), t)$.[13] A different initial process for dS yields a different PDE, as per the exercise below.

---

[13]There are many solutions to the PDE. For example, if V solves this PDE, then so to does $2 \times V$, and so too does $-V$. We seek a particular solution to the PDE that satisfies the initial conditions and boundary conditions for the problem at hand. These conditions will be similar to the economic restrictions appearing in sections 3.4 and 3.5. See chapter 7 and section 9.2.1.

Exercise: Use Itô's Lemma (equation 4.7) to prove that for a stock bleeding a continuous dividend at rate ρ,

$$dS = (\mu - \rho)Sdt + \sigma Sdw,$$

the Black-Scholes PDE is given by

$$\frac{\partial V}{\partial t} + \frac{1}{2}\sigma^2 S^2 \frac{\partial^2 V}{\partial S^2} + (r - \rho)S\frac{\partial V}{\partial S} - rV = 0.$$

Hint: Be sure to account for the dividend bleed using $d\Pi = dV - dS \cdot \Delta - \rho Sdt \cdot \Delta$ in place of equation 4.9 in the Merton hedging argument (e.g., see Wilmott [1998, p77]).

4.5   The Complex Answer: Non-Traditional Methods

In section 4.1, I asked "...can we forecast the expected payoff to an option and then discount this at a CAPM-generated rate?" The simple answer to the question was "no," because of the time-varying and path-dependent discount rate. This led us to risk-neutral pricing with riskless discount rates. The complex answer to the question, however, is "yes," and there are two approaches.

The first approach is to find a single required rate of return on an option that can be used to discount projected payoffs in the real world. Cox and Rubinstein (1985, pp323–324) give enough information to derive a closed-form formula for this real-world expected return on a European-style option.[14] You need, however, both the current option value and the real-world return on the underlying to implement the formula.

The second approach (the one originally adopted by Black and Scholes) is to accept that the discount rate is time-varying and path-dependent. In this case, the valuation must be performed in time steps: either discrete steps in, for example, a binomial framework (as in Arnold and Crack [2003] and Arnold, Crack, and Schwartz [2008]), or in continuous time using a special instantaneous version of the CAPM that holds only over time steps each of an instant (as in Black and Scholes [1973]). Arnold and Crack (2003) demonstrate that DCF using CAPM-generated discount rates for each different possible real-world option payoff leads to exactly the same valuation as using risk-neutral discounting of real-world payoffs. The tree of possible option payoffs is exactly the same in both cases. What changes between the real and risk-neutral worlds is the discount rates and the probabilities of seeing states of the world that produce the payoffs.

Ironically, to execute the second approach, a risk-neutral option valuation has to be performed first to find the intermediate path-dependent discount rates—because the discount rates depend upon the degree of leverage embedded in the option, and

---

[14]I thank Mark Rubinstein for pointing out the Cox and Rubinstein citation, and for telling me about a related but different concept: Mark Garman's "fugit" of an option (Garman [1989]). The fugit is the risk-neutral expected time until exercise.

that depends upon the option value, the stock price, the option delta, and the option beta at that point in time (see footnote 3 on p68 for a related formula and also the discussion in Arnold and Crack [2003]).

Chapter 5

Numerical Option Pricing: Monte Carlo

5.1 Do I Need to Know This?

This book is about Black-Scholes pricing, and about using it in the real world. So, you may ask why you should be reading a chapter about Monte Carlo methods. You can, in fact, skip all the numerical methods parts (this chapter, chapter 6, and section 7.5) without loss of continuity. I do believe, however, that reading this chapter gives you a much better feel for the data-generating process that Black-Scholes pricing assumes, for what it means to take an expected value in both the real and risk-neutral worlds, and for why American option pricing is complex.

5.2 Monte Carlo Methods

Monte Carlo, in the Principality of Monaco, is famous for its casinos. Casinos are famous for games of chance in which different possible random outcomes lead to different possible payoffs. Monte Carlo methods are so named because they use computer-simulations of independent realizations of random variables. In option pricing, the simulations are of possible price paths of the underlying asset (in a hypothetical risk-neutral world). Each simulated price path generates an option payoff. The average of these payoffs estimates the expected payoff. This average is then discounted (at riskless rate r) to estimate option value.

Monte Carlo methods are good for European-style options, but they do not work for American-style options (Boyle [1977]).[1] Monte Carlo methods are suited to path-dependent option valuation because each simulated path determines uniquely the payoff.[2] Lattice methods do not have this simple property because multiple paths

---

[1]Lattice methods (see chapter 6) give the present value (PV) of the option at each node, allowing comparison of PV and intrinsic value so you know whether to exercise. A Monte Carlo gives you the PV of the option only at the initial node and thus does not allow such intermediate comparisons.

[2]A path-dependent option is one for which the payoff depends not only upon the final underlying asset price, but also upon the path followed by the underlying asset price during the life of the option.

lead to a single node—see also footnote 2 on page 89.

We create the data for a Monte Carlo simulation. It follows that these data are so well behaved that the strongest statistical laws apply: Khinchine's Strong Law of Large Numbers and the Lindeberg-Levy Central Limit Theorem. These are the statistical engines that drive Monte Carlo pricing. Risk-neutral pricing is the financial engine.

Khinchine's Strong Law of Large Numbers (SLLN) says that if the sample $X_1, X_2, \ldots, X_n, \ldots$ are IID[3] with $E(X_i) = \mu$ (a finite number) for each i, then, with probability one

$$\bar{X}_n \equiv \frac{1}{n} \sum_{i=1}^{n} X_i \to \mu, \text{ as } n \to \infty.$$

That is, in plain English, the sample mean approaches the true mean as the sample size increases.

The Lindeberg-Levy Central Limit Theorem (CLT) says that if the sample $X_1, X_2, \ldots, X_n, \ldots$ are IID with $E(X_i) = \mu$, and if $\text{var}(X_i) = \sigma^2$ (a finite number) for each i, then

$$\frac{\sqrt{n}(\bar{X}_n - \mu)}{\sigma} \to Z \sim N(0, 1), \text{ as } n \to \infty.$$

That is, in plain English, the sample mean is approximately normally distributed with distribution $N\left(\mu, \frac{\sigma^2}{n}\right)$ for large n.[4]

5.3 Monte Carlo in Science

In the physical sciences, Monte Carlo simulation is used to estimate the expected value (i.e., the mean) of a random variable. Many random variables with the same probability density are simulated, and their average is the estimate of the mean of the random variable (based on the SLLN). The simulation also produces a measure of how close the average is to the true mean (based on the CLT). The precision increases as the number of simulation trials increases.

Monte Carlo in science is useful for solving analytically intractable integral calculus problems. For example, suppose that $W \sim N(0, 1)$ (i.e., W is distributed standard normal). Suppose that $g(\cdot)$ is the "weird function," given in equation 5.1 and illustrated in figure 5.1:

$$g(w) = [\Gamma(|w|, \pi)]^e + \frac{1}{10} \max(w, 0) - e^{-\frac{\sqrt{\exp(w)}}{[1+\sin(|w|)]}} + 3, \qquad (5.1)$$

where $\Gamma(\cdot, \cdot)$ is the incomplete gamma function,[5] e is Euler's number, $\pi = 3.14159...$, and $\exp(x) \equiv e^x$.

---

[3]"IID"=independent and identically distributed. That is, each observation in the sequence is statistically independent of each other observation, and each is drawn from the same statistical distribution.

[4]It follows that as $n \to \infty$, then $\frac{\sigma^2}{n} \to 0$, and thus $\bar{X}_n \to \mu$ (consistent with the SLLN).

[5]The incomplete gamma function is defined as $\Gamma(x, \nu) \equiv \frac{1}{\Gamma(\nu)} \int_{s=0}^{x} s^{\nu-1} e^{-s} ds$, for $x > 0$ (Abramowitz and Stegun [1972, p260]).

How can I find the solution to the integral $\mu_g \equiv E[g(W)]$ given in equation 5.2?

$$
\begin{aligned}
\mu_g &= E[g(W)] \\
&= \int_{-\infty}^{+\infty} g(w) \frac{1}{\sqrt{2\pi}} e^{-\frac{1}{2}w^2} dw \\
&= \int_{-\infty}^{+\infty} \left\{ [\Gamma(|w|, \pi)]^e + \frac{1}{10} \max(w, 0) - e^{-\frac{\sqrt{\exp(w)}}{[1+\sin(|w|)]}} + 3 \right\} \frac{1}{\sqrt{2\pi}} e^{-\frac{1}{2}w^2} dw \quad (5.2)
\end{aligned}
$$

Now, suppose you are talented enough to spend 10 hours completing the two-dozen pages of calculus needed to solve equation 5.2 analytically. Did you make any errors? Who is going to check your proof for you? How much extra time do you need if I change one term, say $\sin(|w|)$ to $\tan(|w|)$? The beauty of Monte Carlo methods is that they circumvent the problems inherent in each of these questions. Indeed, if you can complete the analytical proof, then a Monte Carlo technique is probably the best way to check it.

How do we find $\hat{\mu}_g$? Well, suppose I sample random numbers w_i from the standard normal distribution of W, and estimate $\mu_g = E[g(W)]$ using $\hat{\mu}_g = \frac{1}{n} \sum_{i=1}^n g(w_i)$. The $g(w_i)$ are IID, so the SLLN says that with probability one, $\hat{\mu}_g = \frac{1}{n} \sum_{i=1}^n g(w_i) \longrightarrow \mu_g$. Standard sample statistics tell us that $\widehat{\sigma_n^2} = \frac{1}{n} \sum_{i=1}^n [g(w_i) - \hat{\mu}_g]^2$ is a good estimator of $\text{var}[g(W)]$, so the CLT yields $\hat{\mu}_g$ as approximately $N(\mu_g, \frac{\widehat{\sigma_n^2}}{n})$ for large n, and a 95% confidence interval for μ_g is

$$
\left[\hat{\mu}_g - 1.96 \sqrt{\frac{\widehat{\sigma_n^2}}{n}}, \quad \hat{\mu}_g + 1.96 \sqrt{\frac{\widehat{\sigma_n^2}}{n}} \right].
$$

A short computer program[6] estimates the answer accurately in less than seven seconds: $\hat{\mu}_g = 2.5388$ with a standard error of 0.0003, and a 95% confidence interval of [2.5382, 2.5395]—see table 5.1.

Compared to the 10 hours needed to write the two-dozen pages of calculus to solve the analytical problem in equation 5.2, it is easy to write this code, it is easy to check it (you can probably do it yourself even if you do not understand MATLAB), it runs quickly, and it is also easy to adjust. For example, you can easily change "sin" to "tan" and rerun the code, all in less than 15 seconds. That is the power of Monte Carlo methods!

---

[6]MATLAB language for the Monte Carlo in the last line of table 5.1:

```
n=400000;   w=randn(n,1); aw=abs(w); g=((gammainc(aw,pi)).^exp(1)) + 0.1*max(w,0) -
exp(-sqrt(exp(w))./(1+sin(aw))) + 3; mug=mean(g); sg=std(g)/sqrt(n);
```

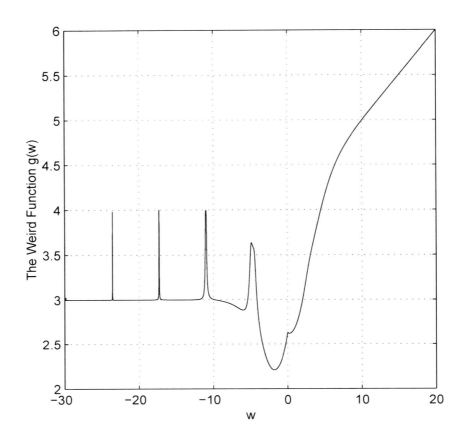

Figure 5.1: The Weird Function $g(\cdot)$

Note: The figure plots $g(w) = [\Gamma(|w|, \pi)]^e + \frac{1}{10}\max(w, 0) - e^{-\frac{\sqrt{\exp(w)}}{[1+\sin(|w|)]}} + 3$, where $\Gamma(\cdot, \cdot)$ is the incomplete gamma function, e is Euler's number, π is pi, and $\exp(x) \equiv e^x$. This is the function whose expected value relative to a standard normal is calculated via Monte Carlo simulation in table 5.1 on page 83.

Table 5.1: Monte Carlo Estimate of $E[g(W)]$ for the Weird Function

Monte Carlo Estimation of $\hat{\mu}_g$			
$\hat{\mu}_g$	$\sqrt{\frac{\widehat{\sigma_n^2}}{n}}$	n	seconds
2.6672	0.0489	10	0.00
2.5502	0.0183	100	0.00
2.5326	0.0069	1,000	0.01
2.5371	0.0021	10,000	0.14
2.5385	0.0007	100,000	1.69
2.5387	0.0005	200,000	3.36
2.5388	0.0003	400,000	6.73

Note: This table shows a Monte Carlo simulation converging to a solution to the integral $\mu_g \equiv E[g(W)]$ given in equation 5.2. $\hat{\mu}_g$ estimates μ_g. $\sqrt{\widehat{\sigma_n^2}/n}$ estimates the standard error of the estimator, n is the number of trials within the simulation, and "seconds" is the number of seconds taken on an old PC.

Op Quiz: Figure 5.1 is a graph of the weird function $g(w)$. In section 5.3, we discussed analytical and numerical techniques for working out $E[g(W)]$ where W is standard normal. Do you understand this well enough to see, by simply looking at figure 5.1 and using your knowledge of the standard normal density, that $E[g(W)]$ must be approximately 2.55?

Answer: W is extremely unlikely to be smaller than -3 or larger than $+3$, and the bulk of the probability mass of W falls between -2 and $+2$. In this range, eyeballing the plot, $g(w)$ takes values between about 2.3 and 2.8. The middle of this range is roughly 2.55.

5.4 Monte Carlo for Options

Our basic option valuation equation $V(t) = e^{-r(T-t)} E_t^*[V(T)]$ (equation 4.3) is a discounted expected payoff in a risk-neutral world (i.e., a discounted mean payoff). The random variable is the terminal option payoff $V(T)$. The mean of $V(T)$ is to be estimated via Monte Carlo.[7] We then discount this mean using riskless rate r.

---

[7]I recommend Hunter and Stowe (1992) as an introduction to Monte Carlo methods for options. They review standard option pricing and discuss path-dependent options. Note, however, that their equation M1 reads $S_{t+1} = S_t e^{r - \frac{\sigma^2}{2}\Delta t + S\sigma\epsilon\sqrt{\Delta t}}$, but should read $S_{t+1} = S_t e^{(r - \frac{1}{2}\sigma^2)\Delta t + \sigma\epsilon\sqrt{\Delta t}}$.

5.4.1 Overview of the Method

We use a computer to simulate a possible path for a stock price over the life of the option from time t to time T in a hypothetical risk-neutral world (details for this "simulation trial" appear in section 5.4.2). Calculate and record the payoff to the option for this first sample path. Call it $V(T)_1$. Now perform a second simulation trial and record a second payoff: $V(T)_2$. Repeat until we have recorded $V(T)_1, V(T)_2, \ldots V(T)_n$.

The average $\overline{V(T)}_n \equiv \frac{1}{n} \sum_{i=1}^{n} V(T)_i \longrightarrow E_t^*[V(T)]$, as $n \to \infty$ (by the SLLN). It follows that

$$\widehat{V(t)} \equiv e^{-r(T-t)} \overline{V(T)}_n = e^{-r(T-t)} \frac{1}{n} \sum_{i=1}^{n} V(T)_i$$

is our estimator of option value, because $\widehat{V(t)} \longrightarrow e^{-r(T-t)} E_t^*[V(T)]$ as $n \longrightarrow \infty$.

Our estimator is of the form $\hat{V} = a\bar{V}_n$ (where a is the discount factor). It follows that if $[L, U]$ is a 95% confidence interval for $\bar{V}_n$, then $[aL, aU]$ is a 95% confidence interval for $\hat{V} = a\bar{V}_n$ using simple properties of random variables. A 95% confidence interval for $V(t)$ is thus (via the CLT)

$$\left[e^{-r(T-t)} \left(\overline{V(T)}_n - 1.96 \sqrt{\frac{\widehat{\sigma_n^2}}{n}} \right), \ e^{-r(T-t)} \left(\overline{V(T)}_n + 1.96 \sqrt{\frac{\widehat{\sigma_n^2}}{n}} \right) \right],$$

where $\widehat{\sigma_n^2} \equiv \frac{1}{n} \sum_{i=1}^{n} [V(T)_i - \overline{V(T)}_n]^2$.

5.4.2 Generating Stock Price Paths

The sample stock price paths are simulated so that they approximately follow a geometric Brownian motion (GBM) random walk. We break up the life of the option from time t to time T into J equally spaced time steps $t_j = t + j(\Delta t)$, for $j = 0, 1, 2, \ldots, J$, where $\Delta t \equiv \frac{T-t}{J}$. Thus, $t_0 = t$, and $t_J = T$. Then we simulate the sample stock price path using:[8]

$$S(t_{j+1}) = S(t_j) e^{\left[\left(r - \frac{1}{2}\sigma^2 \right)(\Delta t) + \sigma \sqrt{(\Delta t)} \, \epsilon_{j+1} \right]},$$

for $j = 0, 1, 2, \ldots, J - 1$, where $S(t_0) = S$ (initial stock price), and $\epsilon_1, \epsilon_2, \ldots, \epsilon_J$ are IID $N(0, 1)$.

5.4.3 Monte Carlo Put Option Example

Consider a two-month European put option on Black and Decker (BDK) struck at $X = \$45$. BDK closed recently at \$41.75. We shall ignore BDK's dividends. Based on the most recent two months of daily continuously compounded stock returns, let us assume that $\hat{\sigma} = 0.34$ (section 8.7.1 shows how to estimate historical volatility). Let us also assume that the shortest term safe interest rate is 0.055 (simple), or

---

[8]Looking ahead, this is a discretization of equation 8.2 in the risk-neutral world.

0.0535 (continuously compounded). There are 365 calendar days in a year, and 61 over the next two months (yes, you have to count). Let (Δt) represent one day (so $\Delta t = \frac{1}{365}$). Then the first simulation trial looks as follows:

$$
\begin{aligned}
S(t_0) &= \$41.75 \\
S(t_{j+1}) &= S(t_j)e^{\left[(0.0535 - \frac{1}{2} \times 0.34^2)(\frac{1}{365}) + 0.34\sqrt{\frac{1}{365}}\,\epsilon_{j+1}\right]} \\
&\quad \text{for } j = 0, 1, 2, \ldots, J-1, \text{where} \\
&\quad \epsilon_1, \epsilon_2, \ldots, \epsilon_J \sim \text{ IID } N(0,1), \\
V(T)_1 &= \max(\$45 - S(T_J), 0), \text{where } J = 61.
\end{aligned}
$$

Each simulation trial yields a payoff $V(T)_i$. The average of these payoffs converges to the Black-Scholes put price (\$4.08) as the number of trials increase (see figure 5.2). Typically, you use at least 10,000 trials.

The example is for a plain vanilla European put, so that we can compare the convergence to a known limit. In practice, the Monte Carlo technique is for exotic options where no pricing formula exists.

Exercise: Section 5.4.2 describes the evolution of stock price paths in the Monte Carlo method. It assumes that

$$
S(t_{j+1}) = S(t_j)e^{\left[(r - \frac{1}{2}\sigma^2)(\Delta t) + \sigma\sqrt{(\Delta t)}\,\epsilon_{j+1}\right]},
$$

where $\epsilon_{j+1} \sim N(0,1)$. Prove that

$$
E_{t_j}^*[S(t_{j+1})|S(t_j)] = S(t_j)e^{r(\Delta t)}.
$$

That is, that the expected value of the stock price one step ahead in the risk-neutral world, conditional upon where it is now, is just the current price grossed up by the riskless rate.

Hint: Plug in the formula for $S(t_{j+1})$ in terms of $S(t_j)$ and the standard normal ϵ_{j+1}. Multiply by the standard normal pdf and collect terms in the exponent, completing the square if necessary. Demonstrate that $S(t_j)e^{r(\Delta t)}$ pops out, leaving a pdf that integrates to one.

5.4.4 Variance Reduction

One problem with Monte Carlo is that it is slow. This becomes less of a problem as technology advances. Several "variance reduction techniques" exist, however, to improve the accuracy of numerically estimated option prices (other than simply using more simulation trials in a Monte Carlo, or a finer mesh in the lattice technique).

The "antithetic variable technique" calculates $\widehat{V(t)}$ in the usual way using the ϵ_j's, but also calculates $\widehat{V(t)}'$ using $-\epsilon_j$'s (which are also IID $N(0,1)$ because of

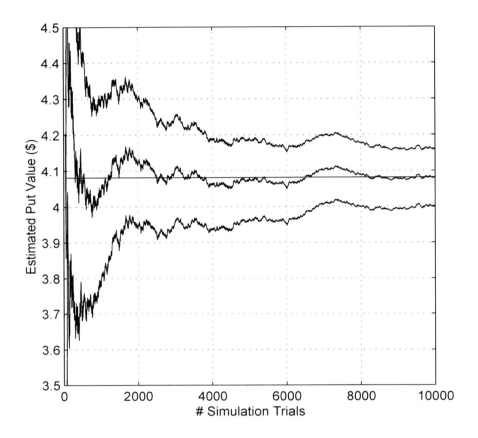

Figure 5.2: Monte Carlo European Put Valuation and 95% C.I.

Note: This is for $S = \$41.75$, $T - t = \frac{61}{365}$, $X = \$45$, $r = 0.0535$, $\sigma = 0.34$, and $J = 61$ steps of $\Delta t = \frac{1}{365}$. The picture also gives the 95% confidence interval for the put value estimator. The Black-Scholes European-style put value of $\$4.08$ is indicated.

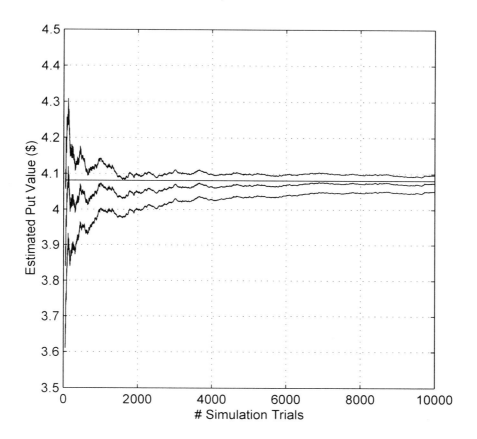

Figure 5.3: Monte Carlo European Put Valuation Using Antithetic Variable Technique

Note: This is for $S = \$41.75$, $T - t = \frac{61}{365}$, $X = \$45$, $r = 0.0535$, $\sigma = 0.34$, and $J = 61$ steps of $(\Delta t) = \frac{1}{365}$. The picture also gives the 95% confidence interval for the antithetic variable put value estimator. The Black-Scholes European-style put value of $4.08 is indicated.

the symmetry of the normal). The average $[\widehat{V(t)} + \widehat{V(t)}']/2$ is more accurate, and converges more quickly, than $\widehat{V(t)}$. See figure 5.3.

The "control variate technique" is for valuing derivative **A** (which has no analytic valuation formula) when there exists derivative **B** similar to **A**, for which a formula exists. For example, suppose **A** is an exotic arithmetic average Asian option, and **B** is a geometric average Asian option (see the formula in Haug [2007, p183]). Calculate both $\hat{V}_A$, and $\hat{V}_B$ using the Monte Carlo, and then find V_B using the analytic formula. Then $\hat{V}_A + (V_B - \hat{V}_B)$ is a better estimator of V_A than is $\hat{V}_A$.

5.4.5 Drift and Dividends

The exercise above asks you to show that if

$$S(t_{j+1}) = S(t_j)e^{\left[(r - \frac{1}{2}\sigma^2)(\Delta t) + \sigma\sqrt{(\Delta t)}\,\epsilon_{j+1}\right]},$$

where $\epsilon_{j+1} \sim N(0,1)$, then $E_{t_j}^*[S(t_{j+1})|S(t_j)] = S(t_j)e^{r(\Delta t)}$. Thus, this really is a model of stock prices evolving with a riskless drift in a risk-neutral world. To incorporate dividends paid at continuous rate ρ into our Monte Carlo, we simply change the data-generating process to

$$\overset{\text{new term}}{\underset{\downarrow}{}}$$
$$S(t_{j+1}) = S(t_j)e^{\left[\,(r - \rho - \frac{1}{2}\sigma^2)(\Delta t) + \sigma\sqrt{(\Delta t)}\,\epsilon_{j+1}\right]},$$

for $j = 0, 1, 2, \ldots, J-1$, where $S(t_0) = S$ (initial stock price), and $\epsilon_1, \epsilon_2, \ldots, \epsilon_J$ are IID $N(0,1)$. With continuous dividends at rate ρ, we have the result

$$E_{t_j}[S(t_{j+1})|S(t_j)] = S(t_j)e^{(r-\rho)(\Delta t)},$$

and the required return (and thus the discount rate) r is now made up of dividends at rate ρ plus capital gains at rate $r - \rho$.

Chapter 6

Numerical Option Pricing: Lattice/Binomial

6.1 Do I Need to Know This?

Let me repeat that although this book is about Black-Scholes option pricing, and you can skip this chapter without loss of continuity, reading it may help even if you do not want to use numerical methods to price options. In particular, this chapter should give you a better feel for risk-neutral probabilities, for the transformation from the risk-neutral world to the real world, for replication arguments, for later approximations to Black-Scholes pricing, and for differences between European and American-style option pricing.

6.2 Lattice Pricing I: One-Step Model

Lattice methods break the life of the option up into discrete equal time steps in a hypothetical risk-neutral world. At each step, the underlying asset value can jump to a finite number of new possible values (typically two or three). Binomial option pricing (i.e., two possible stock price values one step ahead) first appears in Sharpe (1978, pp366–371), but it is not well developed there.[1] Cox, Ross, and Rubinstein (1979) and Rendleman and Bartter (1979) develop binomial option pricing as it is known today. Cox, Ross, and Rubinstein (1979) apply risk-neutral valuation and a limiting argument to arrive at the Black-Scholes formula. Cox and Rubinstein (1985) provide a nice treatment of binomial option pricing.

We build a tree of possible stock prices from time t to time T in a risk-neutral world. We then work backwards from time T using risk-neutral valuation (and riskless discounting) to deduce the initial value of the derivative. Lattice methods are good for both American-style and European-style options, but are not so good for path-dependent options.[2]

---

[1] Note that Parkinson (1977) uses a binomial approximation to the normal to allow numerical integration for pricing the American put.

[2] Hull and White (1993) do, however, present an efficient procedure for valuing path-dependent

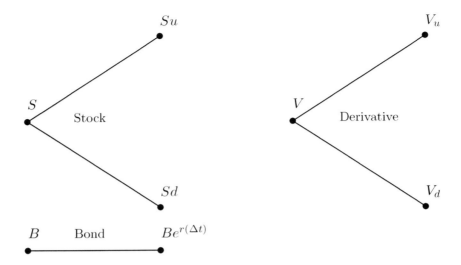

Figure 6.1: Lattice Pricing: Evolution of Stock, Bond, and Derivative

Note: From time t to time T (i.e., over the time step Δt), the stock is modelled as going either up or down using multiplicative growth factors u and d. If the stock goes up, the derivative pays off V_u (that is a subscript); if the stock goes down, the derivative pays off V_d. The bond is riskless; so, its payoff is the same in both the up and down states.

We begin with a simple one-step model. There are three assets: a stock, a riskless bond, and a European-style derivative. We seek the value of the derivative.

Assume that the stock price is S at time t, and then either rises to $S \times u$, or falls[3] to $S \times d$ at time T. Let $\Delta t = T - t$, then an investment of B dollars in the riskless bond at time t grows to be worth $Be^{r(\Delta t)}$ dollars at time T. If S, u, and d are known, then the value of the derivative at time T can be deduced for both states of the world. Label these as "V_u" in the up state, and "V_d" in the down state, as in figure 6.1. For example, if the derivative is a European-style call option with strike X, then, because T is the expiration date, $V_u = \max(0, S \times u - X)$, and $V_d = \max(0, S \times d - X)$, which are both functions of known quantities. We value the derivative at time t by valuing a portfolio that replicates the time-T payoffs to the derivative. We construct this replicating portfolio by holding positions in the stock and the bond. We buy Δ shares of stock and invest B dollars in the riskless bond (Δ and B are to be determined; they may be positive or negative). The portfolio of stock and bond costs $S\Delta + B$ at time t, and must grow to have time-T value $Su\Delta + Be^{r(\Delta t)}$ in the up state, and $Sd\Delta + Be^{r(\Delta t)}$ in the down state—see figure 6.2.

If the portfolio of stock and bond is to replicate the time-T payoff to the derivative,

---

options. The procedure is involved, because you need to know the path followed to arrive at any node (this is clear in a Monte Carlo, but not clear in a lattice).

[3]Although the binomial method presented here sets $d < 1$, this is only for convenience, and d need not be less than 1 as long as $d \leq e^{r(\Delta t)} \leq u$. See the discussion later in this section.

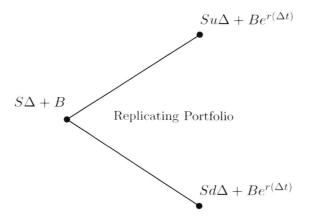

$$Su\Delta + Be^{r(\Delta t)}$$

$$S\Delta + B$$

Replicating Portfolio

$$Sd\Delta + Be^{r(\Delta t)}$$

Figure 6.2: Lattice Pricing: Evolution of the Replicating Portfolio

Note: The portfolio that replicates the derivative begins with Δ shares of stock and \$$B$ invested in the riskless bond. S grows to either $S \times u$ in the up state or $S \times d$ in the down state at time T; \$$B$ invested in the bond grows to $Be^{r(\Delta t)}$ regardless of the state at time T. Do not confuse the Δ shares of stock with the time step length (Δt)—it should be clear from the context.

then its payoffs must be the same as the payoffs to the derivative in both states of the world. That is, equations 6.1 must hold.

$$\text{Derivative Payoffs} \left\{ \begin{array}{ccc} V_u & = & Su\Delta + Be^{r(\Delta t)} \\ V_d & = & Sd\Delta + Be^{r(\Delta t)} \end{array} \right\} \text{Portfolio Payoffs} \qquad (6.1)$$

We know V_u, V_d, S, u, d, r, and Δt (see the numerical example on page 95 to make this concrete), so equations 6.1 are two equations in two unknowns (Δ and B). A small amount of linear algebra yields the particular Δ and B that solve the equations. These are given in equations 6.2 and 6.3:

$$\Delta^{\dagger} = \frac{V_u - V_d}{S(u - d)} \qquad (6.2)$$

$$B^{\dagger} = \frac{uV_d - dV_u}{e^{r(\Delta t)}(u - d)} \qquad (6.3)$$

Exercise: Solve the linear algebra problem of two equations (equations 6.1) in two unknowns (Δ and B) to arrive at equations 6.2 and 6.3.

The portfolio with Δ and B from equations 6.2 and 6.3 replicates the payoff to the option. No-arbitrage arguments imply that the value of the derivative at time t must equal the start-up cost of the replicating portfolio. This yields equation 6.4.

$$V = S\Delta^{\dagger} + B^{\dagger} \qquad (6.4)$$

Plugging the values we obtained for $\Delta^\dagger$ and $B^\dagger$ from equations 6.2 and 6.3 into the no-arbitrage result of equation 6.4 yields, after some algebra, equations 6.5 and 6.6:

$$V = e^{-r(\Delta t)}\left[\pi^* V_u + (1 - \pi^*)V_d\right],\tag{6.5}$$

$$\text{where } \pi^* = \frac{e^{r(\Delta t)} - d}{u - d},\tag{6.6}$$

$$\text{and } \Delta t = \text{the time step.}$$

Exercise: Show that plugging our particular values $\Delta^\dagger$ and $B^\dagger$ from equations 6.2 and 6.3 into the no-arbitrage result in equation 6.4 yields equations 6.5 and 6.6.

This is risk-neutral pricing. The (implicit) "risk-neutral probability" of an up move in the stock appears as π^*. This is not the actual probability of a price move, but the probability of such a move in a risk-neutral world (i.e., a world where the stock price process with the bond as numeraire follows a martingale). If you work out the discounted expected value of the stock under the risk-neutral probabilities, you find that it is just S. Thus, you could have deduced that $\pi^* = \frac{e^{r(\Delta t)}-d}{u-d}$ directly.

Exercise: Prove algebraically that if π^* in equation 6.6 is interpreted as a probability, then the one-step (i.e., $\Delta t = T - t$) binomial model describes stock price drift upward at rate r:
$$E_t^*[S(T)] = S(t)e^{r(T-t)}.$$

Hint: $E_t^*[S(T)] = [\pi^* S(t)u + (1 - \pi^*)S(t)d]$, where $\pi^* = \frac{e^{r(\Delta t)}-d}{u-d}$. Now substitute for π^*, collect terms, and simplify.

In equilibrium, we need $d \le e^{r(\Delta t)} \le u$. If not, then returns to the riskless bond strictly dominate, or are strictly dominated by returns to the stock, and the less attractive of the two assets will be sold short in unlimited quantities to purchase the other asset with unlimited profit; that is not an equilibrium. This result, combined with equation 6.6, implies that $0 \le \pi^* \le 1$, just like a probability. To emphasize the expected DCF nature of this interpretation, equation 6.5 is repeated as equation 6.7, where I have, somewhat loosely, labelled the risk-neutral probabilities "expected."

$$V = \underset{\uparrow}{e^{-r(\Delta t)}} \,[\, \overset{\text{expected}}{(\pi^*)}\, \underset{\uparrow}{V_u} + (1-\pi^*)\, \overset{\text{expected}}{V_d}\,]\tag{6.7}$$

discounted · payoff · payoff

Note that this is a change of probability only. The risk-neutral model of asset price levels is identical to the real-world model (i.e., the same potential asset price outcomes for bond, stock, and derivative). It is only the implicit probabilities of the up and down states that have adjusted to allow a stock price drift upwards at rate r (see the last exercise).

6.3 Lattice Pricing II: *J*-Step Model

I recall John Cox noting in class at MIT that the one-step binomial model is certainly a poor representation of stock price behavior, but that by allowing many small steps, we obtain a model that has much better properties.

In practice, we break the life of the option up into J small time steps from time t to time T. We label these time steps t_j as follows: $t_j = t + j(\Delta t)$, for $j = 0, 1, 2, \ldots, J$, where $(\Delta t) \equiv \frac{T-t}{J}$. Thus, $t_0 = t$, and $t_J = T$.

At each step, the stock price is modelled as per the one-step case:

$$S(t_{j+1}) = \left\{ \begin{array}{ll} S(t_j) \times u\,; & \text{with prob. } \pi^*, \\ S(t_j) \times d\,; & \text{with prob. } (1-\pi^*), \end{array} \right.$$

for $j = 0, 1, 2, \ldots, J-1$, where $\pi^* = \frac{e^{r(\Delta t)} - d}{u - d}$. See figure 6.3 for the two-step case.

6.3.1 Choosing *u* and *d*—and Deducing π^*

So, how do we choose u and d in practice? We choose u and d so that they describe the evolution of possible stock prices in a fashion that approximates the GBM assumed by Black and Scholes. The following is an heuristic argument that should not be taken literally.

1. We shall deduce u and d as multiplicative stock price growth factors of the form $e^{(\text{return})}$ for appropriately chosen "return," where that return is the continuously compounded total (not annualized) return over the time period (Δt).

2. For ease of calculation,[4] I want to choose $u = \frac{1}{d}$. If $u = e^{+(\text{return})}$, this implies that $d = e^{-(\text{return})}$.

3. In the risk-neutral world, our numerical method approximates a GBM with stock return over time step (Δt) distributed as $N[(r - \frac{1}{2}\sigma^2)(\Delta t), \sigma^2(\Delta t)]$ (look ahead to table 8.1 for details). Thus, we must, through choice of u and d, approximate a normally distributed total rate of return that has standard deviation $\sigma \sqrt{(\Delta t)}$. We do not worry about the mean return yet—our subsequent choice of π^* will give us the correct mean return.

4. **Little-known fact:**[5] Suppose R is normally distributed with mean zero, and standard deviation λ. Then, conditional on R being above zero, the expected value of R is approximately $+\lambda$; and, conditional on R being below zero, the expected value of R is approximately $-\lambda$. Thus, the continuous random

---

[4]Advanced aside: Note that this does not necessarily imply a "recombining tree." You get recombination if the option price is path-independent, regardless of u and d. Further details are beyond the scope of this book.

[5]The exact result is $X \sim N(0, \lambda^2)$ implies $E(X|X > 0) = \lambda\sqrt{\frac{2}{\pi}} \approx 0.80 \cdot \lambda$. This is a special case of equation 2.7 on page 28.

variable R could be modelled roughly as the discrete random variable R_{discrete} as in equation 6.8.

$$R_{\text{discrete}} = \begin{cases} +\lambda\,; & \text{prob } \frac{1}{2} \\ -\lambda\,; & \text{prob } \frac{1}{2} \end{cases} \tag{6.8}$$

> **Exercise:** Demonstrate that the normally distributed continuous random variable $R \sim N(0, \lambda^2)$ and the discrete random variable R_{discrete} (from equation 6.8) have the same mean and variance.

5. We conclude that, in order to get the correct volatility, we should choose $u = e^{+\sigma\sqrt{(\Delta t)}}$ and $d = e^{-\sigma\sqrt{(\Delta t)}}$ (with probabilities one-half) to approximate stock price evolution in the real world. The real-world drift rate is irrelevant for pricing the option when the underlying process is a geometric Brownian motion (Merton [1992]).

6. With u and d so chosen, we may now deduce the implicit risk-neutral probabilities π^* that produce drift rate r:

$$\begin{aligned} E^*[S(t + (\Delta t))] &= S(t)e^{r(\Delta t)} \\ &= \pi^* S(t)u + (1 - \pi^*)S(t)d \\ \Rightarrow e^{r(\Delta t)} &= \pi^* u + (1 - \pi^*)d \\ \Rightarrow \pi^* &= \frac{e^{r(\Delta t)} - d}{u - d} \end{aligned}$$

Thus, our choice of u and d trickles down to the implicit probability π^*, correcting the risk-neutral drift. So, we need not worry about drift when choosing u and d.

7. These choices for u and d are the same as those made by Cox, Ross, and Rubinstein (1979). To be exhaustive, however, you should know that the conditions on the binomial parameters that guarantee convergence to a log-normally distributed stock price process in continuous time leave one degree of freedom open to the researchers. Cox, Ross, and Rubinstein (1979) choose one of arbitrarily many possible definitions of the parameters in their limiting arguments. Other choices are available (see Tian [1993]). Note, however, that although many other choices for u and d give appropriate convergence in the limit as step sizes go to zero, Cox, Ross, and Rubinstein's choice is the only one that is consistent with risk-neutral pricing in discrete time (Nawalkha and Chambers [1995]).

With u and d as known functions of σ and Δt, and with π^* a known function of u, d, r, and Δt, we can now work backwards through the stock price tree, discounting the terminal option payoffs using equations 6.5 and 6.6 to get initial option value.

In the case of a European call or put, after some algebra, we can derive an explicit binomial option pricing formula. Let us leave this formula until section 8.3.3, though, both because it provides a nice interpretation of Black-Scholes option pricing, and because more algebra is inappropriate until numerical examples are presented.

6.3.2 Binomial Valuation Example

Let us value a two-month European put option on Black and Decker (BDK) struck at $45. BDK closed recently at $41.75. Let us ignore BDK's dividends. Based on the most recent two months of daily continuously compounded stock returns, $\hat{\sigma} = 0.34$ (section 8.7.1 shows how to estimate historical volatility). Let us assume that the shortest-term safe interest rate is 0.055 (simple), or 0.0535 (continuously compounded). There are 12 months in a year, so $T - t = \frac{2}{12}$. Let (Δt) represent one month (so $(\Delta t) = \frac{1}{12}$).

We calculate $u = 1.1031$, $d = 0.9065$, and $\pi^* = 0.4982$. We use u and d to build the stock price tree, find the final option values, and discount back using $V = e^{-r(\Delta t)} [\pi^* V_u + (1 - \pi^*) V_d]$. The tree in figure 6.3 shows the two time steps and the numbers: the estimated put price is $4.2786.

From Black-Scholes, however, we can calculate the option price to be $4.08. We overpriced by 5%. So, how many time steps do we need, and how small should (Δt) be? Figure 6.4 shows our binomial lattice pricing as the number of time steps within two months increases (and the length of the time step correspondingly decreases).

Actual Job Interview Question: Suppose that the riskless rate is zero. Suppose that a stock is at $100, and one year from now will be at either $130, or $70, with probabilities 0.80 and 0.20, respectively. There are no dividends. What is the value of a one-year European call with strike $110?

Taken from "Heard on The Street: Quantitative Questions from Wall Street Job Interviews," ©2008 Timothy Falcon Crack. See advertisement on last page of this book.

Answer: If you said $16 (an 80% chance of getting $20), then you are wrong. Go back to equations 6.5 and 6.6 and try again. The correct answer is $10.

Note: Looking at figure 6.4, we see that the number returned by the binomial lattice valuation bounces up and down as you increment the number of steps in the valuation. Thus, a simple method to improve accuracy is to take the average of the valuations arrived at by using, say, 50 and 51 steps, respectively. I think this variance reduction method was first published by Mark Rubinstein.

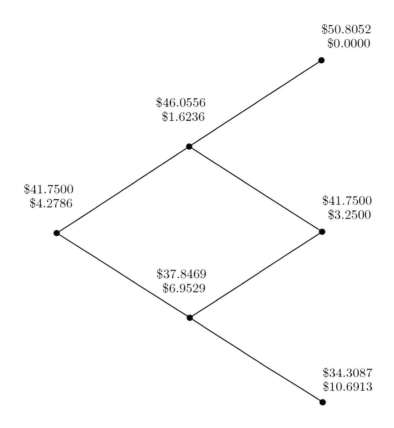

$50.8052
$0.0000

$46.0556
$1.6236

$41.7500
$4.2786

$41.7500
$3.2500

$37.8469
$6.9529

$34.3087
$10.6913

Figure 6.3: Lattice Pricing: Two-Step Tree, European Put

Note: This figure shows a European put binomial lattice valuation with $S = \$41.75$, $T - t = \frac{2}{12}$, $X = \$45$, $r = 0.0535$, $\sigma = 0.34$, and two time steps of $(\Delta t) = \frac{1}{12}$. The upper number in each pair is the stock value, starting at $\$41.75$ and evolving through time using $u = e^{+\sigma\sqrt{(\Delta t)}}$ and $d = e^{-\sigma\sqrt{(\Delta t)}}$. The lower number in each pair is the European put value. The put values terminate at the final nodes as $\max[0, X - S(T)] = \max(0, \$45 - S)$, and are discounted backwards through the tree using risk-neutral pricing $V = e^{-r(\Delta t)}\left[\pi^* V_u + (1 - \pi^*) V_d\right]$ at each step.

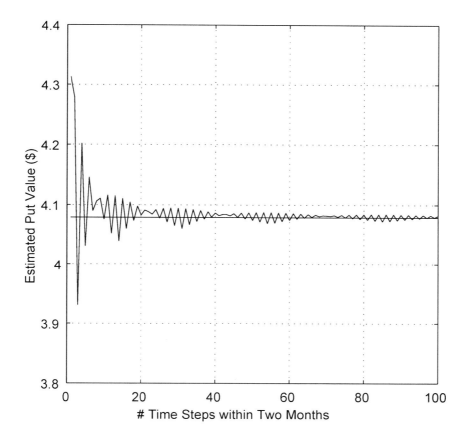

Figure 6.4: Lattice Pricing: European Put $J \longrightarrow \infty$

Note: This figure shows a European put binomial lattice valuation with $S = 41.75, $T - t = \frac{2}{12}$, $X = \$45$, $r = 0.0535$, $\sigma = 0.34$, and time steps of $(\Delta t) = \frac{2}{12\,J}$, where J (the number of time steps within two months) is on the horizontal. The Black-Scholes European put value of $4.08 is indicated. Typically, at least 30 time steps within the option's life are required for accuracy.

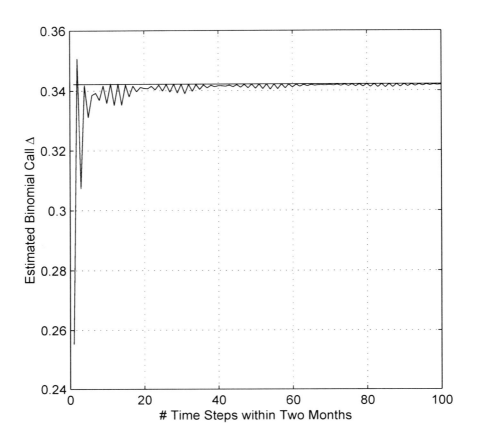

Figure 6.5: Lattice Pricing: European Call $\Delta_t^\dagger \to N(d_1)$

Note: This figure shows the value of $\Delta^\dagger = \frac{V_u - V_d}{S(u-d)}$, using only the first time step, estimated for a European call with $S = \$41.75$, $T - t = \frac{2}{12}$, $X = \$45$, $r = 0.0535$, $\sigma = 0.34$, and time steps of $(\Delta t = \frac{2}{12J})$, where J (the number of time steps within two months) is on the horizontal. $\Delta^\dagger$ approaches the Black-Scholes European call's $\Delta = N(d_1) = 0.3422$ as J (the number of steps) increases. See the op quiz on page 102 for a related exercise.

6.4 Lattice Pricing III: American Options

Lattice methods extend naturally to American-style options. As you work backwards through the tree, you pause at each node, and ask "should I pull the trigger?" Is it more valuable to kill the option now through exercise, or to hold it for the next time step? The former is worth the intrinsic value (IV); the latter is worth the discounted expected payoff.

At each node, the American option value is the maximum of two quantities:

$$V = \max\left\{\text{IV}, e^{-r(\Delta t)}\left[\pi^* V_u + (1 - \pi^*)V_d\right]\right\}, \text{ where}$$
$$\text{IV} = \text{ intrinsic value.}$$

Figure 6.6 is a numerical example for an American put with the same parameters as the European put example in figure 6.3. Figure 6.7 compares the values of the J-step American and European put valuations as the number of time steps with the option life $J \longrightarrow \infty$.

6.5 Adjusting for Dividends

If the underlying pays continuous dividends at rate ρ, then the lattice of stock prices has drift of only $r - \rho$, instead of r. The only change is that $\pi^* = \frac{e^{(r-\rho)(\Delta t)} - d}{u - d}$ replaces our previous π^*. We still discount at the required rate of return r.

If the underlying pays a lump-sum dividend d_1 at time τ during the life of the option, then you proceed as follows:

1. Model the growth of the ex-dividend process S^* using a lattice (where $S^*(t) = S(t) - d_1 e^{-r(\tau-t)}$ initially).

2. Use the terminal values of the S^* tree to calculate the terminal option values.

3. Add the values of the dividends back into the stock price tree prior to the ex-dividend dates. Thus, at time $t + j(\Delta t) < \tau$, you replace $S^*[t + j(\Delta t)]$ by $S^*[t + j(\Delta t)] + d_1 e^{-r(\tau-t-j(\Delta t))}$.

4. Work backwards through the tree discounting the option values using risk-neutral valuation. If the option is American style, then you calculate comparative intrinsic values using the cum-dividend price of the stock prior to the ex-dividend date.

5. This is a recombining tree, but some methods for accommodating the dividend are not recombining. See Hull (2000, pp398–400) for details.

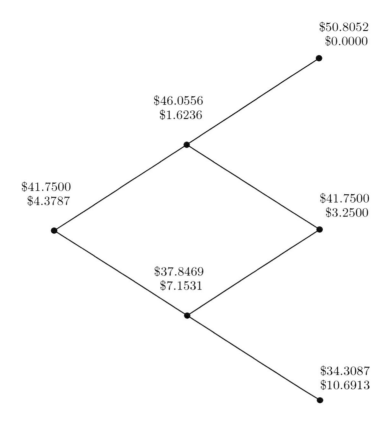

$50.8052
$0.0000

$46.0556
$1.6236

$41.7500
$4.3787

$41.7500
$3.2500

$37.8469
$7.1531

$34.3087
$10.6913

Figure 6.6: Lattice Pricing: American Put, Two-Step Tree

Note: The upper number in each pair is the stock value, starting at $41.75 and evolving through time using $u = e^{+\sigma\sqrt{(\Delta t)}}$ and $d = e^{-\sigma\sqrt{(\Delta t)}}$. The lower number in each pair is the American put value. The put values terminate at the final nodes as $\max[0, X - S(T)] = \max(0, \$45 - S)$, then are discounted backwards through the tree using risk-neutral pricing and comparing to intrinsic value (IV):

$$V = \max\left\{\text{IV}, e^{-r(\Delta t)}\left[\pi^* V_u + (1 - \pi^*)V_d\right]\right\}$$

In this example, early exercise (or sale) is optimal at the node where $S = \$37.8469$. Exercise (or sale) at this node yields $7.1531, whereas the DCF is only $6.9529 in the analogous node in figure 6.3.

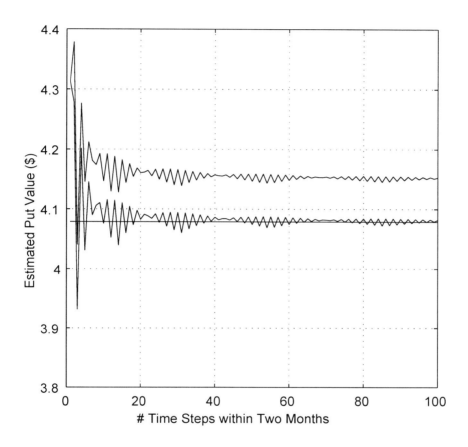

Figure 6.7: Lattice Put Valuation (American versus European)

Note: Valuation of an American and a European put using $S = \$41.75$, $T - t = \frac{2}{12}$, $X = \$45$, $r = 0.0535$, $\sigma = 0.34$, and time steps of ($\Delta t = \frac{2}{12\,J}$), where J (the number of time steps within two months) is on the horizontal. The Black-Scholes European put value of \$4.08 is indicated. Both the European and American option valuations converge, but an exact, closed-form formula for what the American put value converges to is still an unsolved problem.

Op Quiz: Figure 6.5 shows $\Delta^\dagger = \frac{V_u - V_d}{S(u-d)} \to N(d_1)$ as the number of time steps within two months $J \to \infty$ for a European call binomial lattice valuation problem. What happens to $\Delta^\dagger = \frac{V_u - V_d}{S(u-d)}$ in the European put binomial lattice valuation problem above as the number of time steps within two months goes to infinity? You may need to study chapter 8 before answering.

Answer: In the case of the European put, $\Delta^\dagger = \frac{V_u - V_d}{S(u-d)}$ converges to $-N(-d_1)$ (i.e., the delta of the European put).

Chapter 7

Partial Differential Equations

7.1 Do I Need to Know This?

The "Black-Scholes equation" is a partial differential equation (PDE). The Black-Scholes pricing formula is a particular solution to this PDE. Black (1989) tells the story of searching for the solution to the PDE so that he could price options. You can leave this short chapter out without loss of continuity, but reading it helps you to better understand where the Black-Scholes formula comes from and how the PDE that predates it provides economic intuition for some of the consequences of hedging options positions. Skip to section 7.6 if you have no high level mathematics.

7.2 PDEs 101

PDEs are typically the preserve of physical scientists. The famous "diffusion equation," $\frac{\partial u}{\partial \tau} = \frac{\partial^2 u}{\partial x^2}$, can be used to describe how changes in temperature u are related to changes in time τ, and distance x through, for example, a metal bar with one end held at a constant temperature. Loosely speaking, ∂u, $\partial \tau$, and ∂x are small changes in temperature, time, and distance, respectively, and the ratio $\frac{\partial u}{\partial \tau}$, for example, is a relative change in u versus τ (like a slope on a graph of u versus τ).

To solve for the particular $u(\tau, x)$ that describes the diffusion of heat through the bar as a function of time τ and distance x, you need boundary and initial conditions describing behavior at the boundaries, or at $\tau = 0$, respectively, for your particular bar.[1] For example, is heat applied to one end of the bar only, or to both? Is the heat constant at each end of the bar [so, $u(\tau, x_1) = U_1$, and $u(\tau, x_2) = U_2$]? Is one end insulated, so that $\frac{\partial u(\tau, x)}{\partial x} = 0$ when $x = x_2$? The diffusion equation can also describe how liquids mix (e.g., perfume diffusing through the air in a room with the passage of time and the distance from source). Farlow (1993) is an excellent book on PDEs. He presents good intuition and diagrams, with no finance.

---

[1]We should note that, analogously, if c satisfies the Black-Scholes PDE, then so too do $2c$, $\frac{1}{3}c$, $-5c$, etc. Satisfying the PDE may be a necessary condition for deriving the value of a derivative, but it not a sufficient condition. Sensible boundary and initial conditions must also be satisfied.

7.3 Where Do Financial PDEs Come From?

Sections 4.4.1 (p73) and 4.4.3 (p76) demonstrate how to generate financial PDEs by hedging arguments and by martingale arguments, respectively. We arrive, in those sections, at the Black-Scholes PDE for a stock paying no dividends:

$$\frac{\partial V}{\partial t} + \frac{1}{2}\sigma^2 S^2 \frac{\partial^2 V}{\partial S^2} + rS\frac{\partial V}{\partial S} - rV = 0, \qquad (7.1)$$

and the Black-Scholes PDE for a stock paying continuous dividends as rate ρ:

$$\frac{\partial V}{\partial t} + \frac{1}{2}\sigma^2 S^2 \frac{\partial^2 V}{\partial S^2} + (r - \rho)S\frac{\partial V}{\partial S} - rV = 0. \qquad (7.2)$$

Note that these PDEs are associated with the data-generating process for the underlying stock, and not with any particular option. That is, whether the option is a put or a call, for example, the PDE is the same. It is the boundary conditions that determine the type of option whose price is a solution to the PDE. Some example boundary conditions are given in section 7.4, following.

With Black-Scholes, we usually solve the PDE by walking backwards from the final payoff boundary in much the same way as we walk backwards through the tree in binomial option pricing.[2] This requires a change of variables. We turn the Black-Scholes equation (equation 7.1), which is a backward parabolic PDE, into a forward parabolic PDE, so final conditions for the backward equation become initial conditions for the forward equation. See Musiela and Rutkowski (1997, p118), Wilmott et al. (1997, section 4.4), Farlow (1993, Lessons 1 and 41), and section 7.4, following, for details.

Exercise: Consider two pathological derivatives. The first is an investment of B dollars into the bond at time 0, and has value $V(S,t) = Be^{rt}$ at time t; the second is an investment of S dollars at time 0 into a stock bleeding continuous dividends at rate ρ (with dividends reinvested back into the stock), and has value $V(S,t) = S(t)e^{\rho t}$ at time t. Show that in the case of the bond, $V(S,t) = Be^{rt}$ satisfies both equations 7.1 and 7.2. Show that in the case of the stock, $V(S,t) = S(t)e^{\rho t}$ satisfies equation 7.2. Write out $V(S,t)$ for the case of an investment of S dollars at time 0 into a stock that pays no dividends, and show that $V(S,t)$ satisfies equation 7.1 in that case.

7.4 Transforming the PDE

Numerical solution of PDEs is beyond the scope of this book. Indeed, discussing PDEs at all is pushing the envelope. Some limited discussion of how you go about solving a PDE numerically is in order, however, because the change of variables and tentative steps toward solution provide some economic intuition, and remove barriers to entry for those who want to investigate further.

---

[2]Indeed, some forms of numerical solution to the Black-Scholes PDE can be shown to be mathematically equivalent to some forms of lattice pricing. See Hull (2000, p422).

The Black-Scholes equation for a stock bleeding a continuous dividend yield ρ is given in equation 7.2. It is easier to solve the forward diffusion equation than the backward Black-Scholes equation; so, we make the change of variables from (S, t) to (x, τ) described in equations 7.3–7.7:

$$S \quad = \quad Xe^x, \tag{7.3}$$

$$t \quad = \quad T - \frac{\tau}{\frac{1}{2}\sigma^2}, \quad \text{(thereby reversing time)}, \tag{7.4}$$

$$V(S, t) \quad = \quad Xu(x, \tau)e^{-\frac{1}{2}(\iota_2 - 1)x - [\frac{1}{4}(\iota_2 - 1)^2 + \iota_1]\tau}, \quad \text{where} \tag{7.5}$$

$$\iota_1 \quad = \quad \frac{r}{\frac{1}{2}\sigma^2}, \quad \text{and} \tag{7.6}$$

$$\iota_2 \quad = \quad \frac{(r - \rho)}{\frac{1}{2}\sigma^2}. \tag{7.7}$$

Plugging equations 7.3–7.7 into equation 7.2 transforms the Black-Scholes equation into the diffusion equation shown in equation 7.8 (see the exercise following if you have the mathematics skills):

$$\frac{\partial u}{\partial \tau} = \frac{\partial^2 u}{\partial x^2} \tag{7.8}$$

Exercise: Let $\kappa(x, \tau) \equiv -\frac{1}{2}(\iota_2 - 1)x - [\frac{1}{4}(\iota_2 - 1)^2 + \iota_1]\tau$, and use the chain rule results in equations 7.9–7.11, as follows,

$$\frac{\partial V}{\partial t} \quad = \quad \frac{\partial V}{\partial x} \cdot \frac{\partial x}{\partial t} + \frac{\partial V}{\partial \tau} \cdot \frac{\partial \tau}{\partial t}, \tag{7.9}$$

$$\frac{\partial V}{\partial S} \quad = \quad \frac{\partial V}{\partial x} \cdot \frac{\partial x}{\partial S} + \frac{\partial V}{\partial \tau} \cdot \frac{\partial \tau}{\partial S}, \quad \text{and} \tag{7.10}$$

$$\frac{\partial^2 V}{\partial S^2} \quad = \quad \frac{\partial}{\partial x}\left[\frac{\partial V}{\partial S}\right] \cdot \frac{\partial x}{\partial S} + \frac{\partial}{\partial \tau}\left[\frac{\partial V}{\partial S}\right] \cdot \frac{\partial \tau}{\partial S}, \tag{7.11}$$

to demonstrate that equations 7.3–7.7 yield equations 7.12–7.14:

$$\frac{\partial V}{\partial t} \quad = \quad -\frac{1}{2}\sigma^2\left\{\frac{\partial u}{\partial \tau} - u\left[\frac{1}{4}(\iota_2 - 1)^2 + \iota_1\right]\right\} \cdot Xe^{\kappa(x, \tau)} \tag{7.12}$$

$$\frac{\partial V}{\partial S} \quad = \quad \left\{\frac{\partial u}{\partial x} - u\frac{1}{2}(\iota_2 - 1)\right\} \cdot \frac{Xe^{\kappa(x, \tau)}}{S} \tag{7.13}$$

$$\frac{\partial^2 V}{\partial S^2} \quad = \quad \left\{\frac{\partial^2 u}{\partial x^2} - \iota_2\frac{\partial u}{\partial x}\right.$$
$$\left. +u\left[\frac{1}{4}(\iota_2 - 1)^2 + \frac{1}{2}(\iota_2 - 1)\right]\right\} \cdot \frac{Xe^{\kappa(x, \tau)}}{S^2} \tag{7.14}$$

Now plug equations 7.12–7.14 into the Black-Scholes PDE, equation 7.2, cancel out the S terms, divide by $\frac{1}{2}\sigma^2 Xe^{\kappa(x, \tau)}$, label $\frac{r}{\frac{1}{2}\sigma^2}$ as ι_1, label $\frac{(r - \rho)}{\frac{1}{2}\sigma^2}$ as ι_2, and collect and cancel terms to arrive at the diffusion equation: equation 7.8.

The payoff function for the option (i.e., large t) determines the initial conditions (i.e., small τ) for $u(x, \tau)$. The boundary conditions for the option (i.e., small S and large S) determine the conditions at infinity for $u(x, \tau)$, that is, as $x \to \pm\infty$. For a European-style call, the initial and boundary conditions are (in terms of x and τ) given by equations 7.15–7.17 (see the exercise following):

$$u(x,0) = \max\left(e^{\frac{1}{2}(\iota_2+1)x} - e^{\frac{1}{2}(\iota_2-1)x}, 0\right) \qquad (7.15)$$

$$\lim_{x\to+\infty} u(x,\tau) \sim \left(e^x - e^{-\tau\iota_1}\right)e^{\frac{1}{2}(\iota_2-1)x+\left[\frac{1}{4}(\iota_2-1)^2+\iota_1\right]\tau} \qquad (7.16)$$

$$\lim_{x\to-\infty} u(x,\tau) = 0 \qquad (7.17)$$

Exercise: Equation 7.16 describes the boundary behavior of $u(x,\tau)$ as x gets large and positive. How is it derived? From equation 7.3, we see that $x \to +\infty$ implies $S \to +\infty$. We know from discussions in section 3.6.3 that for large S, the call value is $S - PV(X)$. That is, $V(S,t) \sim S - Xe^{-r(T-t)} = Xe^x - X = X(e^x - e^{-r(T-t)})$. Equation 7.5, however, says that $V(S,t) = Xu(x,\tau)e^{-\frac{1}{2}(\iota_2-1)x-\left[\frac{1}{4}(\iota_2-1)^2+\iota_1\right]\tau}$. Equating these two expressions, cancelling X, using equations 7.4 and 7.6 to rewrite $r(T-t)$ as $\tau\iota_1$, and collecting terms yields equation 7.16. Now use the functional form of the payoff to a European call to deduce equation 7.15 via similar arguments.

7.5   PDE Solution by Finite Differences

The basic idea underlying finite-difference methods is to replace the partial derivatives in PDEs by finite-difference approximations; that is, to replace infinitesimal quantities by small finite quantities. We can rewrite the diffusion equation, equation 7.8, replacing the partial derivatives on each side with approximate differences that look like slopes and change in slopes for discrete steps $\delta\tau$ and δx, respectively, to arrive at equation 7.18 as a discretized version of equation 7.8:

$$\frac{u(x,\tau+\delta\tau) - u(x,\tau)}{\delta\tau} \approx \frac{\left[\frac{u(x+\delta x,\tau)-u(x,\tau)}{\delta x}\right] - \left[\frac{u(x,\tau)-u(x-\delta x,\tau)}{\delta x}\right]}{\delta x}$$

$$= \frac{u(x+\delta x,\tau) - 2u(x,\tau) + u(x-\delta x,\tau)}{(\delta x)^2} \qquad (7.18)$$

Proceeding in this fashion, we approximate the partial derivatives on a grid over discretized time intervals, and discretized stock value intervals. We may rearrange equation 7.18 to solve for $u(\cdot,\cdot)$ within the assumed grid as a recursive function of values of $u(\cdot,\cdot)$ one step closer to the boundary. Boundary conditions are then used to start the recursion, and you work backwards to find the initial value of the function $u(x,\tau)$. The details are well beyond the scope of this text. For a full explanation, see Brennan and Schwartz (1978), Farlow (1993, Lesson 38), Hull (2000), Wilmott et al. (1993), or Wilmott et al. (1997).

Once your computer algorithm has solved the diffusion equation in terms of the non-dimensional $u(x,\tau)$, the values of the option $V(S,t)$, in terms of financial variables, may be recovered using equation 7.19:[3]

$$V = X^{\frac{1}{2}(1+\iota_2)} S^{\frac{1}{2}(1-\iota_2)} e^{-\frac{1}{8}[(\iota_2-1)^2 + 4\iota_1]\sigma^2(T-t)} \times u\left(\ln\left(\frac{S}{X}\right), \frac{1}{2}\sigma^2(T-t)\right) \qquad (7.19)$$

7.6 PDE Interpretation: Greeks 101

When an investment bank sells a derivative security to a corporate client, the bank is left with a short position in that security. Most banks do not want to remain exposed to this speculative position. The bank makes money by charging a markup and offlaying their risk by using a trading strategy that replicates a long position in the derivative. Varying degrees of complexity exist for the replicating strategy.

Suppose that an investment bank sells a call option on a stock. If the bank wants to replicate a long position in this option, then it needs to create a "synthetic derivative" that matches the original option to some degree. Ignoring the markup, at the very least the bank wants to replicate the value of the derivative (i.e., the *height* of the plot in figure 3.4 at today's stock price). Of course, as the stock price changes, the bank's synthetic derivative is not much of a hedge if it remains equal to the initial value of the short position. The bank can create a better hedge by replicating both the height of the plot of option value and its local sensitivity to the changing stock price (i.e., the *slope*). This is a good hedge, but if the plot of the option value has a great deal of curvature, for example if the option is near the money and close to maturity, then the bank may also wish to replicate the *curvature* of the plot of option value as a function of stock price. That is, the bank may wish to replicate each of height, slope, and curvature of the plot of option value as a function of stock price.

In mathematics, a "Taylor series expansion" is a sum of terms of increasing order that can be used to approximate a function. The first three terms are related directly to height, slope, and curvature of the function to be approximated; each term brings with it none of the previous (e.g., slope without height, curvature without height or slope, etc.). The more terms you take from the Taylor series expansion, the more accurate is the approximation to the original function. This is analogous to creating more and more complex trading strategies to replicate more and more characteristics of the original option value as a function of the underlying price.

If we let $V(S,t)$ denote option value, then the slope of the plot of option value with respect to stock price is known as "delta" and ($\Delta \equiv \frac{\partial V}{\partial S}$); the curvature is known as "gamma" and ($\Gamma \equiv \frac{\partial^2 V}{\partial S^2}$). These are two of the "Greeks" referred to in the title of this section. If the bank replicates only value and slope of the short option, this is known as a "delta hedge." Delta hedging usually uses only the underlying stock together with borrowing or lending (which we may think of as selling or buying bonds, respectively). The replicating portfolio of stock and bond is managed through time, with proportions typically being adjusted on a daily basis, or perhaps twice daily if there is a lot of convexity. This is one example of a dynamic replicating

---

[3]Wilmott et al. (1993) and Wilmott et al. (1997) misstate this recovery function.

strategy as discussed in section 4.2 (p68). If the bank also replicates the curvature of the short option, then this is known as "delta-gamma hedging," or simply gamma hedging. Gamma hedging usually requires that an option be added to the dynamic replicating strategy to help replicate the curvature of the option that was shorted. We discuss these hedges in more detail and with examples in section 8.8.

You demonstrated in the exercise on page 104 that investments in both the stock and the bond satisfy the Black-Scholes PDE. You will be asked to prove in section 8.3.7 that the Black-Scholes formula for calls or puts also satisfies the Black-Scholes PDE. Delta-gamma hedging of stock options usually involves trading in these very instruments: the stock, the bond, and another option, either a call or a put which is used to help replicate curvature. If a bank shorts a stock option and then enters a delta-gamma hedge, the bank has a position in four instruments: the short option, the stock, the bond, and another option. Each of these positions satisfies the Black-Scholes PDE. It follows that the overall net position of short option plus long replicating portfolio must, as a sum of the parts, also satisfy the Black-Scholes PDE. However, as a hedged position, we know that the value of the short option is replicated by the value of the replicating portfolio, as is the slope and the curvature. The bank is short the option and long the replicating portfolio; so if W now represents the net value of the hedged position, then $W = 0$, $\frac{\partial W}{\partial S} = 0$, and $\frac{\partial^2 W}{\partial S^2} = 0$. We know that W, as the sum of parts that satisfy the Black-Scholes PDE, also satisfies it; so, with continuous dividends at rate ρ,

$$\frac{\partial W}{\partial t} + \frac{1}{2}\sigma^2 S^2 \frac{\partial^2 W}{\partial S^2} + (r - \rho)S\frac{\partial W}{\partial S} - rW = 0. \qquad (7.20)$$

The second, third, and fourth terms on the LHS of equation 7.20 are zero, so we conclude that $\frac{\partial W}{\partial t} = 0$. That is, if you delta-gamma hedge the short option, you create an overall position that does not decay in value simply with the passage of time. That is, the time decay characteristics of the replicating portfolio used to delta-gamma hedge match the time decay characteristics of the short option. This is know as a "theta hedge," and you get it for free when you delta gamma hedge.

The derivatives appearing in the Black-Scholes PDE are the theta (Θ), gamma (Γ), and delta (Δ), respectively. The Black-Scholes PDE in equation 7.20 may thus be rewritten to recognize explicitly the hedge parameters, as in equation 7.21:

$$\Theta + \frac{1}{2}\sigma^2 S^2 \Gamma + (r - \rho)S\Delta - rV = 0 \qquad (7.21)$$

As a final note, if you price your option using numerical techniques, then you cannot use analytical calculus to derive the Greeks. You can, however, find each of them via simple numerical techniques. For example, if $V(\widehat{S}, t)$ is your numerical estimate of option value at today's stock price (via Monte Carlo, lattice, or numerical PDE solution), then for small δS,

$$\Delta = \frac{\partial V}{\partial S} \approx \frac{V(\widehat{S + \delta S}, t) - V(\widehat{S - \delta S}, t)}{(S + \delta S) - (S - \delta S)} = \frac{V(\widehat{S + \delta S}, t) - V(\widehat{S - \delta S}, t)}{2\delta S}.$$

Op Quiz: Options that decay rapidly in value tend also to have significant curvature. That is, large negative Θ is often accompanied by large positive Γ. An at-the-money call close to maturity is a prime example. Are Θ and Γ always of opposing sign? Why or why not? Restrict your answer to plain vanilla options.

Answer: The last two terms of the PDE, $(r - \rho)S\Delta - rV$, tend to offset to some extent. The entire PDE adds to zero, so that leaves $\Theta + \frac{1}{2}\sigma^2 S^2 \Gamma$ taking a value close to zero. The coefficient $\frac{1}{2}\sigma^2 S^2 > 0$, so this means that Θ and Γ are typically going to be of opposite signs. Not only that, but their magnitudes are going to be correlated. For example, if Θ is large and negative then Γ is probably large and positive. There are two exceptions among plain vanilla puts and calls. First, a deep in-the-money European-style put has positive Θ, and will also have positive Γ unless it is so deep in-the-money that the Γ is zero. This is illustrated in the lower plot in figure 3.3 on page 59 for stock price between approximately \$20 and \$30. In this region, the plot of put price has positive curvature (because the slope is negative and is increasing towards zero as we read from left to right), but put value must decay upwards toward instrinsic value as maturity approaches, so, Θ is positive. Second, a deep in-the-money European-style call on a dividend-paying stock can be priced below intrinsic value (if dividend yield is high enough), and have both positive Θ and positive Γ. I encourage you to download the spreadsheet Greeks tool mentioned in section 10.3 to explore the Greeks.

Op Quiz: We demonstrated above that a short option that is delta-gamma hedged is also automatically theta hedged. What do you conclude about the time decay of the net value of the hedged position if the short option is delta hedged only, and not gamma hedged?

Answer: We know the value W of the net hedged position satisfies the Black-Scholes PDE. If the short option is delta hedged only, then $W = 0$ and $\frac{\partial W}{\partial S} = 0$. Plugging these into the PDE, equation 7.20, we conclude that

$$\frac{\partial W}{\partial t} = -\frac{1}{2}\sigma^2 S^2 \frac{\partial^2 W}{\partial S^2}.$$

However, a delta hedge contains only stock and bond, neither of which contains any curvature with respect to stock price (the plots of stock or bond value versus stock price are straight lines with slope 1 and 0, respectively). If V is the value of the short option (a positive number), then any curvature in W comes from V alone. It must be that

$$\frac{\partial W}{\partial t} = -\frac{1}{2}\sigma^2 S^2 \frac{\partial^2 V}{\partial S^2}.$$

That is, the time decay in the overall delta hedged position is driven solely by the degree of curvature of the short option. The very reasonable conclusion is that when the gamma (i.e., the curvature of option price with respect to stock price) is large, you have an incentive to gamma hedge both because you are not hedged against large moves in the underlying, but also because large gamma typically implies large theta for the overall delta hedged position. We discuss this in more detail in section 8.8.

Chapter 8

Analytical Option Pricing: Black-Scholes

8.1 Black-Scholes Assumptions

Black and Scholes (1973) assume two fundamental assets: a bond with price $B(\cdot)$, and a stock with price $S(\cdot)$. The price of a third asset, a European-style call option on the stock maturing at time T, is to be derived from the price of the other two assets. Black and Scholes also assume that there are no T-costs or taxes, all securities are perfectly divisible (so you can buy one-tenth of a share if you wish), the stock pays no dividends during the life of the option, security trading is continuous in time (so if you can trade at two points in time, you can also trade at any time between those two points), security trading is continuous in price (so there are no eighths, sixteenths, or decimals, but arbitrarily fine price resolution), both the stock and riskless bond may be sold short with no restrictions and no margins, and the riskless interest rate r is constant.

How do the price of the stock and the bond evolve through time? That is, what are the functional forms of the data-generating processes? We discussed a GBM random walk in the stock price with predictable and random components in section 4.4.1. This GBM is the price process assumed by Black and Scholes to help price their European-style call option.

When an option pricing formula does exist, the combination of the assumptions about market frictions (T-costs, taxes, etc.), the assumed data-generating process, the type of option (plain vanilla call, plain vanilla put, or exotic), and the exercise style (American, European, or other) determine uniquely what that formula is. For example, you can get a different formula if you assume a different exercise style (e.g., section 9.1.2), or a different data-generating process (e.g., section 9.2.1), or consider an exotic call option (e.g., sections 9.2.2 and 9.2.3), or make some mix of different assumptions. Different options need not, however, have different option pricing formulae; see the Key Point on page 138.

We assume a base observation at time 0, that now is time t, and that the option matures at time T. The prices of the bond and the stock are assumed to grow as in equations 8.1 and 8.2 for any $0 \le t \le T$:

$$B(t) = \exp(rt) \tag{8.1}$$

$$S(t) = S(0)\,\exp\left\{\left(\mu - \frac{1}{2}\sigma^2\right)t + \sigma w(t)\right\} \tag{8.2}$$

The term $w(t)$ in equation 8.2 is a standard Brownian motion; its exponentiation in the equation produces a GBM in stock price.[1,2] The constants r, μ, and σ are the instantaneous risk-free rate per annum, the instantaneous drift rate of the stock price per annum, and the instantaneous volatility of continuously compounded returns on the stock, respectively.

Among the properties of the standard Brownian motion $w(t)$ are that it is initially equal to zero almost everywhere (i.e., with probability one) (equation 8.3), it is normally distributed with variance t (equation 8.4), and it has normal increments (equation 8.5).

$$w(0) = 0, \text{ a.e.,} \tag{8.3}$$

$$w(t) \sim N(0,t), \text{ and} \tag{8.4}$$

$$w(t) - w(s) \sim N(0, t-s), \; t > s. \tag{8.5}$$

We use equation 8.2 to calculate the ratio of $S(T)$ to $S(t)$ (i.e., the "price relative") in equation 8.6:

$$\frac{S(T)}{S(t)} = \frac{S(0)\,\exp\{(\mu - \frac{1}{2}\sigma^2)T + \sigma w(T)\}}{S(0)\,\exp\{(\mu - \frac{1}{2}\sigma^2)t + \sigma w(t)\}}$$

$$= \exp\left\{\left(\mu - \frac{1}{2}\sigma^2\right)(T-t) + \sigma[w(T) - w(t)]\right\} \tag{8.6}$$

Taking the natural log of both sides of equation 8.6 yields equation 8.7:

$$\ln\left(\frac{S(T)}{S(t)}\right) = \left(\mu - \frac{1}{2}\sigma^2\right)(T-t) + \sigma[w(T) - w(t)] \tag{8.7}$$

From equation 8.4, the increment $w(T) - w(t)$ is distributed normal $N(0, T-t)$, so, equation 8.7 implies equation 8.8

$$\ln\left(\frac{S(T)}{S(t)}\right) \sim N\left(\left(\mu - \frac{1}{2}\sigma^2\right)(T-t),\; \sigma^2(T-t)\right) \tag{8.8}$$

---

[1]You may apply Itô's Lemma (equation 4.7 on page 74) to $B(t)$ and $S(t)$ and write (in the symbolic notation of stochastic calculus) that $dS(t) = \mu S(t)dt + \sigma S(t)dw(t)$ and $dB(t) = rB(t)dt$. These imply $E[S(t)|S(0)] = S(0)e^{\mu t}$ (consult table 2.1 on page 24 or do the calculus). For additional details on Itô's Lemma, see Hull (2000) and Merton (1992).

[2]A GBM in stock price yields an arithmetic Brownian motion (ABM) in continuously compounded stock returns. See Harrison (1985) for mathematical details of Brownian motion. Brownian motion is named after the botanist Robert Brown, who noticed in 1827 that pollen (or almost any fine insoluble substance) exhibits random motion when suspended in water (Brown [1828]). The mathematics of this "Brownian motion" did not come until Bachelier (1900) and Einstein (1905). The standard Brownian motion, $w(t)$, is an "arithmetic" Brownian motion. If you exponentiate the standard Brownian motion, to get $e^{w(t)}$, you get a "geometric" Brownian motion (GBM). The terms "arithmetic" and "geometric" refer to additive and multiplicative growth, respectively.

From equation 8.7 (and the properties of logs) it can also be seen that

$$\ln[S(T)] = \ln[S(t)] + \left(\mu - \frac{1}{2}\sigma^2\right)(T-t) + \sigma[w(T) - w(t)],$$

and, therefore, that, if $S(t)$ is known,

$$\ln[S(T)] \sim N\left(\ln[S(t)] + \left(\mu - \frac{1}{2}\sigma^2\right)(T-t),\ \sigma^2(T-t)\right). \tag{8.9}$$

What is the probability distribution of terminal stock price $S(T)$ under these assumptions? Well, if $\ln[S(T)/S(t)]$ is normal, it follows that the price relative $S(T)/S(t)$ is lognormal. Thus, the terminal price $S(T)$, conditional on $S(t)$, must also be lognormal. All of this information is summarized in tables 8.1 and 8.2.[3]

Now look at a concrete example. Suppose that the current stock price is $S(t) = \$40$, the instantaneous stock price drift is $\mu = 0.16$ per annum, the standard deviation of continuously compounded stock returns is $\sigma = 0.20$ per annum, $T = 1.0$ (i.e., one year), and $t = 0.5$ (so $T - t = 0.5$, and there are six months to maturity). Plugging all of these into tables 8.1 and 8.2 yields table 8.3.

The probability density functions for continuously compounded return X and price relative Y given in table 8.3 are illustrated in figures 2.3 and 2.4 (on pages 20 and 22, respectively). The distribution of terminal stock price $S(T)$ is illustrated in figure 8.1.

Why is there a rightward shift of approximately $+1$ in going from figure 2.3 (for continuously compounded return X) to figure 2.4 (for price relative Y)? It is because $Y = S(T)/S(t)$ is just one plus the simple rate of return on the stock, and simple and continuously compounded returns are close for small values; that is, for small X, Y is roughly $X + 1$.

In my example, the mean, median, and mode of $S(T)$, conditional on $S(t) = \$40$, are all above \$40 (see table 8.3). This is because of the drift upward from time t to time T. If the volatility term σ^2 is very large, the median and mode can fall below \$40. However, the ordering of the mean, median, and mode remains unchanged. In particular, the median of a lognormal distribution is always below its mean. It follows that, more often than not, the realized value of a lognormal random variable falls below its expected value. Thus, more often than not, the terminal stock price $S(T)$ falls below its expected value (expectation taken at time t). These results are a direct consequence of positive skewness. That is, the long right tail drags up the mean of the distribution, but with little probability mass.

---

[3]Table 8.1 is obtained by plugging $\nu = \left(\mu - \frac{1}{2}\sigma^2\right)(T-t)$ and $\lambda^2 = \sigma^2(T-t)$ into table 2.1 on page 24 (where ν and λ^2 come from equation 8.8); table 8.2 is deduced in turn from the last column in table 8.1. Note that some authors denote the mean of the distribution of $X = \ln[S(T)/S(t)]$ as "$\mu^* \times \tau$," where $\mu^* = \mu - \frac{1}{2}\sigma^2$, and τ is time to expiration. This may be consistent with mathematical convention, but it causes confusion here. I choose to denote the mean of X as "$\left(\mu - \frac{1}{2}\sigma^2\right)(T-t)$," and my notation is consistent with the representation of the underlying process as $dS(t) = \mu S(t)dt + \sigma S(t)dw(t)$.

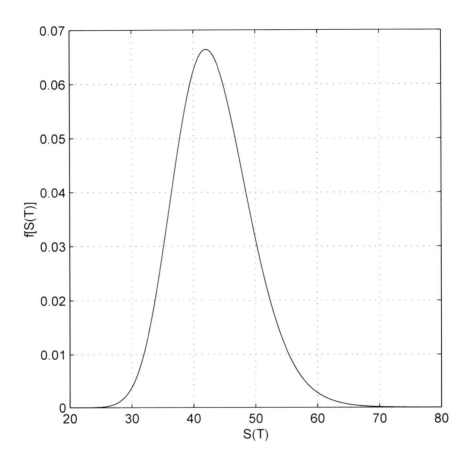

Figure 8.1: Lognormal Distribution of $S(T)$

Note: The lognormal probability density function $f[S(T)]$ for the final stock price $S(T)$ is plotted for the particular parameter values $S(t) = \$40$, $\mu = 0.16$, $\sigma = 0.20$, $T = 1.0$ (one year), and $t = 0.5$ (so $T - t = 0.5$, and there are six months to maturity). The functional form is

$$f[S(T)] = \frac{1}{\sqrt{2\pi}\,\lambda S(T)} e^{-\frac{1}{2}\left(\frac{\ln(S(T))-\nu}{\lambda}\right)^2},$$

where $\nu = 3.75887945$ and $\lambda^2 = 0.02$ are derived from reverse transformations—an exercise for the reader.

Table 8.1: Distribution of Return and Price Relative (Black-Scholes)

	Normal $X = \ln\left(\frac{S(T)}{S(t)}\right)$	Lognormal $Y = \frac{S(T)}{S(t)}$
MEAN	$\left(\mu - \frac{1}{2}\sigma^2\right)(T-t)$	$e^{\mu(T-t)}$
MEDIAN	$\left(\mu - \frac{1}{2}\sigma^2\right)(T-t)$	$e^{\left(\mu - \frac{1}{2}\sigma^2\right)(T-t)}$
MODE	$\left(\mu - \frac{1}{2}\sigma^2\right)(T-t)$	$e^{\left(\mu - \frac{3}{2}\sigma^2\right)(T-t)}$
VARIANCE	$\sigma^2(T-t)$	$e^{2\mu(T-t)}\left(e^{\sigma^2(T-t)} - 1\right)$
STD. DEV.	$\sigma\sqrt{T-t}$	$\sqrt{e^{2\mu(T-t)}\left(e^{\sigma^2(T-t)} - 1\right)}$
LIMITS	$-\infty < X < +\infty$	$0 \leq Y < +\infty$

Note: Black and Scholes assume that, conditional upon $S(t)$, continuously compounded return $X = \ln[S(T)/S(t)]$ is distributed normal, and thus that the price relative $Y = S(T)/S(t)$ is distributed lognormally. Replace μ with r to get risk-neutral distributions.

8.1.1 A Note on Concavity and Geometric Averages

Simple algebra implies that

$$1 + \frac{S(T) - S(t)}{S(t)} = \frac{S(T)}{S(t)}.$$

It follows from the "MEAN" row in table 8.1, therefore, that equation 8.10 holds:

$$E\left[\ln\left(1 + \frac{S(T) - S(t)}{S(t)}\right)\right] = E\left[\ln\left(\frac{S(T)}{S(t)}\right)\right] = \left(\mu - \frac{1}{2}\sigma^2\right)(T-t) \qquad (8.10)$$

However, from the same row in table 8.1, equation 8.11 must hold:

$$\ln\left[E\left(1 + \frac{S(T) - S(t)}{S(t)}\right)\right] = \ln\left[E\left(\frac{S(T)}{S(t)}\right)\right] = \mu(T-t) \qquad (8.11)$$

Thus, the expected value of the continuously compounded return, equation 8.10, is less than the continuously compounded expected return, equation 8.11. Mathematically, $\ln(\cdot)$ is a nonlinear function, and $E(\cdot)$ is a linear operator. In other words, the average of the log is less than the log of the average because the logarithm function is concave. Economically, the continuously compounded return per unit time is expected to produce growth in a stock price that gives a simple return exceeding the original continuously compounded return (arithmetic averages exceed geometric averages). For further details, see the discussion in Hull (2000, pp240–241), and my discussion of averages in Crack (2008, p208).

Table 8.2: Distribution of Terminal Stock Price (Black-Scholes)

	Lognormal $S(T)$
MEAN	$S(t)e^{\mu(T-t)}$
MEDIAN	$S(t)e^{\left(\mu-\frac{1}{2}\sigma^2\right)(T-t)}$
MODE	$S(t)e^{\left(\mu-\frac{3}{2}\sigma^2\right)(T-t)}$
VARIANCE	$S^2(t)e^{2\mu(T-t)}\left(e^{\sigma^2(T-t)}-1\right)$
STD. DEV.	$\sqrt{S^2(t)e^{2\mu(T-t)}\left(e^{\sigma^2(T-t)}-1\right)}$
LIMITS	$0 \leq S(T) < +\infty$

Note: Black and Scholes assume that, conditional upon $S(t)$, the terminal stock price $S(T)$ is distributed lognormally. Replace μ with r to get risk-neutral distributions.

8.2 Black-Scholes Derivation

There are many ways to derive the Black-Scholes formula. For example, you can take the continuous limit of a binomial tree (see section 8.3.3); you can take straight expected values under a risk-neutral probability measure (see section 4.4.2 and later in this section); you can "change numeraire" as well as probability measure, apply Itô's Lemma, and derive a PDE with boundary conditions (as in section 4.4.3); you can arrive at the same PDE using Merton-type hedging arguments (see section 4.4.1 and section 9.2.1); and you can use an instantaneous-CAPM derivation to derive an equilibrium version of the model (this was Black and Scholes' original derivation of the model). These, and other techniques, lead to the Black-Scholes formulae given in equations 8.17 and 8.18 on p120.[4] In this section, I present a derivation of the Black-Scholes formula using straight expected values under a risk-neutral probability measure.

From equation 8.6 on page 112, it is deduced that the terminal stock price, $S(T)$, may be written as in equation 8.12:

$$\begin{aligned} S(T) &= S(t)\,\exp\left\{\left(\mu-\frac{1}{2}\sigma^2\right)(T-t)+\sigma[w(T)-w(t)]\right\} \\ &= S(t)\,\exp\left\{\left(\mu-\frac{1}{2}\sigma^2\right)(T-t)+\sigma\mathcal{W}\right\}, \end{aligned} \qquad (8.12)$$

where $\mathcal{W} \equiv [w(T) - w(t)]$ is distributed as normal $N(0, T - t)$ under the usual probability measure.

---

[4]Note that a mathematically-equivalent representation of the Black-Scholes formula uses simple interest rate $r' \equiv e^r - 1$.

Table 8.3: Continuously Compounded Returns, Price Relative, and Terminal Stock Price: Example

	Normal $X = \ln\left(\frac{S(T)}{S(t)}\right)$	Lognormal $Y = \frac{S(T)}{S(t)}$	Lognormal $S(T)$
MEAN	0.07	1.08328707	43.33148271
MEDIAN	0.07	1.07250818	42.90032725
MODE	0.07	1.05127110	42.05084386
VARIANCE	0.02	0.02370649	37.93038741
STD. DEV.	0.14142136	0.15396913	6.15876509
LIMITS	$-\infty < X < +\infty$	$0 \leq Y < +\infty$	$0 \leq S(T) < +\infty$

Note: This table presents a numerical example for continuously compounded return X, price relative Y, and terminal stock price $S(T)$. The current stock price is $S(t) = \$40$, the instantaneous stock price drift is $\mu = 0.16$ per annum, the standard deviation of continuously compounded stock returns is $\sigma = 0.20$ per annum, $T = 1.0$ (i.e., one year), and $t = 0.5$ (so $T - t = 0.5$, and there are six months to maturity). Consult tables 8.1 and 8.2 for the formulae underlying the numbers.

It can be shown that $w(t)$ (a standard Brownian motion under the usual probability measure) may be written as $w(t) = w^*(t) - \left(\frac{\mu-r}{\sigma}\right) t$, where $w^*(t)$ is a standard Brownian motion under the risk-neutral probability measure.[5] Substituting $w(t) = w^*(t) - \left(\frac{\mu-r}{\sigma}\right) t$ into equation 8.12 yields

$$
\begin{aligned}
S(T) &= S(t) \exp\left\{\left(r - \frac{1}{2}\sigma^2\right)(T-t) + \sigma[w^*(T) - w^*(t)]\right\} \\
&= S(t) \exp\left\{\left(r - \frac{1}{2}\sigma^2\right)(T-t) + \sigma\mathcal{W}^*\right\},
\end{aligned}
\tag{8.13}
$$

where $\mathcal{W}^* \equiv [w^*(T) - w^*(t)] \sim N(0, T-t)$ under the risk-neutral probability measure.[6]

---

[5]This is Girsanov's Theorem. For mathematical details on Girsanov's Theorem, see Girsanov (1960), Karatzas and Shreve (1997), or Métivier (1982); for option pricing applications, see Harrison and Pliska (1981) or Merton (1992). I recommend Nawalkha and Beliaeva (2007) for its easy to follow introduction to high-level mathematical finance.

[6]If you are uncomfortable with the Girsanov Theorem transformation, but comfortable with the concept of a risk-neutral world, then let the differential equation $dS(t) = rS(t)dt + \sigma S(t)dw^*(t)$, with instantaneous drift r, be your starting point. Now apply Itô's Lemma to $S(t) = S(0)\exp\left\{\left(r - \frac{1}{2}\sigma^2\right)t + \sigma w^*(t)\right\}$ to satisfy yourself that this is the solution to that differential equation. Compare this with footnote 1 on page 112.

The conversion from the usual probability measure (real-world probabilities) to the risk-neutral probability measure (risk-neutral world probabilities) allows the option to be priced via a straightforward discounted expected payoff calculation. The present value of a security in a risk-neutral world is the discounted value of its expected payoffs, with discounting at the riskless rate and with expectations taken under the risk-neutral measure. The same σ is used in both the real and risk-neutral worlds.[7]

Distributional results for continuously compounded returns, price relative, and terminal stock price are presented in tables 8.1 and 8.2. These results do not hold under the risk-neutral probability measure. However, we need only replace μ by r in tables 8.1 and 8.2 to get the distributional properties of these random variables under the risk-neutral probability measure. Black-Scholes pricing is performed with respect to the risk-neutral distributions.

The price of the call option at time t is the discounted expected payoff to the call option, where E^* denotes expectation taken under the risk-neutral probability measure. The expectation is taken conditional on information at time t; that is, conditional on $S(t)$, as in equation 8.14:

$$c(t) = e^{-r(T-t)} \, E^* \left\{ \max[S(T) - X, 0] \mid S(t) \right\} \tag{8.14}$$

Let "v" play the part of $\mathcal{W}^*$ distributed $N(0, T - t)$ in equation 8.13 and substitute equation 8.13 into equation 8.14 to yield equation 8.15:

$$c(t) = e^{-r(T-t)} \int_{v=-\infty}^{+\infty} \left(S(t) e^{(r - \frac{1}{2}\sigma^2)(T-t) + \sigma v} - X \right)^+ f_V(v) \, dv \tag{8.15}$$

Note that I have used the conventional (United States) notation "$(\cdot)^+$" to denote $\max(\,\cdot\,, 0)$. Note also that $f_V(v)$ is the pdf of v.

The terminal stock price, $S(T)$, is lognormally distributed, conditional on $S(t)$, and v is normally distributed.[8] Equation 8.15 is simply the expectation of a nonlinear function of a normal random variable, v, taken with respect to its pdf. With $v \sim N(0, T - t)$, it follows from equation 2.1 (p19) that the pdf of v is given by equation 8.16:

$$f_V(v) = \frac{1}{\sqrt{2\pi} \, \sqrt{T - t}} e^{-\frac{1}{2} \left(\frac{v}{\sqrt{T-t}} \right)^2} \tag{8.16}$$

Now substitute equation 8.16 for $f_V(v)$ in equation 8.15 to get the call option value

$$c(t) = e^{-r(T-t)} \int_{v=-\infty}^{+\infty} \left(S(t) e^{(r - \frac{1}{2}\sigma^2)(T-t) + \sigma v} - X \right)^+$$

$$\times \frac{1}{\sqrt{2\pi} \, \sqrt{T - t}} e^{-\frac{1}{2} \left(\frac{v}{\sqrt{T-t}} \right)^2} \, dv.$$

---

[7]Note, however, that in models that incorporate higher-order moments such as skewness and kurtosis in the underlying data-generating process (via stochastic volatility, with or without jumps), σ is not necessarily the same in the real and risk-neutral worlds, and higher-order moments can also differ (see sections 9.4.1 and 9.4.2 for discussion of jumps and stochastic volatility, respectively; and Arnold and Crack [2003] for an alternative pricing approach).

[8]You should review equation 8.13 to check that the relationship between $S(T)$ and $v \equiv \mathcal{W}^*$ is as it should be between a lognormal and a normal random variable.

To simplify, let $\epsilon = v/\sqrt{T-t}$ so that $d\epsilon = \frac{dv}{\sqrt{T-t}}$ and the call option value becomes

$$c(t) = e^{-r(T-t)} \int_{\epsilon=-\infty}^{+\infty} \left(S(t)e^{\left(r-\frac{1}{2}\sigma^2\right)(T-t)+\sigma\epsilon\sqrt{T-t}} - X \right)^+ \frac{1}{\sqrt{2\pi}} e^{-\frac{1}{2}\epsilon^2} \, d\epsilon.$$

Let ϵ_0 be such that $\left(S(t)e^{\left(r-\frac{1}{2}\sigma^2\right)(T-t)+\sigma\epsilon_0\sqrt{T-t}} - X \right) = 0$, then

$$\epsilon_0 = \frac{1}{\sigma\sqrt{T-t}} \left\{ \ln\left(\frac{X}{S(t)}\right) - \left(r - \frac{1}{2}\sigma^2\right)(T-t) \right\}.$$

The formula for $c(t)$ simplifies slightly because the integrand, and thus the integral, are each identically zero when $\epsilon < \epsilon_0$.

$$c(t) = e^{-r(T-t)} \int_{\epsilon=\epsilon_0}^{+\infty} \left(S(t)e^{\left(r-\frac{1}{2}\sigma^2\right)(T-t)+\sigma\epsilon\sqrt{T-t}} - X \right) \frac{1}{\sqrt{2\pi}} e^{-\frac{1}{2}\epsilon^2} \, d\epsilon$$

We now split the integrand, and thus the integral, into two components:

$$\begin{aligned} c(t) &= e^{-r(T-t)} \int_{\epsilon=\epsilon_0}^{+\infty} S(t)\, e^{\left(r-\frac{1}{2}\sigma^2\right)(T-t)+\sigma\epsilon\sqrt{T-t}} \frac{1}{\sqrt{2\pi}} e^{-\frac{1}{2}\epsilon^2} d\epsilon \\ &\quad - e^{-r(T-t)} \int_{\epsilon=\epsilon_0}^{+\infty} X \, \frac{1}{\sqrt{2\pi}} e^{-\frac{1}{2}\epsilon^2} \, d\epsilon \end{aligned}$$

Collect terms and simplify:

$$\begin{aligned} c(t) &= S(t) \int_{\epsilon=\epsilon_0}^{+\infty} \frac{1}{\sqrt{2\pi}} e^{-\frac{1}{2}\sigma^2(T-t)+\sigma\epsilon\sqrt{T-t}-\frac{1}{2}\epsilon^2} \, d\epsilon \\ &\quad - Xe^{-r(T-t)} \int_{\epsilon=\epsilon_0}^{+\infty} \frac{1}{\sqrt{2\pi}} e^{-\frac{1}{2}\epsilon^2} \, d\epsilon \end{aligned}$$

Notice that the exponent in the integrand of the first term is a scaled perfect square satisfying

$$-\frac{1}{2}\sigma^2(T-t) + \sigma\epsilon\sqrt{T-t} - \frac{1}{2}\epsilon^2 = -\frac{1}{2}(\epsilon - \sigma\sqrt{T-t})^2 = -\frac{1}{2}\epsilon'^2,$$

where $\epsilon' \equiv \epsilon - \sigma\sqrt{T-t}$. Now substitute ϵ' into the first integral to simplify the expression for $c(t)$:

$$\begin{aligned} c(t) &= S(t) \int_{\epsilon'=\epsilon_0-\sigma\sqrt{T-t}}^{+\infty} \frac{1}{\sqrt{2\pi}} e^{-\frac{1}{2}\epsilon'^2} \, d\epsilon' \\ &\quad - Xe^{-r(T-t)} \int_{\epsilon=\epsilon_0}^{+\infty} \frac{1}{\sqrt{2\pi}} e^{-\frac{1}{2}\epsilon^2} \, d\epsilon \end{aligned}$$

The integrands are standard normal pdfs (i.e., equation 2.1 with $\nu = 0$ and $\lambda = 1$). Therefore, the integrals involve standard normal cdfs (see section 2.2.4). The option value $c(t)$ may now be written in terms of the cumulative standard normal function $N(\cdot)$ as follows:

$$c(t) = S(t) \left[1 - N(\epsilon_0 - \sigma\sqrt{T-t})\right] - Xe^{-r(T-t)} \left[1 - N(\epsilon_0)\right]$$

Recall from section 2.2.4, the property of the cumulative standard normal function: $[1 - N(z)] = N(-z)$. This may be used to simplify $c(t)$:

$$c(t) = S(t)N(-\epsilon_0 + \sigma\sqrt{T-t}) - Xe^{-r(T-t)}N(-\epsilon_0)$$

It is straightforward algebraic manipulation to demonstrate that if

$$\epsilon_0 = \frac{1}{\sigma\sqrt{T-t}} \left\{ \ln\left(\frac{X}{S(t)}\right) - \left(r - \frac{1}{2}\sigma^2\right)(T-t) \right\},$$

then

$$-\epsilon_0 + \sigma\sqrt{T-t} = \frac{\ln\left(\frac{S(t)}{X}\right) + (r + \frac{1}{2}\sigma^2)(T-t)}{\sigma\sqrt{T-t}},$$

and

$$-\epsilon_0 = \frac{\ln\left(\frac{S(t)}{X}\right) + (r - \frac{1}{2}\sigma^2)(T-t)}{\sigma\sqrt{T-t}}.$$

If we label the latter two terms as d_1 and d_2, respectively, we get the Black-Scholes formula for the price of a standard European call on a non dividend-paying stock:

$$
\begin{aligned}
c(t) &= S(t)N(d_1) - e^{-r(T-t)}XN(d_2), \text{ where} &&(8.17)\\
d_1 &= \frac{\ln\left(\frac{S(t)}{X}\right) + (r + \frac{1}{2}\sigma^2)(T-t)}{\sigma\sqrt{T-t}}, \text{ and}\\
d_2 &= d_1 - \sigma\sqrt{T-t}.
\end{aligned}
$$

The put price is similarly shown to be

$$p(t) = e^{-r(T-t)}XN(-d_2) - S(t)N(-d_1). \qquad (8.18)$$

The Black-Scholes formula was first published in Black and Scholes (1972), though Black and Scholes (1973) is the better-known citation. The formula appeared in the classroom at MIT as early as 1971.

8.3 Black-Scholes Interpretations and Intuition

8.3.1 Interpretation I: Recipe for Replication

We discussed option replication in sections 4.2 and 7.6. In section 7.6 we discussed the height, slope, and curvature of the plot of option value versus underlying stock price and noted that, like a Taylor series expansion, the more option characteristics we replicate, the better the hedge. We noted that the simplest hedge—a delta hedge—replicates only height and slope.

$$c(t) = \overbrace{S(t)\,\underbrace{N(d_1)}_{\Delta}}^{\text{stock position}} - \overbrace{e^{-r(T-t)}X\,N(d_2)}^{\text{bond position}}$$

borrowing

Figure 8.2: Black-Scholes Replication: Call; No Dividends

Note: This is a summary of the replication argument in section 8.3.1 for a call on a stock that pays no dividends. Δ is the delta of the call; it is the number of units of stock to be held in a continuously rebalanced portfolio that replicates the payoff to the call. The negative bond position corresponds to the borrowing.

The term $N(d_1)$ in the Black-Scholes call formula is the "delta," denoted "Δ," of a call option on a stock that does not pay dividends. $N(d_1)$ is equal to $\frac{\partial c(t)}{\partial S(t)}$ and is thus the slope of the plot of option price versus stock price. It is also the number of units of stock you must hold in a continuously rebalanced portfolio that replicates the payoff to the call. That is, $N(d_1)$ is the number of units of stock that you must hold when using the dynamic self-financing replicating strategy mentioned in section 4.2 (p68).

The second term in the Black-Scholes call formula, $e^{-r(T-t)}X\,N(d_2)$, is the value of your borrowing in a continuously rebalanced portfolio that replicates the payoff to the call on a non dividend-paying stock. Figure 8.2 summarizes the Black-Scholes replication strategy.

Actual Job Interview Question: You are long a call option on MITCO stock. You have delta hedged your position. You hear on the radio that the CEO of MITCO has just been arrested for running a massive Ponzi scheme. The stock price plunges $10. How do you adjust your hedge (qualitatively)? That is, do you borrow and buy stock or sell stock and lend? Explain carefully.

Taken from "Heard on The Street: Quantitative Questions from Wall Street Job Interviews," ©2008 Timothy Falcon Crack. See advertisement on last page of this book.

Answer: Borrow and buy stock. If you got it wrong, then ask yourself how the replicating portfolio changes (i.e., delta falls, so less stock is needed in the replicating portfolio). Then ask yourself whether you are long or short the replicating portfolio (you are short here). So, you need to reduce your short stock position. You do this by buying back (i.e., covering) some of the short stock.

8.3.2 Interpretation II: DCF, Cost/Benefit

Our basic risk-neutral option valuation formula (equation 4.3 on page 70) is $V(t) = e^{-r(T-t)}E_t^*[V(T)]$, where $V(T)$ is final payoff and the expectation is taken in a risk-neutral world (indicated by the asterisk). We derived the Black-Scholes formula using this formula in section 8.2. This basic valuation formula is just a DCF in the risk-neutral world, so we should be able to break the Black-Scholes formula down into costs and benefits that are weighed against each other.

Key Points:

- *The Black-Scholes call pricing formula for options on a stock that pays no dividends is given by*

$$
\begin{aligned}
c(t) &= S(t)N(d_1) - e^{-r(T-t)}XN(d_2), \ \text{where} \\
d_1 &= \frac{\ln\left(\frac{S(t)}{X}\right) + (r + \frac{1}{2}\sigma^2)(T-t)}{\sigma\sqrt{T-t}}, \ \text{and} \\
d_2 &= d_1 - \sigma\sqrt{T-t}.
\end{aligned}
$$

- *The first term, $S(t)N(d_1)$, is the discounted expected benefit of owning the option, with expectations taken under the "risk-neutral" probability measure.*

- *The second term, $e^{-r(T-t)}XN(d_2)$, is the discounted expected cost of owning the option, with expectations taken under the risk-neutral probability measure. $N(d_2)$ is the (risk-neutral) probability that the option finishes in-the-money; X is your cost if it does; and $e^{-r(T-t)}$ is the discounting factor.*

- *Taken together, the two terms that comprise the Black-Scholes formula represent a DCF analysis that weighs costs and benefits.*

Why is $N(d_2)$ the risk-neutral probability that the call option finishes in-the-money? To answer this, first rewrite d_2 as follows:[9]

$$
d_2 = -\left(\frac{\ln\left(\frac{X}{S(t)}\right) - (r - \frac{1}{2}\sigma^2)(T-t)}{\sigma\sqrt{T-t}}\right) = -\left(\frac{R^* - MEAN}{SD}\right) = -Z^*, \quad (8.19)
$$

where $Z^* \equiv \frac{R^* - MEAN}{SD}$, and

- $R^* \equiv \ln\left(\frac{S(T)}{S(t)}\right)\Big|_{S(T)=X} = \ln\left(\frac{X}{S(t)}\right)$ is the smallest continuously compounded return required of the stock over the life of the option if the option is to finish at-the-money (i.e., where final stock price $S(T)$ equals X),

- $MEAN \equiv (r - \frac{1}{2}\sigma^2)(T-t)$ is the risk-neutral expected continuously compounded return on the stock over the life of the option (see table 8.1 on page 115), and

---

[9]I use the property of logarithms that $\ln(A) = -\ln\left(\frac{1}{A}\right)$, for any $A > 0$.

- $SD \equiv \sigma\sqrt{T-t}$ is the standard deviation of the continuously compounded return on the stock over the life of the option (see table 8.1 on page 115).

The quantity R^* just defined is a particular value of the normally distributed $R \equiv \ln\left(\frac{S(T)}{S(t)}\right)$. The ratio $Z^* = \frac{R^* - MEAN}{SD}$ is a particular value of the standard normally distributed $Z = \frac{R - MEAN}{SD}$. The ratio Z^* is thus a regular Z-score, and $N(Z^*)$ tells how likely it is that $R \leq R^*$ (i.e., that $S(T) \leq X$ and the call finishes at-the-money or worse in the risk-neutral world). By definition, $N(d_2)$ satisfies $N(d_2) = N(-Z^*) = 1 - N(Z^*)$, and is therefore the probability that the call finishes in-the-money (i.e., that $S(T) > X$) in the risk-neutral world. See the exercise on page 128.

Op Quiz: The Black-Scholes put pricing formula for options on a stock that pays no dividends is given by

$$p(t) = e^{-r(T-t)}XN(-d_2) - S(t)N(-d_1), \text{ where}$$

$$d_1 = \frac{\ln\left(\frac{S(t)}{X}\right) + (r + \frac{1}{2}\sigma^2)(T - t)}{\sigma\sqrt{T-t}}, \text{ and}$$

$$d_2 = d_1 - \sigma\sqrt{T-t}.$$

Which parts of the put formula represent the discounted expected benefits and the discounted expected costs of owning the put option?

Answer: The first term, $e^{-r(T-t)}XN(-d_2)$, is the discounted expected benefit of put option ownership. The second term, $S(t)N(-d_1)$, is the discounted expected cost of put option ownership. $N(-d_2)$ is the risk-neutral probability that the put finishes in-the-money.

Note that $d_1 = d_2 + \sigma\sqrt{T-t}$. The difference between d_1 and d_2 involves both the volatility, σ, and the time to expiration, $\sqrt{T-t}$. Conditional on the option finishing in-the-money, the future cost to exercising is fixed at X, but the future benefit, $S(T)$, is random. The additional term, $\sigma\sqrt{T-t}$, accounts for this additional randomness in the benefit compared to the cost. In fact, $N(d_1)$ has a risk-neutral probabilistic interpretation: The same argument that demonstrates that $N(d_2) = P^*(S(T) \geq X)$ also demonstrates that $N(d_1) = P^*\left(S(T) \geq Xe^{-\sigma^2(T-t)}\right)$, where P^* denotes a risk-neutral probability.[10] That is, P^* denotes probability in a world where the stock price process with the bond as numeraire follows a martingale. See also section 8.3.4 where $N(d_1)$ has a stock-numeraire probabilistic interpretation.

---

[10]I thank Victor W. Goodman for this result. Any errors are mine.

Exercise 1: You buy a straddle struck at $40 (i.e., a long call and a long put both with strike price $X = \$40$). Assume the position costs $3, that the options are European style, and that you hold the position until maturity. Under the Black-Scholes assumptions, prove that the real-world probability that you make a profit on this trade (ignoring the time value of money on the $3) is just

$$P(\text{profit}) = N(-Z_\mu(43)) + N(Z_\mu(37)), \text{ where}$$

$$Z_\mu(H) = \frac{\ln\left(\frac{H}{S(t)}\right) - (\mu - \frac{1}{2}\sigma^2)(T-t)}{\sigma\sqrt{T-t}}$$

$S(t)$ is today's stock price, and μ is the real-world continuously compounded return on the stock per annum.

Exercise 2: Satisfy yourself that if $S \longrightarrow \infty$, then $N(d_1) \longrightarrow 1$, and $N(d_2) \longrightarrow 1$. It follows that if $S \longrightarrow \infty$, then $c(t) \sim S - PV(X)$. Now, what happens to $N(d_1)$, $N(d_2)$, and $c(t)$ if $S \longrightarrow 0$?

8.3.3 Interpretation III: Binomial Limit

Black-Scholes pricing is the limit of plain vanilla European binomial option pricing as the step size gets smaller and the number of steps gets larger—as discussed in section 6.3. This may be demonstrated numerically (as illustrated in figure 6.4 on page 97); it may also be proved algebraically as follows.

For a fixed maturity of option, say six months, very small step sizes go hand in hand with very many steps. The stock price can therefore follow a path through the binomial tree that looks much like the random walk assumed by Black and Scholes. In the limit as step size goes to zero, and the number of steps goes to infinity, the possible paths through the binomial tree are GBMs.

Consider a two-step tree—like that in figure 6.3 on page 96. Let V_{uu}, V_{ud}, and V_{dd} be the values of an option at the terminal nodes. Let V_u and V_d be the intermediate option values. Then, applying equation 6.5 (p92) to each node, we get equations 8.20–8.22 (where $\pi^* = [e^{r(\Delta t)} - d]/(u - d)$ is the risk-neutral probability of an up move as in equation 6.5):

$$V_u = e^{-r(\Delta t)}\left[\pi^* V_{uu} + (1 - \pi^*)V_{ud}\right] \tag{8.20}$$

$$V_d = e^{-r(\Delta t)}\left[\pi^* V_{ud} + (1 - \pi^*)V_{dd}\right] \tag{8.21}$$

$$V = e^{-r(\Delta t)}\left[\pi^* V_u + (1 - \pi^*)V_d\right] \tag{8.22}$$

We may use equation 8.20 and equation 8.21 to substitute for V_u and V_d, respectively, in equation 8.22. Doing so, and collecting terms, yields equation 8.23:

$$V = e^{-2r(\Delta t)}\left[(\pi^*)^2 V_{uu} + 2\pi^*(1 - \pi^*)V_{ud} + (1 - \pi^*)^2 V_{dd}\right] \tag{8.23}$$

More generally, for a J-step tree, the same process of discounting the terminal payoffs and then working back through the tree using recursive substitution to solve for the initial V, yields the general binomial option pricing formula in equation 8.24:

$$V = e^{-Jr(\Delta t)} \left[\sum_{j=0}^{J} \binom{J}{j} (\pi^*)^j (1 - \pi^*)^{J-j} V_{u^j d^{J-j}} \right], \qquad (8.24)$$

where $\binom{J}{j} \equiv \frac{J!}{j!(J-j)!}$ is the usual binomial coefficient (see section 2.5.3, p35), and $V_{u^j d^{J-j}}$ is the terminal payoff to the option after j "ups" and $J - j$ "downs." To avoid confusion, note that in equation 8.23, $\Delta t = (T-t)/2$, but that in equation 8.24 the more general $\Delta t = (T - t)/J$ is used.

The terminal payoff to a European call after j up steps and $J - j$ down steps is $V_{u^j d^{J-j}} = \max[0, S(T) - X] = \max[0, Su^j d^{J-j} - X]$. We may plug this into the general formula, equation 8.24, to obtain the binomial option pricing formula specific to a European call—equation 8.25:

$$
\begin{aligned}
V &= e^{-r(T-t)} \left[\sum_{j=a}^{J} \binom{J}{j} (\pi^*)^j (1 - \pi^*)^{J-j} [Su^j d^{J-j} - X] \right] \\
&= S \left[\sum_{j=a}^{J} \binom{J}{j} (\pi^*)^j (1 - \pi^*)^{J-j} \left(\frac{u^j d^{J-j}}{e^{r(T-t)}} \right) \right] \\
&\qquad\qquad - Xe^{-r(T-t)} \left[\sum_{j=a}^{J} \binom{J}{j} (\pi^*)^j (1 - \pi^*)^{J-j} \right] \\
&= S\Phi[a; J, \bar{\pi}] - Xe^{-r(T-t)}\Phi[a; J, \pi^*], \qquad (8.25)
\end{aligned}
$$

where a is the minimum number of upward moves needed to place the call in-the-money at expiration,[11] $\bar{\pi} \equiv (ue^{-r(\Delta t)})\pi^*$, and Φ is the complimentary binomial distribution $\Phi[a; J, \lambda] \equiv \left[\sum_{j=a}^{J} \binom{J}{j} \lambda^j (1 - \lambda)^{J-j} \right]$, which is just one minus the binomial cdf.

Exercise: Prove that $1 - \bar{\pi} = (de^{-r(\Delta t)})(1 - \pi^*)$. This is required to derive equation 8.25.

After some algebra, it may be demonstrated that the binomial option pricing formula for the European call, equation 8.25, tends to the Black-Scholes European call formula as $J \to \infty$ and $(\Delta t) \to 0$ (Cox, Ross, and Rubinstein [1979]; Cox and Rubinstein [1985, pp196–208]; Tian [1993]). Implicit within this approximation is that a binomial distribution is being used to approximate the normal distribution assumed by Black and Scholes (as mentioned in section 2.5.3, p35).

We already know that π^* in equation 8.25 is the risk-neutral probability on an up move in the binomial tree. That is, π^* is the probability of a stock price rise within the binomial framework when the stock price process with the bond as numeraire

---

[11]So, a is the smallest non-negative integer greater than $\ln[X/(S(t)d^J)]/\ln(u/d)$ (Cox and Rubinstein [1985, p178]). Compare R^* to a in equation 8.19 on page 122.

follows a martingale. What may come as a surprise is that $\bar{\pi} \equiv (ue^{-r(\Delta t)})\pi^* = u[1 - de^{-r(\Delta t)}]/(u - d)$ in equation 8.25 is the probability of a stock price rise within the binomial framework when the bond price process with the stock as numeraire follows a martingale (see the exercise below). This is an example of a competing numeraire with an associated equivalent martingale measure, albeit in the discrete case.

The Black-Scholes terms $N(d_1)$ and $N(d_2)$ have discrete-time counterparts in $\Phi[a; J, \bar{\pi}]$ and $\Phi[a; J, \pi^*]$, respectively, in equation 8.25 (see the Op Quiz on page 102 and figure 6.5 on page 98 for numerical examples). These counterparts, combined with the competing bond-numeraire and stock-numeraire probabilities embedded within equation 8.25, lead to bond-numeraire and stock-numeraire probabilistic interpretations of $N(d_1)$ and $N(d_2)$, discussed in section 8.3.4.

Exercise (difficult): Demonstrate that if $\bar{\pi} \equiv (ue^{-r(\Delta t)})\pi^* = u[1 - de^{-r(\Delta t)}]/(u - d)$ is the probability of an up move in the binomial framework, then

$$\bar{E}\left[\frac{B(t + \Delta t)}{S(t + \Delta t)} \,\bigg|\, \frac{B(t)}{S(t)}\right] = \frac{B(t)}{S(t)}, \qquad (8.26)$$

where $\bar{E}$ denotes expectations taken with respect to the probabilities $\bar{\pi}$. That is, under the probabilities $\bar{\pi}$, the bond, de-trended by the stock, follows a martingale in the binomial framework. Compare equation 8.26 with equation 4.4 in section 4.4 on page 71.

8.3.4   Interpretation IV: Stock-Numeraire

Section 8.3.3 discussed the discrete case of the competing-numeraire equivalent martingale probabilities π^* and $\bar{\pi}$ corresponding to the binomial case of the risk-neutral and stock-numeraire worlds, respectively.[12] Just as we showed in section 8.3.2 that $N(d_2) = P^*(S(T) > X)$, we show here that $N(d_1) = \bar{P}(S(T) > X)$, where P^* and $\bar{P}$ are the risk-neutral and stock-numeraire equivalent martingale measures, respectively. That is, P^* and $\bar{P}$ are the probability measures under which, respectively, the stock de-trended by the bond and the bond de-trended by the stock follow martingales (see Musiela and Rutkowski [1992, pp114, 120–121] for deep details including Radon-Nikodym derivatives).

Begin with the bond and stock price processes assumed by Black and Scholes (1973), as shown in equations 8.1 and 8.2 on page 112. We now ask what does equation 8.26 imply about the stock's drift μ, when applied to the stock and bond price processes in equations 8.1 and 8.2? Plugging equations 8.1 and 8.2 into equation 8.26, replacing w (a standard Brownian motion under P) in equation 8.2 with $\bar{w}$ (a standard Brownian motion under $\bar{P}$), and using time t and time 0 (in place of

---

[12]I thank Scott Chaput for contributions to this section. Any errors are mine.

time $t + \Delta t$ and time t), equation 8.26 is transformed into equation 8.27:

$$\bar{E}\left[\frac{B(t)}{S(t)} \,\middle|\, \frac{B(0)}{S(0)}\right] = \frac{B(0)}{S(0)}$$

$$\Rightarrow \bar{E}\left[\frac{e^{rt}}{S(0)e^{(\mu - \frac{1}{2}\sigma^2)t + \sigma\bar{w}(t)}} \,\middle|\, \frac{1}{S(0)}\right] = \frac{1}{S(0)}$$

$$\Rightarrow e^{(r - \mu + \frac{1}{2}\sigma^2)t} \bar{E}\left[e^{-\sigma\bar{w}(t)}\right] = 1 \qquad (8.27)$$

However, $e^{-\sigma\bar{w}(t)}$ in this equation is lognormal because $-\sigma\bar{w}(t) \sim N(0, \sigma^2 t)$ under $\bar{P}$ by the properties of a standard Brownian motion (see p112). It follows from table 2.1, on page 24, that $\bar{E}\left[e^{-\sigma\bar{w}(t)}\right] = e^{0 + \frac{\sigma^2 t}{2}}$, and plugging this into equation 8.27, we deduce that $e^{(r - \mu + \sigma^2)t} = 1$ under $\bar{P}$. It follows that[13] $\mu = r + \sigma^2$, if we are to have $[B(t)/S(t)]$ follow a martingale under $\bar{P}$. Let us now calculate $\bar{P}(S(T) > X)$ using this μ.

$$
\begin{aligned}
\bar{P}(S(T) > X) &= \bar{P}\left(\frac{S(T)}{S(t)} > \frac{X}{S(t)}\right) \\[2mm]
&= \bar{P}\left(\frac{S(0)e^{\left[(\mu - \frac{1}{2}\sigma^2)T + \sigma\bar{w}(T)\right]}}{S(0)e^{\left[(\mu - \frac{1}{2}\sigma^2)t + \sigma\bar{w}(t)\right]}} > \frac{X}{S(t)}\right) \\[2mm]
&= \bar{P}\left(\frac{e^{\left[(r + \frac{1}{2}\sigma^2)T + \sigma\bar{w}(T)\right]}}{e^{\left[(r + \frac{1}{2}\sigma^2)t + \sigma\bar{w}(t)\right]}} > \frac{X}{S(t)}\right) \\[2mm]
&= \bar{P}\left(e^{\left[(r + \frac{1}{2}\sigma^2)(T - t) + \sigma[\bar{w}(T) - \bar{w}(t)]\right]} > \frac{X}{S(t)}\right) \\[2mm]
&= \bar{P}\left\{\left[\left(r + \frac{1}{2}\sigma^2\right)(T - t) + \sigma[\bar{w}(T) - \bar{w}(t)]\right] > \ln\left(\frac{X}{S(t)}\right)\right\} \\[2mm]
&= \bar{P}\left([\bar{w}(T) - \bar{w}(t)] > \frac{\ln\left(\frac{X}{S(t)}\right) - \left(r + \frac{1}{2}\sigma^2\right)(T - t)}{\sigma}\right) \\[2mm]
&= \bar{P}\left(\bar{V} > \frac{\ln\left(\frac{X}{S(t)}\right) - \left(r + \frac{1}{2}\sigma^2\right)(T - t)}{\sigma}\right) \\[2mm]
&= \bar{P}\left(\frac{\bar{V}}{\sqrt{T - t}} > \frac{\ln\left(\frac{X}{S(t)}\right) - \left(r + \frac{1}{2}\sigma^2\right)(T - t)}{\sigma\sqrt{T - t}}\right), \qquad (8.28)
\end{aligned}
$$

where $\bar{V} \equiv \bar{w}(T) - \bar{w}(t) \sim N[0, (T - t)]$, by the properties of a standard Brownian motion (see p112). Now define $\bar{Z} \equiv \bar{V}/\sqrt{T - t}$. By definition, $\bar{Z}$ is distributed

---

[13]Note that the statement "$\mu = r + \sigma^2$" assumes that the data-generating process is $S(t) = S(0)\exp\left[\left(\mu - \frac{1}{2}\sigma^2\right)t + \sigma\bar{w}(t)\right]$, where $\bar{w}(t)$ is a standard Brownian motion under $\bar{P}$. You cannot plug $\mu = r + \sigma^2$ directly into equation 8.2 on page 112, because the Brownian motion term is then mis-specified.

©2009 Timothy Falcon Crack   127

standard normal under $\bar{P}$. Equation 8.28 thus yields equation 8.29, which leads to equation 8.30 via Z-score arguments:

$$
\begin{aligned}
\bar{P}(S(T) > X) &= \bar{P}\left(\bar{Z} > \frac{\ln\left(\frac{X}{S(t)}\right) - \left(r + \frac{1}{2}\sigma^2\right)(T-t)}{\sigma\sqrt{T-t}}\right) \quad (8.29)\\
&= \bar{P}\left(\bar{Z} > -\left[\frac{\ln\left(\frac{S(t)}{X}\right) + \left(r + \frac{1}{2}\sigma^2\right)(T-t)}{\sigma\sqrt{T-t}}\right]\right)\\
&= \bar{P}(\bar{Z} > -d_1)\\
&= 1 - N(-d_1)\\
&= N(d_1), \quad (8.30)
\end{aligned}
$$

where I used the property of logarithms that $-\ln(A) = \ln\left(\frac{1}{A}\right)$, for any $A > 0$, and the property of the cumulative standard normal that $1 - N(-z) = N(z)$.

> **Exercise:** Prove that $N(d_2) = P^*(S(T) > X)$ by replicating equations 8.28, 8.29, and 8.30 for the P^* risk-neutral measure.

We now have the symmetrical results that $N(d_1) = \bar{P}(S(T) > X)$ and $N(d_2) = P^*(S(T) > X)$, where $\bar{P}$ and P^* are the stock-numeraire and risk-neutral equivalent martingale measures, respectively. That is, as stated earlier, $\bar{P}$ and P^* are the probability measures under which, respectively, the bond de-trended by the stock and the stock de-trended by the bond follow martingales.

> **Exercise 1:** The Black-Scholes put pricing formula for an option on a stock that pays no dividends is given by
>
> $$
> \begin{aligned}
> p(t) &= e^{-r(T-t)}XN(-d_2) - S(t)N(-d_1), \text{ where}\\
> d_1 &= \frac{\ln\left(\frac{S(t)}{X}\right) + (r + \frac{1}{2}\sigma^2)(T-t)}{\sigma\sqrt{T-t}}, \text{ and}\\
> d_2 &= d_1 - \sigma\sqrt{T-t}.
> \end{aligned}
> $$
>
> Use calculus to confirm that $\Delta \equiv \frac{\partial p(t)}{\partial S(t)} = -N(-d_1)$.
>
> **Exercise 2:** In the case where the stock pays continuous dividends at rate ρ, Merton (1973) extends the basic Black-Scholes formula by replacing $S(t)$ by $S(t)e^{-\rho(T-t)}$. Perform this replacement for the call, rewrite the formula, and recalculate the call option delta to confirm that it now equals $e^{-\rho(T-t)}N(d_1)$. The interpretation is simple: The replicating strategy now needs slightly fewer shares because dividends that leak out may be reinvested to create more shares. See section 8.5.1 (p139) for the full formulae.

Do not lose sight of the fact that $N(d_1)$ and $N(d_2)$ are just numbers. The probabilistic interpretations we place on them aid our understanding, and, in the case of the bond-numeraire argument, allow us to use the risk-neutral technique to price

$$c(t) = \overbrace{\underbrace{S(t)}_{PV_S} \underbrace{N(d_1)}_{\bar{P}(in)}}^{\text{stock position}} - \overbrace{\underbrace{[e^{-r(T-t)}X]}_{PV_B} \underbrace{N(d_2)}_{P^*(in)}}^{\text{bond position}}$$

Figure 8.3: Competing-Numeraire Symmetry Black-Scholes Summary

Note: This figure summarizes the competing-numeraire symmetry results of section 8.3.4 for a call on a stock with no dividends. The first term is the stock term; the second is the bond term. First term: $S(t)N(d_1)$ is the stock position in a replicating portfolio (see section 8.3.1, p120); PV_S is the present value of time-T stock price $S(T)$; and $\bar{P}(in) = \bar{P}(S(T) > X)$ is the probability that the call finishes in the money in the stock-numeraire world in which the bond price de-trended by the stock price follows a martingale under $\bar{P}$. Second term: $-e^{-r(T-t)}XN(d_2)$ is the bond position in a replicating portfolio (see section 8.3.1); PV_B is the present value of a discount bond with face value X that matures at time T; and $P^*(in) = P^*(S(T) > X)$ is the probability that the call finishes in the money in the risk-neutral world in which the stock price de-trended by the bond price follows a martingale under P^*.

options more broadly. The original Black-Scholes instantaneous CAPM and Merton hedge arguments do not, however, contain these probabilistic interpretations; Black, Scholes, and Merton were not aware of these interpretations until several years after they had derived their original results (see section 4.4.2, p75).

You may have seen the risk-neutral equivalent martingale measure result that $N(d_2) = P^*(S(T) > X)$, but not the stock-numeraire equivalent martingale measure result, $N(d_1) = \bar{P}(S(T) > X)$. I think this is for historical reasons. The risk-neutral equivalent martingale measure evolved naturally out of work conducted by Cox and Ross (see Cox and Ross [1976]). This work, in turn, built on the search, 10 to 15 years earlier, for a solution to the discount rate puzzle for option pricing (e.g., Sprenkle [1961] and Samuelson [1965]). The arrival of risk-neutral discounting solved the discount rate puzzle and was carried forward vigorously. In particular, in the risk-neutral measure world, we have the result that $E^*[S(T)|S(t)] = S(t)e^{r(T-t)}$, and this holds for *every* security in the risk-neutral world including options. In the stock-numeraire world, however, we have the result that $\bar{E}[S_i(T)|S_i(t)] = S_i(t)e^{(r+\sigma_i^2)(T-t)}$ for stock i, and this is security-specific. Although the former appears intuitively more simple than the latter,[14] the Black-Scholes formula can be derived just as easily under the stock-numeraire equivalent martingale measure as it is under the risk-neutral equivalent martingale measure; You just have to discount the option payoff using the stock numeriare. For an example of this, you can attempt the proof mentioned at the end of the op quiz on page 135.

---

[14]...simpler because option returns are still path-dependent random variables in the stock-numeriare world and this is unlike risk-neutral-world DCF, which simplifies matters tremendously (as shown in sections 4.1–4.3, pp67–70).

> **Exercise:** Figure 8.3 presents competing-numeraire symmetry results as an interpretation of the Black-Scholes call formula. Write down the analogous result for the Black-Scholes put formula.

A summary of the competing-numeraire symmetry results appears in figure 8.3. The summary draws on results from section 8.3.1. The stock position in the replicating portfolio of section 8.3.1 is composed of the present value of future stock price and the probability that the call finishes in-the-money if the stock is used as numeraire (where the bond price so de-trended follows a martingale under $\bar{P}$). Similarly, and symmetrically, the bond position in the replicating portfolio is composed of the present value of a future discount bond price and the probability that the call finishes in-the-money if the discount bond is used as numeraire (where the stock price so de-trended follows a martingale under P^*). Be sure to see the stock-numeraire op quiz (p135) for another representation of the Black-Scholes formula.

8.3.5 Interpretation V: Digital (Binary) Options

The payoff to a standard call option may be broken down into payoffs to two exotic options: a "digital (or 'binary') asset-or-nothing option" and a "digital (or 'binary') cash-or-nothing option." The European digital asset-or-nothing pays $S(T)$ if $S(T) > X$, and zero otherwise; hence its name. It is worth $S(t)N(d_1)$ today. The European digital cash-or-nothing with "bet" size H pays H if $S(T) > X$, and zero otherwise; hence its name. It is worth $He^{-r(T-t)}N(d_2)$. If $H = X$, then a long digital asset-or-nothing, combined with a short digital cash-or-nothing exactly replicates the payoff to a call.

> **Exercise:** Draw the payoff diagrams (terminal cash flow to option on the vertical versus terminal price of underlying stock on the horizontal) to both digital options. Note that for $S(T) > X$, the asset-or-nothing dominates the cash or nothing, and thus a regular call (i.e., long asset-or-nothing and short cash-or-nothing with bet size $H = X$) is never worth less than zero.

8.3.6 Interpretation VI: Conditional Payoffs

The first term in the Black-Scholes formula for a call on a non dividend-paying stock is $S(t)N(d_1)$, where $d_1 \equiv \left[\ln(S/X) + \left(r + \frac{1}{2}\sigma^2\right)(T-t)\right] / \left(\sigma\sqrt{(T-t)}\right)$. Could it be that equation 8.31 holds?

$$S(t)N(d_1) \stackrel{?}{=} e^{-r(T-t)}E^*[S(T)|S(T) > X] \tag{8.31}$$

The answer is "no," even though the present value of the digital asset-or-nothing option is $S(t)N(d_1)$, and this option does indeed pay off $S(T)$ when $S(T) > X$. Let us apply some simple economic intuition to prove that equation 8.31 is false before working out the correction.

Suppose X is \$100 and that $S(t)$ is around \$100. Consider a six-month option. Between now and expiration, the stock price could go up or down, so there must be a roughly 50% chance that the option will finish in-the-money. From section 8.3.2 it follows that $N(d_2)$ is roughly 0.50. $N(d_1)$ is roughly the same as $N(d_2)$ by definition, so $N(d_1)$ is also roughly 0.50. With $S(t) \approx \$100$ and $N(d_1) \approx 0.50$, it follows that the digital asset-or-nothing option is valued at $S(t)N(d_1) \approx \$50$, thus fixing the LHS of equation 8.31.

What about the RHS of equation 8.31; i.e., $e^{-r(T-t)}E^*[S(T)|S(T) > X]$? Well, in my example, $E^*[S(T)|S(T) > X]$ is the expected value of the terminal stock price conditional upon the stock price being above \$100. This must be a number above \$100 by definition; something like \$105, say. Discounting it back means that $e^{-r(T-t)}E^*[S(T)|S(T) > X]$ must be a number of the order of \$100. With $S(t)N(d_1) \approx \$50$ and $e^{-r(T-t)}E^*[S(T)|S(T) > X] \approx \$100$, the RHS of equation 8.31 is roughly twice the LHS in this case. It follows that $S(t)N(d_1) \neq e^{-r(T-t)}E^*[S(T)|S(T) > X]$.

The asset-or-nothing option that pays off $S(T)$ if $S(T) > X$ and nothing otherwise does *not* have payoff "$S(T)|S(T) > X$." Rather, it has payoff $I_X[S(T)]$, where $I_X(\cdot)$ is an indicator function defined as follows:

$$I_X(x) \equiv \begin{cases} x; & \text{if } x > X, \\ 0; & \text{otherwise.} \end{cases}$$

That is, the digital asset-or-nothing option has payoff

$$I_X[S(T)] = \begin{cases} S(T); & \text{if } S(T) > X, \\ 0; & \text{otherwise,} \end{cases} \tag{8.32}$$

and this is not the same as $S(T)|S(T) > X$.

If we repeat the portion of the calculus used in section 8.2 (p116) to arrive at the first term $S(t)N(d_1)$ in the Black-Scholes call formula, we can confirm that equation 8.33 holds:

$$S(t)N(d_1) = e^{-r(T-t)}E^*\{I_X[S(T)]\}, \tag{8.33}$$

with $I_X[S(T)]$ as given in equation 8.32. As a simple analogy, consider a random variable Y, defined as follows:

$$Y = \begin{cases} 1; & \text{with probability } 0.20 \\ 2; & \text{with probability } 0.20 \\ 3; & \text{with probability } 0.20 \\ 4; & \text{with probability } 0.20 \\ 5; & \text{with probability } 0.20 \end{cases}$$

Clearly, $E(Y|Y > 3) = 4.5$. Now consider a transformation of Y analogous to the payoff to an asset-or-nothing option that pays off Y if $Y > 3$, but zero otherwise;

label this U (for payoff in the upper part of the distribution):

$$U \equiv \max(Y, 0) = \begin{cases} 0; & \text{with probability } 0.20 \\ 0; & \text{with probability } 0.20 \\ 0; & \text{with probability } 0.20 \\ 4; & \text{with probability } 0.20 \\ 5; & \text{with probability } 0.20 \end{cases}$$

Clearly, $E(U) = E[\max(Y, 0)] = 1.8$ and this differs from $E(Y|Y > 3)$. The random variable U exists and has payoffs equal to zero when $Y \leq 3$. These zero payoffs and their probabilities are taken into account when finding $E(U) = E[\max(Y, 0)]$, but are ignored when calculating $E(Y|Y > 3)$ because the conditional distribution $Y|Y > 3$ takes values only when $Y > 3$ and is undefined otherwise. Thus, the conditional probability distribution $Y|Y > 3$ needs to be grossed up so that the probabilities sum to one. That is,

$$Y|Y > 3 = \begin{cases} 4; & \text{with probability } 0.50 \\ 5; & \text{with probability } 0.50. \end{cases}$$

The relationship is that $E(Y|Y > 3) = \frac{E(U)}{P(Y>3)} = \frac{1.80}{0.40} = 4.50$. Using the earlier indicator function notation, we may write $E(U) = E[I_3(Y)]$, and we may deduce equation 8.34:

$$E(Y|Y > 3) = \frac{E[I_3(Y)]}{P(Y > 3)} \tag{8.34}$$

If we replace Y by $S(T)$, and 3 by X, in equation 8.34, and multiply through by $e^{-r(T-t)}$, we deduce equation 8.35 as the correction to equation 8.31:

$$e^{-r(T-t)}E^*[S(T)|S(T) > X] = \frac{e^{-r(T-t)}E^*\{I_X[S(T)]\}}{P^*(S(T) > X)} = \frac{S(t)N(d_1)}{N(d_2)}, \tag{8.35}$$

where we have used the fact that

$$S(t)N(d_1) = e^{-r(T-t)}E^*\{I_X[S(T)]\}, \text{ and}$$
$$N(d_2) = P^*(S(T) > X).$$

The denominator, $N(d_2)$, in equation 8.35 is absent in equation 8.31. This absence explains the earlier numerical example being out by a rough factor of two, because $N(d_2) \approx 0.50$ implies $\frac{1}{N(d_2)} \approx 2$.

Riskless drift in the risk-neutral world implies $E^*[S(T)] = S(t)e^{r(T-t)} = F(t)$, where $F(t)$ is the forward price. If we multiply both sides of equation 8.35 by $e^{r(T-t)}$, we can use this result to deduce equation 8.36 relating the conditional and unconditional expectations of $S(T)$ to the forward price $F(t)$:

$$\begin{aligned} E^*[S(T)|S(T) > X] &= \frac{e^{r(T-t)}S(t)N(d_1)}{N(d_2)} \\ &= E^*[S(T)]\frac{N(d_1)}{N(d_2)} \\ &= F(t)\frac{N(d_1)}{N(d_2)} \end{aligned} \tag{8.36}$$

Equation 8.36 is interesting for several reasons:

- The relationship $d_1 = d_2 + \sigma\sqrt{T-t}$, and the monotonic increasing nature of $N(\cdot)$, imply that $N(d_1) > N(d_2)$, and thus that the multiplier in equation 8.36 satisfies $\frac{N(d_1)}{N(d_2)} > 1$. The multiplier $\frac{N(d_1)}{N(d_2)}$ is an adjustment factor that adjusts upward the unconditional expectation $E^*[S(T)]$ to arrive at the conditional expectation $E^*[S(T)|S(T) > X]$, which is more relevant for option pricing.

- Equation 8.36 can be rearranged to yield equation 8.37:

$$S(t)N(d_1) = e^{-r(T-t)}E^*[S(T)|S(T) > X]N(d_2) \qquad (8.37)$$

Equation 8.37 may be substituted directly into the Black-Scholes call pricing formula (equation 8.17, p120) to yield equation 8.38:

$$c(t) = e^{-r(T-t)}\left\{E^*[S(T)|S(T) > X] - X\right\}N(d_2), \qquad (8.38)$$
$$\text{where } d_2 = \frac{\ln\left(\frac{S(t)}{X}\right) + (r - \frac{1}{2}\sigma^2)(T-t)}{\sigma\sqrt{T-t}}.$$

Key Point: Equation 8.38 gives us another way of looking at Black-Scholes:

$$c(t) = \underbrace{e^{-r(T-t)}}_{\text{discounted}}\underbrace{\left\{E^*[S(T)|S(T) > X] - X\right\}}_{\text{expected net payoff}}\underbrace{N(d_2)}_{P^*(in)}, \qquad (8.39)$$
$$\text{where } d_2 = \frac{\ln\left(\frac{S(t)}{X}\right) + (r - \frac{1}{2}\sigma^2)(T-t)}{\sigma\sqrt{T-t}}.$$

There is risk-neutral probability $P^*(in) = N(d_2)$ that the call option finishes in-the-money. In that case, your risk-neutral expected benefit is $E^*[S(T)|S(T) > X]$, and your risk-neutral expected cost is X. The risk-neutral expected future benefit of call option ownership is $E^*[S(T)|S(T) > X] \cdot N(d_2)$, and this is identical to $e^{r(T-t)}S(t)N(d_1)$.

- If $S(t)$ is very large relative to X, i.e., $X \ll S(t)$, the call is so likely to finish in-the-money that $E^*[S(T)|S(T) > X] \approx E^*[S(T)]$ must hold, and equation 8.36 then implies that $\frac{N(d_1)}{N(d_2)}$ must be very close to one. Indeed, when $X \ll S(t)$, both $N(d_1)$ and $N(d_2)$ are very close to one, and so must be their ratio.

- If the call option is so deep in-the-money that $E^*[S(T)|S(T) > X] \approx E^*[S(T)]$, then equation 8.39 implies that

$$\begin{aligned}c(t) &= e^{-r(T-t)}\left\{E^*[S(T)|S(T) > X] - X\right\}N(d_2)\\ &\approx e^{-r(T-t)}\left\{E^*[S(T)] - X\right\}N(d_2)\\ &= e^{-r(T-t)}[F(t) - X]N(d_2)\\ &\approx e^{-r(T-t)}[F(t) - X], \qquad (8.40)\end{aligned}$$

where $F(t) = E^*[S(T)] = e^{r(T-t)}S(t)$ is the forward price, and the last step follows because $N(d_2) \approx 1$ for deep in-the-money options. That is, a deep in-the-money call has roughly the same expected payoff as a forward contract, where at time T, you agree to pay X and receive today's $F(t)$.

- When X is very large relative to $S(t)$, i.e., $S(t) \ll X$, the call is deep out-of-the-money and it is very unlikely that the stock will finish above X at time T. The conditional expectation $E^*[S(T)|S(T) > X]$, however, ignores any other possibility and grosses up the probability to use a pdf defined only over $S(T) > X$. This means that $E^*[S(T)|S(T) > X]$ must be close to X, but slightly higher. For large X, each extra dollar of X thus increases $E^*[S(T)|S(T) > X]$ by almost exactly a dollar. With $E^*[S(T)|S(T) > X]$ so X-like, equation 8.36 implies that

$$\frac{e^{r(T-t)}S(t)N(d_1)}{N(d_2)} \approx X,$$

and thus that for large X,

$$\frac{N(d_1)}{N(d_2)} \approx \frac{X}{e^{r(T-t)}S(t)} = \frac{X}{F(t)}.$$

The ratio $\frac{N(d_1)}{N(d_2)}$ can thus be arbitrarily large for large X; i.e., for deep out-of-the-money call options.

- For the stock options that I trade, the typical range of values of $\frac{N(d_1)}{N(d_2)}$ is something like 1–1.50.

Exercise: In a similar vein to equation 8.39, demonstrate that equation 8.41 holds for European puts.

$$p(t) = e^{-r(T-t)}\left\{X - E^*[S(T)|S(T) < X]\right\}N(-d_2) \qquad (8.41)$$

$$d_2 = \frac{\ln\left(\frac{S(t)}{X}\right) + (r - \frac{1}{2}\sigma^2)(T-t)}{\sigma\sqrt{T-t}}$$

Hint: Begin by showing that

$$E^*[S(T)|S(T) < X] = \frac{e^{+r(T-t)}S(t)N(-d_1)}{N(-d_2)},$$

then substitute the result into equation 8.18 (p120) for a put. Recall that

$$E^*[S(T)|S(T) < X] = \int_{w=-\infty}^{w_0} S(t)e^{(r-\frac{1}{2}\sigma^2)(T-t)+\sigma w}f_W(w)dw,$$

for w_0 such that $S(t)e^{(r-\frac{1}{2}\sigma^2)(T-t)+\sigma w_0} = X$, where $W \sim N[0,(T-t)]$ is a Brownian motion.

Op Quiz (difficult): Can you use the stock-numeraire results of section 8.3.4 to derive a conditional expectation result analogous to equations 8.39 and 8.41 but ending in $N(d_1)$ for the call and $N(-d_1)$ for the put?

Answer: Yes, we may write $c(t) = \left\{ S(t) - X \cdot \bar{E}\left[\frac{S(t)}{S(T)} \middle| S(T) > X \right] \right\} N(d_1)$, and

$p(t) = \left\{ X \cdot \bar{E}\left[\frac{S(t)}{S(T)} \middle| S(T) > X \right] - S(t) \right\} N(-d_1)$, where $\bar{E}(\cdot)$ is expectation under the stock-numeraire measure. To derive these, note that the option payoff is discounted using the stock-numeraire backwards from time T to time t:

$$c(t) = \bar{E}\left[\underbrace{\frac{S(t)}{S(T)}}_{\text{discount factor (stochastic)}} \underbrace{[S(T) - X]}_{\text{conditional net payoff}} \middle| S(T) > X \right] \underbrace{N(d_1)}_{\bar{P}(in)} \quad (8.42)$$

$$= \bar{E}\left[\frac{S(t)}{S(T)} \cdot S(T) - \frac{S(t)}{S(T)} X \middle| S(T) > X \right] N(d_1) \quad (8.43)$$

$$= \left\{ \underbrace{S(t)}_{\text{PV(benefit)}} - \underbrace{X}_{\text{cost}} \cdot \underbrace{\bar{E}\left[\frac{S(t)}{S(T)} \middle| S(T) > X \right]}_{\text{discount factor}} \right\} \underbrace{N(d_1)}_{\bar{P}(in)} \quad (8.44)$$

Note 1: I thank Andreas Stirnemann for supplying the solution to this op quiz; any errors are mine.

Note 2: We can break up the discount factor, pull out $S(t)$, and write the expression for the call concisely as $c(t) = S(t)\left\{ 1 - X \cdot \bar{E}\left[\frac{1}{S(T)} \middle| S(T) > X \right] \right\} N(d_1)$, but some of the economic intuition is lost; a similar result holds for the put.

Note 3: Comparing equation 8.44 to Black-Scholes, you should be able to deduce that $\bar{E}\left[\frac{S(t)}{S(T)} \middle| S(T) > X \right] = e^{-r(T-t)} \frac{N(d_2)}{N(d_1)}$.

Hint: If you attempt the tedious proof of these results, be sure to use $\mu = r + \sigma^2$ (see p127), and to rescale the conditional pdf by $\bar{P}(in) = N(d_1)$ for the integral (analogous to step (*) on page 27).

8.3.7 Interpretation VII: PDE Solution

The Black-Scholes formulae are solutions to PDEs. We showed in sections 4.4.1 and 4.4.3 that financial PDEs can be generated by hedging arguments and by martingale arguments, respectively. We discussed PDE generation further in section 7.3 and followed up with discussions of solution techniques in sections 7.4 and 7.5, and interpretations in section 7.6. Section 8.8, later in this chapter, also discusses the Greeks and PDEs.

> **Exercise:** We demonstrated in the exercise on page 104 that simple investments in both the stock and the bond satisfy the Black-Scholes PDE. Prove now that Black-Scholes call and put formulae satisfy the Black-Scholes PDE. Be sure to use the original no-dividend version of the Black-Scholes formulae if you use the no-dividend PDE, and the Merton continuous-dividend version of the Black-Scholes formulae (see section 8.5.1) if you use the continuous-dividend PDE.

8.3.8   Interpretation VIII: See figure 3.3

In figure 3.3 (p59), we plotted the value of the European call and put versus the underlying stock price using the Black-Scholes formula. For the call, a tangent line drawn anywhere has slope $N(d_1)$ and intercept $-e^{-r(T-t)}XN(d_2)$. For the put, a tangent line drawn anywhere has slope $-N(-d_1)$ and intercept $e^{-r(T-t)}XN(-d_2)$. See the summaries in equations 8.45 and 8.46:

$$\underbrace{c(t)}_{y\text{-axis}} = \underbrace{S(t)}_{x\text{-axis}}\underbrace{N(d_1)}_{\text{slope}}\underbrace{-e^{-r(T-t)}XN(d_2)}_{\text{intercept}} \tag{8.45}$$

$$\underbrace{p(t)}_{y\text{-axis}} = \underbrace{e^{-r(T-t)}XN(-d_2)}_{\text{intercept}}\underbrace{-N(-d_1)}_{\text{slope}}\underbrace{S(t)}_{x\text{-axis}} \tag{8.46}$$

At first glance, $c(t) = S(t)N(d_1) - e^{-r(T-t)}XN(d_2)$ appears to have the form $c(t) = S \cdot a + b$, where $a = N(d_1)$ and $b = -e^{-r(T-t)}XN(d_2)$. If a and b are not functions of S, then it follows immediately that in the S-c-plane, a and b must be the slope and intercept, respectively, of any tangent line. Note, however, that both $N(d_1)$ and $N(d_2)$ *are* functions of S. It follows that both $a = N(d_1)$ and $b = -e^{-r(T-t)}XN(d_2)$ are functions of S and my statements about slopes and intercepts are *not* immediate, but need to be derived (see the exercise following).

> **Exercise:** Given equation 8.17 (p120), and equation 8.18 (p120), prove that $\frac{\partial c(t)}{\partial S(t)} = N(d_1)$ and $\frac{\partial p(t)}{\partial S(t)} = -N(-d_1)$. Deduce, therefore, that a line drawn tangent to the plot of option value must have these slopes, with intercepts as stated in equations 8.45 and 8.46.

8.4   Approximations to Black-Scholes

The more intuition you have about Black-Scholes pricing, the more likely it is that you can derive approximations to the formula that allow you to distill the essential characteristics.

For example, Cox, Ross, and Rubinstein (1979) use a binomial approximation to the Brownian motion to derive binomial option pricing and the binomial option pricing formula (see my equations 8.24 and 8.25, pages 125 and 125). This provides intuition insofar as providing an approximation to the price process that is easy to understand. A second example is that a deep in-the-money call is worth $c(t) \approx S(t)-$

$e^{-r(T-t)}X$ (see sections 3.6.2–3.6.3 on pp55–57 and equation 8.40 on page133). This approximation is based on the simple observation that high likelihood of exercise removes the $N(d_i)$ terms.

8.4.1 Louis Jean Baptiste Alphonse Bachelier (1900)

Modern option pricing theory derives from the work of Robert Merton, Fischer Black, and Myron Scholes in the very early 1970s. They, in turn, were inspired by Paul Samuelson's work at MIT in the mid- to late-1960s. Samuelson, in turn, was inspired by Louis Bachelier's work around 1900 at the Sorbonne, in Paris. Bachelier derived a closed-form option pricing formula that is closely related to the Black-Scholes formula.

There are many ways to arrive at Bachelier's formula. I derive it first in this section using simple intuition and loose mathematics. I then derive a generalization of it using PDEs in section 9.2.1.

Take an at-the-money call (i.e., $S = X$). Assume $r = 0$ (it is the least important input in Black-Scholes anyway, and it is not far wrong in the US in 2009). With risk-neutral drift zero, there is roughly a fifty-fifty chance that the option expires in-the-money as opposed to being worthless in a risk-neutral world. With $r = 0$, the formula for option value as discounted expected payoff then simplifies to expected payoff, and reduces to equation 8.49:

$$
\begin{aligned}
c(t) &\approx \left(P^*(S \uparrow) \cdot E^*[\text{payoff}|S \uparrow] \right) + \left(P^*(S \downarrow) \cdot E^*[\text{payoff}|S \downarrow] \right) \\
&= \frac{1}{2} \cdot E^*[S(T) - S(t)|S \uparrow] + \frac{1}{2} \cdot [0|S \downarrow] \qquad (8.47) \\
&= \frac{1}{2} \cdot E^*[S(T) - S(t)|S \uparrow] \qquad (8.48) \\
&= \frac{1}{2} \cdot S(t) \cdot E^* \left[\frac{S(T) - S(t)}{S(t)} \middle| S \uparrow \right] \qquad (8.49)
\end{aligned}
$$

For small returns, $[S(T) - S(t)]/S(t) \approx \ln[S(T)/S(t)]$. We may deduce from table 8.1 on page 115 that the continuously compounded rate of return $\ln[S(T)/S(t)]$ is normal with risk-neutral mean $(r - \frac{1}{2}\sigma^2)(T - t)$ and standard deviation $\sigma\sqrt{T-t}$. With r assumed zero, this mean is roughly zero (e.g., $\sigma = 0.30$, and $T - t = 0.5$ implies $\frac{1}{2}\sigma^2(T - t) = 0.0225$). Although it is the continuously compounded return that is distributed normally, not $[S(T)-S(t)]/S(t)$, we shall dispense with formality and use the above-mentioned approximation $[S(T) - S(t)]/S(t) \approx \ln[S(T)/S(t)]$ to drive a special case of equation 2.7 (see p28) as follows:

$$
Y \sim N(0, \lambda^2) \text{ implies } E(Y|Y > 0) = \lambda\sqrt{\frac{2}{\pi}}
$$

This result allows us to replace $E^*\{[S(T) - S(t)]/S(t)| S \uparrow\}$ in equation 8.49 with $\sigma\sqrt{T-t}\sqrt{\frac{2}{\pi}}$, thus yielding equations 8.50 and 8.51.

$$
c(t) \approx \frac{1}{2} \cdot S(t) \cdot \sigma\sqrt{T-t}\sqrt{\frac{2}{\pi}} \qquad (8.50)
$$

$$\Rightarrow c(t) \approx \frac{S(t)\sigma\sqrt{T-t}}{\sqrt{2\pi}} \tag{8.51}$$

Equation 8.51 is very close to Bachelier's option pricing formula. In fact, Bachelier's ABM has the data-generating process $dS = \sigma_A dw$, where σ_A is volatility of price change. If σ is the volatility of returns to the GBM, then the volatility σ_A in the ABM is roughly equal to σS. Replacing σS in equation 8.51 by σ_A yields Bachelier's original 1900 option pricing formula given in equation 8.52:

$$\begin{aligned} c(t) &= \frac{\sigma_A\sqrt{T-t}}{\sqrt{2\pi}} \\ &\approx 0.4 \cdot \sigma_A\sqrt{T-t} \end{aligned} \tag{8.52}$$

Key Point: Louis Bachelier's equation 8.52 is the ABM equivalent of my GBM-derived equation 8.51:

$$\begin{aligned} c(t) &= \frac{\sigma_A\sqrt{T-t}}{\sqrt{2\pi}} \\ &\approx \frac{S(t)\sigma\sqrt{T-t}}{\sqrt{2\pi}}, \\ &\approx 0.4S(t)\sigma\sqrt{T-t}. \end{aligned}$$

For $S = X$, and $r = 0$, Bachelier's formula is within about 2% of Black-Scholes pricing. It works for both puts and calls. It also tells us how at-the-money option values change given changes in $S(t)$, σ, and $T - t$. Be careful—it compares at-the-money options only.

My first book, *Heard on The Street*, (Crack [2008]) contains over 170 quantitative finance job interview questions (see the last page of this book for details). For example, "What is the value of a three-month at-the-money (i.e., $S = X$) call option on a \$100 stock when the σ is 40? Please assume $r = 0$ (it is the least important ingredient anyway) and assume also that the stock pays no dividends. You have 10 seconds to perform the calculation in your head. Now tell me how your answer changes if it is a put." Well, it is 0.40 times \$100 times 0.40 times $\sqrt{0.25}$. We know $\sqrt{0.25} = 0.50$, so multiply in your head... ...equals \$8. For at-the-money options when $r = 0$, the European put and call have the same value. If you go to the Black-Scholes formulae and work it out, you get \$7.97 for the call and for the put. Not a bad approximation! See section 9.2.1 for more general ABM results.

Exercise: Prove that if $S = X$ and $r = 0$ then put-call parity implies $c(t) = p(t)$; that is, the at-the-money European call and put have the same value if interest rates are zero.

I think it may be useful for you to compare equation 8.39 (p133) with equation 8.47 (p137). Both involve a breakdown of option payoff into two cases, one of which is zero. Both involve multiplication of those payoffs by the probability of occurrence, and both involve discounting. Equation 8.39 implicitly drops the zero-payoff case and equation 8.47 discounts at a zero rate, but I do think additional intuition for equation 8.39 can be gained by looking at equation 8.47.

Exercise (difficult): Derive my version of Bachelier's formula, equation 8.51, directly from the Black-Scholes call formula, equation 8.17, by plugging in $S = X$ and $r = 0$, and approximating the height of the standard normal curve by its height at zero (i.e., $1/\sqrt{2\pi}$). **Hint:** If $a > 0$ and small, then $N(a) - N(-a)$ is the area under the standard normal curve from $-a$ to $+a$, and this is roughly rectangular with base $a - (-a) = 2a$ and height $f_Z(z)|_{z=0} = \left.\frac{1}{\sqrt{2\pi}}e^{-\frac{1}{2}z^2}\right|_{z=0} = \frac{1}{\sqrt{2\pi}}$.

Op Quiz: Use my version of Bachelier's option pricing formula, equation 8.51, to deduce what happens to the price of an at-the-money call if (a) time to maturity is multiplied by a factor of four, (b) volatility, σ, doubles, or (c) stock price $S(t)$ goes up 50%.

Answer: The formula is $c(t) \approx 0.40 S(t) \sigma \sqrt{T-t}$. (a) The option price is related to time to maturity through the surd $\sqrt{}$. So, if maturity is four times as far away, then price changes by a factor of $\sqrt{4} = 2$; i.e., it doubles. (b) The option price is linear in volatility, σ, so doubling the volatility doubles the price. (c) If stock price goes up 50%, the option is no longer at-the-money, and Bachelier's formula does not apply. The delta of an at-the-money call is approximately one-half. The delta of a deep in-the-money call is approximately one. If you know the stock went from $40 to $60, say, then the option probably increased by about $0.75 \cdot \$20 = \$15$ (where 0.75 is the average of the deltas of one-half and one, and $\$20 = \Delta S = \$60 - \$40$).

8.5 Immediate Extensions

8.5.1 Index: Merton (1973)

Merton (1973) generalizes the no-dividend Black-Scholes formula to the case of calls and puts on underlying assets paying continuous dividends at rate ρ, as shown in equations 8.53 and 8.54:

$$c(t) = S(t)e^{-\rho(T-t)}N(d_1) - e^{-r(T-t)}XN(d_2), \text{ and} \qquad (8.53)$$

$$p(t) = e^{-r(T-t)}XN(-d_2) - S(t)e^{-\rho(T-t)}N(-d_1), \text{ where} \qquad (8.54)$$

$$d_1 = \frac{\ln\left(\frac{S(t)}{X}\right) + (r - \rho + \frac{1}{2}\sigma^2)(T-t)}{\sigma\sqrt{T-t}}, \text{ and}$$

$$d_2 = \frac{\ln\left(\frac{S(t)}{X}\right) + (r - \rho - \frac{1}{2}\sigma^2)(T-t)}{\sigma\sqrt{T-t}} = d_1 - \sigma\sqrt{T-t}.$$

Merton's model works well for European index options where dividends, although clustered, are closer to continuous than the lump sum payment for an individual stock. If, however, an underlying stock pays lump sum dividends of present value D

during the life of the option, then you may plug $S^* = S - D$ into the Black-Scholes formulae and, in theory, you should use some $\sigma^* > \sigma$ since the ex-dividend process is more volatile (see footnote 2 on page 154).

Exercise: Derive Merton's call pricing formula, equation 8.53, by replacing $S(t)$ with $S(t)e^{-\rho(T-t)}$ throughout the original Black-Scholes call formula, equation 8.17 (p120). You need to use the properties of logarithms and exponentials discussed in chapter 2.

8.5.2 Futures: Black (1976b)

Black (1976b) applies Merton's model to futures options by putting r in place of ρ and assuming that futures prices follow a GBM.

Exercise (difficult): Black assumes that futures options may be priced as if the futures price is the price of a traded asset that bleeds a continuous dividend at rate r. Explain why we can replace ρ by r to price futures options in the risk-neutral world.

8.5.3 FX: Garman and Kohlhagen (1983) and Grabbe (1983)

Garman and Kohlhagen (1983) and Grabbe (1983) apply Merton's model to FX options with the foreign interest rate in place of ρ (recall the discussion of FX in section 2.4.3 (p31) establishing FX as an asset paying a continuous dividend). Thus, the price of USD-denominated call and put options on GBP, for example, are given by equations 8.55 and 8.56, respectively:

$$c(t) = S(t)e^{-r_{GB}(T-t)}N(d_1) - e^{-r_{US}(T-t)}XN(d_2), \text{ and} \qquad (8.55)$$

$$p(t) = e^{-r_{US}(T-t)}XN(-d_2) - S(t)e^{-r_{GB}(T-t)}N(-d_1), \text{ where} \qquad (8.56)$$

$$d_1 = \frac{\ln\left(\frac{S(t)}{X}\right) + (r_{US} - r_{GB} + \frac{1}{2}\sigma^2)(T-t)}{\sigma\sqrt{T-t}}, \text{ and}$$

$$d_2 = \frac{\ln\left(\frac{S(t)}{X}\right) + (r_{US} - r_{GB} - \frac{1}{2}\sigma^2)(T-t)}{\sigma\sqrt{T-t}} = d_1 - \sigma\sqrt{T-t}.$$

Be cautious in placing the interest rates into equations 8.55 and 8.56. For a USD-denominated option on FX, the US interest rate is the discount rate, and the foreign interest rate is the continuous dividend yield on the underlying. Thus, the US rate goes into the discount factor adjacent to the strike, and the GB rate goes into the discount factor adjacent to the price of the underlying. Note that each of $c(t)$, $p(t)$, X, and $S(t)$ are denominated in USD per GBP in equations 8.55 and 8.56.

Exercise: Use the Garman-Kohlhagen formulae, equations 8.55 and 8.56, to prove that $\Delta = e^{-r_{FX}(T-t)}N(d_1)$ for an FX call, and $\Delta = -e^{-r_{FX}(T-t)}N(-d_1)$ for an FX put, where

$$d_1 = \frac{\ln\left(\frac{S(t)}{X}\right) + (r_{DOM} - r_{FX} + \frac{1}{2}\sigma^2)(T-t)}{\sigma\sqrt{T-t}},$$

and r_{DOM} and r_{FX} are the domestic and foreign interest rates respectively. **Hint:** Recall that $\Delta = \frac{\partial c(t)}{\partial S(t)}$ and $\frac{\partial p(t)}{\partial S(t)}$, for a call and put, respectively.

8.6 Application: The Adequation Formula for FX Option Parity

Many people are perplexed by FX forwards and options. They have trouble understanding the symmetry.[15] For example, if you are long a USD-denominated GBP forward, you are agreeing to buy GBP and make payment using USD. You are also, equivalently, agreeing to sell USD and receive payment in GBP. Thus, a long USD-denominated GBP forward is economically identical to a short GBP-denominated USD forward. Similarly, a USD-denominated GBP put must be economically identical to a GBP-denominated USD call.

In the exercise on page 142, I ask you to verify an FX parity relationship, equation 8.57 (the "adequation formula"), between a USD-denominated FX put and an FX-denominated USD call. The relationship described is $Q \cdot p = S \cdot (QX) \cdot c$, where the FX put covers Q units of FX, S and X are in USD/FX, p is the USD/FX price of the put, and c is the FX/USD price of the call. For ease of interpretation, I place Q, redundantly, on both sides of the equation. Before you try the exercise, you must confirm, via dimensional analysis, that equation 8.57 even makes sense. Dimensional analysis means we look at the units in which each side of the equation are expressed, and confirm that they are the same. For example, if the LHS is in GBP/USD and the RHS is in USD/(GBP^2), then something is wrong.

Suppose we have an FX put that gives us the right to sell $Q = 1,000$ GBP at a strike $X = 1.6500$USD/GBP, when the exchange rate is $S = 1.6000$USD/GBP. Assume for the sake of argument that we have already calculated $p = 0.032$USD/GBP. Then, $Qp = SQXc$ (equation 8.57) implies that $c = Qp/(SQX) = 0.012$, but do the dimensions work out? A dimensional analysis of the adequation formula appears in figure 8.4. In our case, c must be in GBP/USD, and both sides are, ultimately, in USD. The units of the LHS and the RHS are consistent, and, having passed this initial test, we may proceed to the exercise.

Why do I have only one σ in the equations in the exercise on page 142? That is, why do I not have σ_{US} and σ_{FX}? The answer is that the σ used is the volatility

---

[15]See Detemple (2001) and Haug (2007, section 1.2) for other symmetry results.

$$\underbrace{Q(\text{GBP})\!\cdot\!p(\text{USD/GBP})}_{\text{USD}} \;=\; S(\text{USD/GBP})\!\cdot\!\underbrace{\underbrace{[Q(\text{GBP})X(\text{USD/GBP})]}_{\text{USD}}}_{\underbrace{}_{\text{GBP}}}\!\cdot\!c(\text{GBP/USD}),$$

Figure 8.4: Dimensional Analysis for the FX Options Adequation Formula

Note: This is a dimensional analysis of the FX option parity relationship given in equation 8.57 (the adequation formula). See the exercise immediately before equation 8.57 for further details.

of continuously compounded returns to a US investor holding FX, and that this is *identical to* the volatility of continuously compounded returns to a foreign investor holding USD. I leave that as an exercise for those of you who like mathematics.

> **Exercise (difficult):** Let an FX put cover Q units of FX, and let S and X be in USD per unit of FX. Then the corresponding USD call covers QX USD, and is priced in FX (so its price is multiplied by (QX) to get total FX price of the call, and by S to convert its total price to USD). Please verify the adequation formula, equation 8.57:
>
> $$\begin{aligned} Q \cdot p &= S \cdot (QX) \cdot c, \text{ where} & (8.57)\\ p &= Xe^{-r_{US}(T-t)}N(-d_2) - Se^{-r_{FX}(T-t)}N(-d_1),\\ c &= S'e^{-r_{US}(T-t)}N(d_1') - X'e^{-r_{FX}(T-t)}N(d_2'),\\ S' &= \frac{1}{S},\\ X' &= \frac{1}{X},\\ d_1' &= \frac{\ln\left(\frac{S'}{X'}\right) + (r_{FX} - r_{US} + \frac{1}{2}\sigma^2)(T-t)}{\sigma\sqrt{T-t}},\\ d_2' &= d_1' - \sigma\sqrt{T-t},\\ d_1 &= \frac{\ln\left(\frac{S}{X}\right) + (r_{US} - r_{FX} + \frac{1}{2}\sigma^2)(T-t)}{\sigma\sqrt{T-t}}, \text{ and}\\ d_2 &= d_1 - \sigma\sqrt{T-t}. \end{aligned}$$

8.7 Black-Scholes Implementation

There are two ways to think about implementation. First, you can collect the numbers for all the raw inputs to Black-Scholes pricing, including an estimate of σ based on historical stock returns, and then use the inputs and the formula to deduce what the option price should be. You will be very lucky if the price that you deduce is within the bid-ask spread, and you will be a fool if you buy or sell the option based on the difference between the calculated price and the price in the marketplace. This method gives insight into how the inputs to Black-Scholes are constructed, but it is largely of academic interest. Second, you can look at what the option price is in the marketplace, then use observed numbers (i.e., interest rate, dividend yield, stock price, etc.) to deduce what volatility number is implicitly being used by the market to price the option. In this case, you place your faith in the market and use the model, populated by a combination of observed and implied parameters, as a guide to which options to trade. Apart from volatility estimation, the two methods agree.

Let me point out here, before we get to chapter 10, that as a trader I make money by identifying mispriced stocks and using options to capitalize on my view. I do not look for mispriced options or academic arbitrage opportunities. Rather, I assume that the market correctly prices options relative to the stock, and I calibrate the option pricing model to fit the market. I then feed my forecast of future stock price and volatility, accounting for deviations of Black-Scholes from reality, into the calibrated model to guide me in my choice of which options to buy or sell.

Black-Scholes pricing requires $S(t)$ (today's stock price), X (the strike), r (an interest rate), $T - t$ (time to maturity), ρ (dividend yield), and σ (volatility). In theory, if you are trading an option, then the stock price $S(t)$ that you use in Black-Scholes is the price that the option dealer in Chicago would trade at to delta hedge his or her resulting option position. So, if you are buying a call, the dealer will buy stock to delta hedge his or her short call. You should therefore use the ask price for the stock as $S(t)$—that is the price he or she is going to pass on to you. In practice, bid-ask spreads are very tight in New York now that stocks trade on decimals. Intraday stock price moves are large enough that whatever you used for $S(t)$ is going to be stale by the time you come to trade the option anyway. Just take the most recent trade price and then revise it if need be when you are ready to trade.

The strike price X is contractually specified. I usually set up a spreadsheet to have a half-dozen strikes to look at. The spacing of the strikes depends on the price of the stock. See section 10.1.1 for institutional details.

In theory, r is a short-term safe interest rate, and it is constant through time—though the theory does goes through with $\bar{r}$ (average r from t to T) in place or r. In practice, you take the continuously compounded yield on a T-bill of maturity closest to that of your option. Eurocurrency rates work too, especially for currency options. In theory, you should choose whether to use a LIBOR or LIBID rate depending upon whether the option dealer who delta hedges your trade is going to be borrowing money (at the LIBOR rate) or lending money (at the LIBID rate).[16]

---

[16]On February 12, 2009, my Bloomberg screen quoted three-month USD LIBOR as 1.23125 and three-month USD LIBID as 1.10625. The quoted LIBOR rate is the official British Banking Association (BBA) fix, but historically "LIBID was considered to be 1/8th or 12.5 basis points below LIBOR. However, we do not believe that this holds true anymore and that the spreads in most currencies would be a lot tighter in today's market environment. However, we have never officially stated the relationship between BBA LIBOR and LIBID and have never provided LIBID

Table 8.4: HP17B/HP19B T-Bill Yield Code

```
T~BILL~YIELD:R=-(365÷N)×LN(1-(N÷36000)×((BID+ASK)÷2))
```

Note: This code is for the HP17B or HP19B, but also works on the HP17BII and HP19BII. This code implements equation 8.58 to estimate the continuously compounded yield on a T-bill using the average of the bid and ask prices.

For example, if you are buying a three-month USD-denominated GBP call option (i.e., the right to buy GBP using USD), then the dealer will hedge by borrowing the denomination and buying the underlying. That is, in this case, the dealer borrows USD (paying r equals three-month USD LIBOR) and buys GBP (yielding ρ equals three-month GBP LIBID). In practice, the dealer hedges using FX futures because they have lower T-costs than physical FX.

You may choose to use USD LIBOR and LIBID in place of T-bill yields, on the grounds that they represent actual borrowing and lending costs (remember that only the US Treasury can borrow at the T-bill yield). In practice, the Black-Scholes model is quite robust to choice of r, and the difference of the bid-ask spread or the credit spread will be of little importance.

Averaging the bid and the ask, the continuously compounded yield on a T-bill with N days to maturity and *Wall Street Journal* bid and ask quotes B and A, respectively, is given in equation 8.58 (Cox and Rubinstein [1985, p255]). HP17B and HP19B code for implementing the equation appears in table 8.4.

$$r = -\frac{365}{N} \ln \left[1 - \frac{N}{36000} \left(\frac{B + A}{2} \right) \right] \tag{8.58}$$

The term to maturity $(T - t)$ is measured in years. Thus, a 24-day option has $T - t = \frac{24}{365}$ (yes, you must count actual days). For long-term options, I usually just use $T - t = M/12$, where M is the number of months to maturity.

Like the interest rate r, the dividend yield ρ is a continuously compounded rate. Stock dividends are quite consistent and predictable from one year to another. They are usually listed on online brokerage Web sites. Remember to continuously compound the number. For example, a $20 stock paying 60 cents in dividends over the next year has a dividend yield of $\rho = \ln(1 + 0.60/20)$ which is slightly lower than $0.60/20$. If dividend yields are very low, whether you continuously compound or not makes little difference.

The volatility σ comes from one of two sources: estimation via historical prices of the underlying or direct inference from prices of related options.

---

fixings. You might still find a few screen pages around e.g., on Bloomberg, who simply take the BBA LIBOR rates and subtract 1/8th mathematically to arrive at a LIBID rate. However, this can lead to all sorts of problems e.g. negative interest rates in the case of JPY..." (personal communication from a BBA Director June 16, 2004).

8.7.1 Method I: Estimate Historical σ

To estimate σ from historical prices, take two to three months of daily data (N observations, let us assume). Some people use as many days back in time as there are days remaining in the life of the option. In my opinion, anything older than six months is too old to be relevant.

Let $R_n \equiv \frac{S(n)-S(n-1)}{S(n-1)}$ denote the simple rate of return on day n, where $S(n)$ is the closing price of the stock on day n. We estimate the daily mean and variance of continuously compounded returns using equations 8.59 and 8.60:

$$\hat{\mu}_d = \frac{1}{N}\sum_{n=1}^{N}\ln(1+R_n) \qquad (8.59)$$

$$\hat{\sigma}_d^2 = \frac{1}{N-1}\sum_{n=1}^{N}\left[\ln(1+R_n)-\hat{\mu}_d\right]^2 \qquad (8.60)$$

The Black-Scholes formula needs annualized σ. We know that the variance of a random walk is linear in time (i.e., variance of the sum of the daily returns is the sum of the variance of the daily returns), so standard deviation, as the square root of variance, increases with the square root of time. Volatility is recognized as being generated on trading days (with 252–254 trading days per annum). Thus, the annual σ is estimated as $\hat{\sigma} = \hat{\sigma}_d\sqrt{252}$, where σ_d is the daily volatility estimate from equation 8.60.

In practice, stock prices do not follow random walks. There is substantial auto-correlation in stock returns. There is significant short-term, negative auto-correlation corresponding to price reversals and microstructure-induced price discreteness, and significant long-term, positive auto-correlation corresponding to price momentum. This means that, for example, using daily, weekly, or monthly returns and grossing up to get annual volatility will give you different answers. Daily observations are favored.

Historically, US stocks priced \$1–\$10 have had annual σ (historical or implied) in the range 30%–100% while stocks priced over \$10 have had annual σ in the range 10%–60%. In late March 2009, I pulled from my Bloomberg terminal historial and implied volatilities on all S&P500 stocks with listed options. The volatility numbers were almost exactly twice the historical numbers. This demonstrates that in times of crisis these volatilities can rise dramatically across the board. A typical $\hat{\sigma}$ in 2009 is 50% per annum (i.e., roughly 3.0% per day).

Exercise: Confirm that $\sigma = 0.50$ per annum implies $\sigma_d \approx 0.03$ per day.

Two common deviations observed using historical estimates of σ are that model estimates are below market prices for near-to-maturity options, and that if variance is estimated to be high (conversely low), model prices are higher (conversely lower) than market prices. The latter may be just an error-in-variables problem. That is, when you estimate volatility to be high, it probably is high; but ex ante you are more likely to have a positive estimation error in your calculation than a negative one. The converse holds for low estimates of volatility.

8.7.2 Method II: Infer Market Forecast σ

Today is the first day in the rest of the life of the option you are analyzing. Market participants price the option using their aggregate forecast of volatility over the remaining life of the option. This is a forward-looking estimate of volatility. History is history, so why look backwards to forecast the future? That is like driving while looking in the rear view mirror. It works in slow markets where not much is happening, but otherwise it makes little sense. It makes more sense to use the market aggregate forecast of volatility. Suppose that $S = \$100$, $X = \$100$, $r = 0.05$, $\rho = 0$, $T - t = 0.5$, and a European call option's price is $12. We may infer, via Black-Scholes (I leave this as an exercise), that the volatility number implicitly being used is $\sigma = 0.386$. This is the "implied volatility," "implied vol," or simply the "vol." Traders often quote and trade options using implied volatilities rather than prices.

Although Black-Scholes is for European options, there is nothing to stop us finding the implied volatility for an American-style option using Black-Scholes. That is, what σ when plugged into the European option pricing formula gives the price we see for the American option in the marketplace? Many traders, myself included, use the Black-Scholes formula to understand how American-style options behave.

I mentioned that when I set up a spreadsheet, I often look at several different strike prices simultaneously. Using the implied volatility to look at my projections of stock price and volatility, I choose the option that gives me the most attractive combination of good upside potential if my most likely forecast is correct, and not too terrible downside performance if my forecast is wrong (see my spreadsheet trading tool in section 10.3). You do need to be wary, however, of differences in implied volatility with the maturity and strike of an option.

Fixing the strike, implied volatilities vary with the maturity of options on a stock. That is, traders use different volatilities to value long-maturity and short-maturity options (Derman and Kani [1994, pp2–3]; Hull [2000, chapter 17]). This is called the "term structure of implied volatility." Fixing maturity, implied volatilities vary with the strike price of the option; this is the "volatility skew" or "volatility smile" (see the discussion in section 9.4.2 and figure 8.5 on page 148). The variation in shape of the skews or smiles changes from month to month, but longer-dated contracts typically have less steep skews, as indicated for S&P500 index calls in figure 8.5. Many traders use a matrix of implied volatility for a cross section of maturity and moneyness, which allows them to pick off the volatility appropriate for their particular pricing problem. This is called matrix pricing.

I am not much concerned about the term structure of volatility. The horizon of my forecast of stock performance usually determines the minimum horizon of the option I want to use, allowing a few months or more as a buffer. My view is usually so short-term, however, that the term structure is irrelevant. The volatility skew, though, does need to be accounted for. You need a different implied volatility for each strike price (see section 10.3).

Op Quiz 1: From your Bloomberg terminal (or working with prices from your online broker), you should see that the implied volatility is not the same for puts and calls on the same underlying with the same maturity and strike. Does this violate European put-call parity?

Answer: If they are European-style options, and you have accounted correctly for bid and ask prices, then yes; but this is very unlikely in practice. If they are American-style options, then no, because there is no reason why they should satisfy European put-call parity.

Op Quiz 2: Suppose that $S = \$100$, $X = \$100$, $r = 0.03$, $\rho = 0$, $T - t = 0.5$, and a European call option is priced at $15. What is the implied volatility?

Answer: The answer must be higher than the 0.386 number mentioned in section 8.7.2, because the option price is higher and r is not important enough to change the answer much. My first guess is 0.50, and I am close: $\hat{\sigma} = 0.5114793$.

Exercise: If you have access to a Bloomberg terminal, enter the line `SPX <INDEX> SKEW <GO>` (see figure 8.5 on page 148). Are the implied volatility smiles different for puts and calls? Why, or why not? Try a big stock like Eastman Kodak: `EK <EQUITY> SKEW <GO>`. If you do not have a Bloomberg terminal, try calculating the implied volatilities of out-of-the-money, at-the-money, and in-the-money puts on a heavily traded stock and plotting the result. My spreadsheet tool allows you to do this easily (see section 10.3). My brokerage's Web site also has analytical tools to do this.

8.8 Synthetic Options: Greeks 102

Suppose that a US investment bank, USIB, sells a tailor-made USD-denominated GBP call option to a UK corporation, UKCorp, so that UKCorp can hedge some USD receivables. This is a pedagogical example only, because UKCorp is more likely to use an exchange-traded GBP call (with lower T-costs and more liquidity than one purchased from an investment bank).

The transaction leaves USIB with a short position in a GBP call. USIB wants to pocket the markup and neutralize the short GBP call exposure by dynamically replicating a long GBP call.[17] The dynamic replication can be standard ("delta hedging"), or more advanced ("delta-gamma hedging"), or more advanced still ("delta-gamma-vega[18] hedging"), and so on, depending upon how much exposure they want to neutralize.

---

[17]In practice, USIB hedges its "derivatives book;" that is, the overall net position.
[18]Sensitivity of a derivative to changing volatility is called "vega."

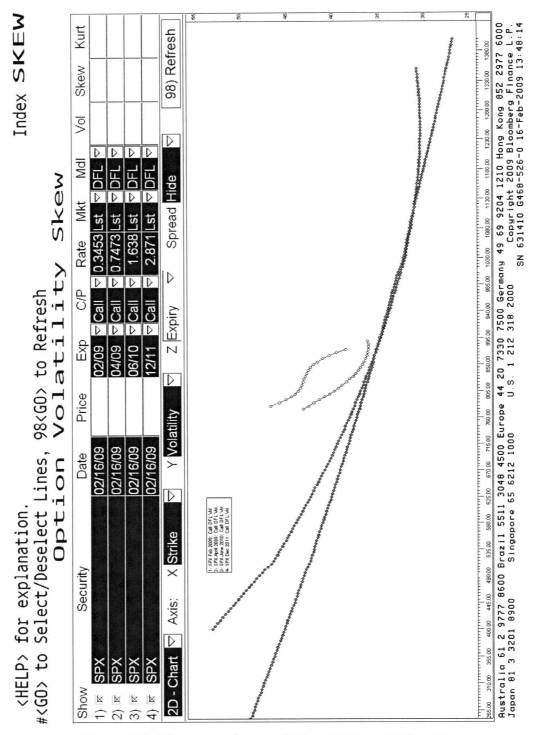

Figure 8.5: Bloomberg Screen: SPX <INDEX> SKEW <GO>

Note: This figure shows implied volatility skews/smiles for S&P500 index options on February 16, 2009. In this case, the order of the curves, reading down the screen, corresponds to the order of the selected maturities, reading down the table (i.e., near-month at the top).

8.8.1 Delta Hedging

To delta hedge the short European GBP call, USIB must go long $\Delta = e^{-\rho(T-t)}N(d_1)$ GBP,[19] and borrow $Xe^{-r(T-t)}N(d_2)$ USD. Remember to multiply both by the number of GBP covered by the call. The delta, Δ, and the borrowing vary through time.

8.8.2 Delta-Gamma (and Theta) Hedging

Delta hedging creates a synthetic derivative that is similar to the real derivative. They have the same value, and the same delta. Thus, the overall position for USIB is of value zero, and is delta-neutral. These two conditions are satisfied by using two assets in the replicating portfolio (underlying and borrowing/lending).

Op Quiz: If USIB sells a USD-denominated GBP call option to a client (i.e., the right to buy GBP using USD), prove that USIB loses for sure on a delta hedge if there is a large move in the underlying. **Hint:** Draw a picture or do the algebra.

Answer: If you plot the picture of the value of the call that was sold and the value of the long synthetic call, you see that the plot of call value has curvature, but that the plot of the value of the synthetic is tangent to the call plot at today's underlying price and has no curvature. A big price move up means the short call increases in value by more than does the replicating portfolio whose value follows the line tangent to the call plot. Similarly, a big price move down sees the short call decrease in value by less than does the replicating portfolio's linear position. USIB is long the linear relationship and short the convexity, so loses in either scenario. Algebraically, if V is value, then overall position value is synthetic less actual: $V_{syn} - V_{call} = 0$, by definition. Similarly, $\frac{\partial V_{syn}}{\partial S} - \frac{\partial V_{call}}{\partial S} = 0$, by definition of a delta hedge. For convexity, however, $\frac{\partial^2 V_{syn}}{\partial S^2} - \frac{\partial^2 V_{call}}{\partial S^2} < 0$ because the call has positive convexity and the synthetic has none. These three quantities are the height, slope, and curvature, respectively, of the plot of the net value of the delta hedged position versus price of the underlying. Thus, at today's underlying price, the plot has value zero, slope zero about that point, but negative convexity. Today's underlying price thus yields the peak of a "value hill" that is flat on top; small changes in price have no effect, but big changes see us sliding down the hill.

For options, "gamma," "convexity," "curvature," and "Γ" are identical in meaning, and refer to the curvature (i.e., rate of change of slope) of the plot of option value as a function of the underlying.[20] That is, $\Gamma \equiv \frac{\partial^2 V}{\partial S^2}$.

Looking at figure 3.3 on page 59, we see that $\Gamma \approx 0$ (i.e., there is no curvature) for deep in-the-money and deep out-of-the-money options, and that Γ is maximized (and positive) near-the-money. This is true for puts and calls.

---

[19]In practice, it would be cheaper for USIB to hedge using GBP futures rather than physical GBP, and a slight adjustment to the number of contracts may be needed.

[20]In bond pricing, "curvature" and "convexity" differ. What we call "convexity" in bond pricing is usually $\frac{\partial^2 P}{\partial y^2} \Big/ P$, where y is yield; whereas curvature is just $\frac{\partial^2 P}{\partial y^2}$.

Neither the underlying nor the borrowing/lending have any convexity as a function of S. Rather, both vary linearly in value for changes in S. However, the call changes nonlinearly for changes in S (i.e., the plot of call value versus S has curvature). Thus, delta hedging alone exposes you to gamma-risk (USIB loses for sure on the hedge if there is a large move in the underlying—as per the op quiz on page 149).

Delta hedging a call option is a first-order approximation to replication of a call option. It is analogous to estimating the change in a bond price using duration only, instead of incorporating bond convexity. If USIB wants its overall position to be value-zero, delta-neutral, and gamma-neutral, it needs to add a third asset to its replicating portfolio. The obvious choice is a readily available security with some gamma of its own: for example, a short-dated, at-the-money, exchange-traded GBP call option.

For a standard European call on a security paying a continuous dividend yield at rate ρ, the gamma is given by equation 8.61:

$$\Gamma = \frac{e^{\left[-\rho(T-t) - \frac{1}{2}d_1^2\right]}}{S\sigma\sqrt{2\pi(T-t)}}, \text{ where} \tag{8.61}$$

$$d_1 = \frac{\ln\left(\frac{S}{X}\right) + (r - \rho + \frac{1}{2}\sigma^2)(T-t)}{\sigma\sqrt{T-t}}.$$

You cannot simply throw a call option into the replicating portfolio, because it contributes some delta of its own that would unbalance the delta hedge. Rather, you need to solve a simple system of equations for the replicating portfolio as shown in equations 8.62:

$$\begin{aligned}
V_C &= N_B B &&+ N_S S &&+ N_\tau V_\tau \\
\Delta_C &= N_B \Delta_B &&+ N_S \Delta_S &&+ N_\tau \Delta_\tau \\
\Gamma_C &= N_B \Gamma_B &&+ N_S \Gamma_S &&+ N_\tau \Gamma_\tau,
\end{aligned} \tag{8.62}$$

where B, S, and τ refer to the borrowing/lending, stock, and traded call, respectively. Let $B = \$1$ invested in bonds (i.e., lent), then N_B, N_S, and N_τ are the unknown number of dollars in borrowing/lending (+ for lending, − for borrowing), number of units of underlying to buy (+ for long, − for short), and number of traded calls to buy (+ for long, − for short), respectively.

We know $\Gamma_B = 0$, $\Gamma_S = 0$, $\Delta_B = 0$, and $\Delta_S = 1$, so we may solve equations 8.62 to find equations 8.63–8.65:

$$N_\tau = \frac{\Gamma_C}{\Gamma_\tau} \tag{8.63}$$

$$\begin{aligned}
N_S &= \Delta_C - N_\tau \Delta_\tau \\
&= \Delta_C - \left(\frac{\Gamma_C}{\Gamma_\tau}\right)\Delta_\tau \tag{8.64}
\end{aligned}$$

$$\begin{aligned}
N_B &= V_C - N_S S - N_\tau V_\tau \\
&= V_C - \left(\Delta_C - \frac{\Gamma_C}{\Gamma_\tau}\Delta_\tau\right)S - \left(\frac{\Gamma_C}{\Gamma_\tau}\right)V_\tau \tag{8.65}
\end{aligned}$$

> **Exercise:** Verify that equations 8.63, 8.64, and 8.65 solve the gamma hedge system, equations 8.62.

In practice, everyone delta hedges, but not everyone gamma hedges. For example, rather than gamma hedge, USIB typically updates its delta hedge every day. This is an attempt to dynamically replicate convexity. In theory, with no T-costs, you can dynamically replicate convexity by updating your delta every instant. In practice, if USIB rebalances its delta hedge too frequently, it is guaranteed one result: a loss! T-costs reduce the frequency with which you can rebalance. Investment banks use delta, gamma, and vega to quantify the level of risk in their portfolios, and adjust their hedges when the exposure becomes unacceptable.

In practice, Γ hedging is done by those who face convexity: those who sell short-term options, sell exotics, or face specific strike "pin risk." Pin risk is the risk associated with being short a near-the-money, close-to-maturity option; your delta flips between zero and one as the option flips from being slightly out-of-the-money to slightly in-the-money. If you are only delta hedging, then you risk getting pinned down with the wrong delta.

We demonstrated in section 7.6 that delta-gamma hedging automatically provides theta hedging. It is worth repeating here in case you skipped chapter 7. Theta, denoted "θ," measures the decay in value of a derivative with the passage of time; it can be of either sign (see the op quiz on page 109). Theta is given by $\theta = \frac{\partial V}{\partial t}$. The Black-Scholes PDE with continuous dividends (equation 7.2, p104) may be rewritten as equation 8.66:

$$\theta + \frac{1}{2}\sigma^2 S^2 \Gamma + (r - \rho)S\Delta - rV = 0 \qquad (8.66)$$

Both the derivative and the replicating portfolio satisfy equation 8.66, so the net hedged position also satisfies it. If you delta-gamma hedge, then $V = 0$, $\Delta = 0$, and $\Gamma = 0$ for the net hedged position. It thus follows from equation 8.66 that $\theta = 0$ for the net hedged position. That is, delta-gamma hedging automatically provides theta hedging. In other words, the time decay characteristics of a synthetic derivative created via the delta-gamma hedge match those of the original derivative.

Unfortunately, delta-gamma hedging produces an overall position that is quite sensitive to changes in volatility. If you want the overall position to have value zero, and be delta-gamma-vega neutral, then a fourth security (most likely a long-dated, at-the-money option) must be added to the replicating portfolio with appropriate rebalancing via a four-equation system of equations analogous to equations 8.62.

Each of the above-mentioned "Greeks" can be estimated using numerical option pricing routines.

Note, finally, that all of the foregoing is based on a Black-Scholes world. The real world is different. This means that a hedged position that is delta-gamma-vega neutral still changes in value with small changes in stock price and/or volatility.

Chapter 9

Beyond Black-Scholes

There exist many option pricing formulae and techniques that go beyond the preceding chapters.[1] Most of these techniques reduce to Black-Scholes pricing when the complexities they model are assumed away. I consider Black-Scholes pricing to be the "80% solution" insofar as the majority of the theoretical intuition that a novice needs to trade options can be gleaned from it.

In chapter 10, I present some practical ad hoc adjustments that allow you to use Black-Scholes pricing even though many of the assumptions underlying it are violated. In this chapter, I present well-known results in American-style option pricing (to contrast with the European-style results), as well as some new formulae that relate to odd cases I have come across and seen nowhere else. The latter formulae include option prices under a general ABM (to generalize the Bachelier formula seen in section 8.4.1, p137 and in contrast to the GBM results of Black-Scholes), and some exotic option formulae (in contrast to the plain vanilla results). I also discuss jump and stochastic volatility models. You may skip this chapter without loss of continuity.

9.1 American-Style Options

Black-Scholes pricing applies to European-style options only. Here is a list of simple points to keep in mind when considering American-style versus European-style option pricing:

- The right to exercise early is what distinguishes an American option from its European counterpart. Any approach to valuation must consider the value of this right.

- Most exchange-traded options are American style. Most over-the-counter (OTC) options are European style (see section 10.1.2). Many financial instruments have American-style option features embedded in them (e.g., call provisions in a corporate bond or Treasury bond).

---

[1]For an excellent compilation of option pricing formulas, computer code, practical advice, and more, I recommend Haug (2007).

- "Early exercise is not optimal" means that an option is worth more alive than dead. That is, you can get more by selling the option than you can by exercising it. If the underlying does not pay dividends, then early exercise is not optimal for a plain vanilla American call: and thus American and European calls have equal value. See restrictions R4 and R8 on pp48–49.

- Early exercise of an American call option is optimal if, and only if, a dividend is about to be paid and it is large enough to replace the interest lost on the strike price, and the loss of the time value of the call. If the dividend is small, or the time to maturity is large, early exercise of an American call is unlikely to be optimal. See the summary in table 3.5 on page 54.

- The benefit to early exercise of an American put is the ability to earn interest on the strike. The cost is that you give up any possible additional payoff (i.e., loss of time value). If it is a protective put, then you also lose dividends.

- The payoff to a put is bounded above by the strike (unlike a call which has unlimited upside). Therefore, if the stock price is low enough (i.e., any potential additional profit on the put is low enough), then early exercise of an American put option may be optimal. Contrast this with a European put where the price can be lower than $X - S$ if the put is deep in-the-money.

- In general, it can be optimal to exercise a plain vanilla American put any time when it is deep in-the-money. This makes analysis so difficult that no exact, closed-form analytical pricing formula exists in this case.

- If early exercise is optimal, then ignoring T-costs, selling the option yields the same payoff as exercising, and you may be indifferent between exercise and sale.

9.1.1 Approximate Analytical Pricing

Pseudo-American Pricing: Black (1975)

Let $c(t, T, S)$ denote the Black-Scholes time-t call price for a European option maturing at time T. Assume the stock pays a dividend d_1 at time $t_1 < T$. An American call matures at time T. Black's pseudo-American call value is

$$C(t) = \max[c(t, t_1, S), \ c(t, T, S^*)],$$

where $S^*(t) = S(t) - PV(d_1)$.[2] The formula can be generalized to the many dividends case.

Given that exercise should rationally occur only at date t_1, or at date T, the option's life ends at one of these two dates (with no intermediate exercise). Thus, we take the maximum of two European option values with these lifespans.

---

[2]For $c(t, T, S^*)$, you may use a slightly higher volatility in the formula: $\sigma^* = \sigma \frac{S}{S - PV(d_1)}$ (Hull [2000, footnote 5, p400]).

Op Quiz (difficult): Black (1975, p41) estimates a pseudo-American call option value as the maximum value of two European-style options maturing at the American-style option's ex-dividend date t_1 and maturity T, respectively. He adjusts the stock price for the latter option by subtracting the present value of dividends. Why is this an approximation only? What does Black ignore?

Answer: Black ignores the compound option (i.e., option on an option; see p157) nature of the problem. An American-style call carries with it the right to give up the remaining life of the option in exchange for a cash flow. This is the right to exchange an option for cash; it is an option on an option with exercise decision reserved until time t_1. Black simplifies by assuming, in essence, that you can deduce now which way that decision will go by identifying the more valuable of the two European-style options. Section 9.1.2 gives the exact answer.

MacMillan (1986) and Barone-Adesi and Whaley (1987)

MacMillan (1986) and Barone-Adesi and Whaley (1987) present approximate option pricing formulae for American puts and American puts and calls, respectively. These papers approximate the following Black-Scholes PDE and then solve it:[3]

$$\frac{\partial V}{\partial t} + \frac{1}{2}\sigma^2 S^2 \frac{\partial^2 V}{\partial S^2} + (r - \rho)S\frac{\partial V}{\partial S} - rV = 0.$$

Both analyses note that if V (American option value) satisfies the PDE, and v (European option value) satisfies the PDE, then the additional value e, where $V = v + e$, also satisfies the PDE. In this case, e is the value of the right to exercise early. The PDE for e is set up, approximated in functional form, and then approximated by removing the derivative with respect to time. This produces an ordinary differential equation that may be solved directly.

9.1.2 Exact Analytical Pricing

Calls: Roll (1977), Geske (1979), Whaley (1981) and the Early Exercise Decision

Consider a stock with price S that pays a single dividend d_1, with ex-dividend date $t_1 < T$. Suppose that it is now time t_1^-, immediately prior to time t_1, that we own an American-style call on the stock with strike X, and that we are trying to decide whether to exercise or not. If we exercise, we receive the stock worth $S(t_1^-)$ and capture the dividend d_1, but we give up X and kill the option; if we do not exercise, we are left holding an American-style call on the ex-dividend stock. Assuming the

---

[3]Note that for American-style options the PDE equality becomes an inequality. The PDE=0 if exercise is not optimal, but the PDE ≤ 0 if early exercise is optimal. This is because of the opportunity loss associated with not exercising optimally. See Wilmott et al. (1993, pp55–61) and Wilmott (1998, pp128–129) for more details.

stock falls by the full value of the dividend, the stock price at time t_1^+, immediately after t_1, is $S(t_1^+) = S(t_1^-) - d_1$. With no dividends remaining, the American-style call is worth the same as a European-style call: $c(S(t_1^+), T - t_1)$. Our decision is therefore whether to exercise for payoff $S(t_1^-) - X = S(t_1^+) + d_1 - X$, or not to exercise and be left holding a call of value $c(S(t_1^+), T - t_1)$.

There is a particular value of the ex-dividend price $S(t_1^+)$ (or equivalently, of the cum-dividend price $S(t_1^-)$ reduced by the dividend d_1) for which we are indifferent between exercising and not exercising. Indifference requires that this particular value equates the two above-mentioned payoffs; that is, it solves equation 9.1:

$$S(t_1^+) + d_1 - X = c(S(t_1^+), T - t_1) \qquad (9.1)$$

We do not need to wait until time t_1 to figure out the solution to equation 9.1. Rather, it can be solved in advance by looking for the particular value $S(t_1^+) = \bar{S}$, say, such that $\bar{S} + d_1 - X = c(\bar{S}, T - t_1)$.[4] This requires an iterative (i.e., trial and error) solution using the Black-Scholes formula. For $S(t_1^+) < \bar{S}$ (i.e., $S(t_1^-) < \bar{S} + d_1$), early exercise and dividend capture are not optimal (the dividend yield is too low—see the box immediately below); for $S(t_1^+) > \bar{S}$ (i.e., $S(t_1^-) > \bar{S} + d_1$), early exercise is optimal.

Subtle Point: I state immediately above that $S(t_1^-) < \bar{S} + d_1$ means the dividend yield is too low for early exercise to be optimal. It looks, however, as if $S(t_1^-) < \bar{S} + d_1$ implies that $S(t_1^-)$ is low relative to d_1, and thus that the dividend yield is high. In fact, if the hurdle $\bar{S} + d_1$ is so high that $S(t_1^-)$ is below it, then d_1, other things being equal, must be small, and the dividend yield must also be small. This is because the hurdle $\bar{S}$ is a function of d_1 (i.e., $\bar{S} = \bar{S}(d_1)$), and an increase in d_1 produces a more than compensating drop in $\bar{S}(d_1)$. Thus, the sum $\bar{S}(d_1) + d_1$ actually *decreases* with increasing d_1. A small dividend, d_1 (and thus a low dividend yield), thus corresponds to a high hurdle, $\bar{S}(d_1) + d_1$, and this makes it more likely that $S(t_1^-)$ will fall below the hurdle. As an exercise, you can differentiate equation 9.1 (evaluated at $S(t_1^+) = \bar{S}(d_1)$) implicitly with respect to d_1 to prove that $\frac{\partial \bar{S}(d_1)}{\partial d_1} \leq -1$, with equality only if the call option is deep out-of-the-money. It follows that for other than the deep out-of-the-money case, $\frac{\partial [\bar{S}(d_1) + d_1]}{\partial d_1} < 0$, as stated.

If $S(t_1^-) > \bar{S} + d_1$, and the call holder exercises early, he or she effectively gives up a European-style call option worth $c(S(t_1^+), T - t_1) = c(S(t_1^-) + d_1, T - t_1)$, in favor of a cash flow of $S(t_1^+) + d_1 - X = S(t_1^-) - X$. It is as though the original American-style stock option holder is short a call option on the European-style call option on the stock (i.e., short an option on an option) and has been assigned an exercise, forcing him or her to give up the option and receive $S(t_1^-) - X$.

An option on an option is referred to as a "compound option." Our compound option observation is a step towards solving the American-style call option pricing

---

[4]Note that if there are no dividends, then $\bar{S} = \infty$, early exercise is never optimal, and this pricing technique yields the Black-Scholes formula.

problem. The above-mentioned short option on the European call option has strike price $S(t_1^-) - X = S(t_1^+) + d_1 - X$; this is, however, an unknown quantity at time t. If we consider instead a compound option with known strike price $\bar{S} + d_1 - X$, and introduce a third option to adjust the payoffs, we can solve the problem.

Consider a portfolio of options composed of the following:

1. A long European-style call option on the stock with strike X and maturity date T (this is the option you lose at date t_1^- if you exercise early; it is also the long-dated option in the Black pseudo-American approximation).

2. A short European-style compound option with option 1 as underlying, strike $\mathcal{X} = \bar{S} + d_1 - X$, and maturity date t_1^+, where $\bar{S}$ solves $\bar{S} + d_1 - X = c(\bar{S}, T - t_1)$.

3. A long European-style call option on the stock with strike $\bar{S}$ and expiration date t_1^+.

It can be shown that if $S(t_1^+) < \bar{S}$ (i.e., $S(t_1^-) < \bar{S} + d_1$), then options 2 and 3 expire worthless, leaving only option 1. Conversely, if $S(t_1^+) > \bar{S}$ (i.e., $S(t_1^-) > \bar{S} + d_1$), then options 2 and 3 expire in-the-money: You are assigned an exercise on option 2 and must deliver option 1, receiving $\bar{S} + d_1 - X$; you exercise option 3 by paying $\bar{S}$ and receiving the stock worth $S(t_1^+)$. The net payoff is $S(t_1^+) + d_1 - X = S(t_1^-) - X$. It follows that the portfolio of three options has the same payoff as the payoff to the American-style call option, and must have the same value.

Exercise: Demonstrate that the payoff to the portfolio of three options in section 9.1.2 is identical to the payoff to the American-style call in the cases where $S(t_1^+) > \bar{S}$ and $S(t_1^+) < \bar{S}$.

If the ex-ante ex-dividend process $S(t) - e^{-r(t_1-t)}d_1$ follows a GBM, then options 1 and 3 may be valued using Black-Scholes; option 2 may be valued using the Geske (1979) compound option pricing formula. The net result is the Roll-Geske-Whaley exact formula for the value of an American call option on a stock paying a single dividend d_1 at time t_1:

$$
\begin{aligned}
C &= (S - d_1 e^{-r\tau_1})N(b_1) + (S - d_1 e^{-r\tau_1})M\left(a_1, -b_1; -\sqrt{\frac{\tau_1}{\tau}}\right) \\
&\quad - Xe^{-r\tau}M\left(a_2, -b_2; -\sqrt{\frac{\tau_1}{\tau}}\right) - (X - d_1)e^{-r\tau_1}N(b_2), \text{ where} \\
a_1 &= \frac{\ln\left(\frac{S - d_1 e^{-r\tau_1}}{X}\right) + (r + \frac{1}{2}\sigma^2)\tau}{\sigma\sqrt{\tau}}, \\
a_2 &= a_1 - \sigma\sqrt{\tau}, \\
b_1 &= \frac{\ln\left[(S - d_1 e^{-r\tau_1})/\bar{S}\right] + (r + \frac{1}{2}\sigma^2)\tau_1}{\sigma\sqrt{\tau_1}}, \\
b_2 &= b_1 - \sigma\sqrt{\tau_1}, \\
\tau_1 &= t_1 - t, \quad \tau = T - t.
\end{aligned}
$$

S is the actual stock price. As in Black's model, σ is the volatility of $S - d_1 e^{-r\tau_1}$. $M(a, b, \rho)$ is the cumulative standard bi-variate normal function.[5] As before, $\bar{S}$ appearing in b_i, solves $c(\bar{S}, T - t_1) = \bar{S} + d_1 - X$, and is thus the ex-dividend upper exercise boundary for the American-style call.

If early exercise is not optimal, $\bar{S} = \infty$, $b_1 = b_2 = -\infty$, and the formula reduces to regular Black-Scholes. Otherwise, $\bar{S} < \infty$, and the call should be exercised at t_1 if $S(t_1^-) > \bar{S} + d_1$.

If there are several dividends, then set t_1 equal to the final ex-dividend date during the life of the option and use the Roll-Geske-Whaley formula, replacing S with the original stock price reduced by the present value of all but the final dividend.

Perpetual American Puts and Calls

A perpetual American-style put or call does not age. It follows that it has no theta (i.e., no time decay). Thus, the PDE becomes an ordinary differential equation (ODE) that may be solved using standard techniques. See Crack (2008) for derivations based on course work taken with Merton, or Merton (1992) for the original results.

Let $\underline{S}$ be the lower exercise boundary for the perpetual American put; then for $S \geq \underline{S} \equiv \frac{\lambda_2 X}{\lambda_2 - 1}$, the perpetual American put is worth (Crack [2008])

$$V(S) = (X - \underline{S})\left(\frac{S}{\underline{S}}\right)^{\lambda_2} = \left(\frac{X}{1 - \lambda_2}\right)\left[\frac{(\lambda_2 - 1)S}{\lambda_2 X}\right]^{\lambda_2}, \text{ where}$$

$$\lambda_2 = \frac{-\left(r - \rho - \frac{1}{2}\sigma^2\right) - \sqrt{\left(r - \rho - \frac{1}{2}\sigma^2\right)^2 + 2\sigma^2 r}}{\sigma^2}.$$

Let $\bar{S}$ be the upper exercise boundary for the perpetual American call; then for $0 \leq S \leq \frac{\lambda_1 X}{(\lambda_1 - 1)} \equiv \bar{S}$, it may be shown that a perpetual American call is worth (Crack [2008])

$$V(S) = \left(\frac{X}{\lambda_1 - 1}\right)\left[\frac{(\lambda_1 - 1)S}{\lambda_1 X}\right]^{\lambda_1}, \text{ where}$$

$$\lambda_1 = \frac{-\left(r - \rho - \frac{1}{2}\sigma^2\right) + \sqrt{\left(r - \rho - \frac{1}{2}\sigma^2\right)^2 + 2\sigma^2 r}}{\sigma^2}.$$

9.2 Some New Formulae

9.2.1 Arithmetic Brownian Motion

We have argued previously that the same option but with different data-generating processes, or the same data-generating processes but with a different option, typically gives rise to different option pricing formulae. Suppose now that instead of a

---

[5]See Haug (2007, p471) for an approximation to $M(\cdot, \cdot, \cdot)$ analogous to those in my appendix, sections A.1 and A.2, for the univariate standard normal.

GBM driving a stock price process (i.e., equation 4.6 on page 74), we have a general ABM as in equation 9.2:

$$dS = \mu dt + \sigma_A dw, \tag{9.2}$$

where σ_A is the volatility of stock price in the ABM, not the volatility of stock returns that we have previously denoted σ.

Equation 9.2 is a poor model of stock price behavior because it admits negative stock prices. For small σ_A, and for initial prices far from zero, however, it should yield option prices close to Black-Scholes.

Equation 9.2 is a generalization of the Bachelier data-generating process; Bachelier assumes the drift μ is zero. In fact, Bachelier assumes that expected returns, in general, should be reduced to zero through competitive market forces; and thus he assumes $\mu = 0$, $r = 0$, and that the expected return on the option is zero. He is, implicitly, assuming both that people are risk-neutral and that the risk-neutral expected return is $r = 0$. Unlike the Cox-Ross and Harrison-Kreps techniques that price options *as if* people are risk-neutral, Bachelier assumes that people *really are* risk-neutral. Under these assumptions, Bachelier derives equation 8.52 for at-the-money options (p138) and repeated here as equation 9.3:

$$c(t) = \frac{\sigma_A \sqrt{T-t}}{\sqrt{2\pi}} \tag{9.3}$$

In my other book, *Heard on The Street* (Crack [2008]), I provide a generalization of Bachelier's option pricing that does not require that the option be at-the-money, but still assumes that $r = 0$. I reproduce my generalization here as equation 9.4:

$$
\begin{aligned}
c(t) &= \sigma_A \sqrt{T-t}\,\left[N'(d) + N(d) \cdot d\right], \\
&= \sigma_A \sqrt{T-t}\,\left[\frac{e^{-\frac{1}{2}d^2}}{\sqrt{2\,\pi}} + N(d) \cdot d\right],
\end{aligned}
\tag{9.4}
$$

$$\text{where} \quad d = \frac{S(t) - X}{\sigma_A \sqrt{T-t}}. \tag{9.5}$$

My option pricing formula, equation 9.4, is mathematically equivalent to equation A.5 in Smith (1976).

Exercise: Substitute $S(t) = X$ into equation 9.4 to arrive at the less general equation 9.3.

Mikhail Voropaev has suggested to me a generalization of my equation 9.4 that does not require $r = 0$ (personal communication June 4, 2003; any errors are mine).[6] His solution requires that we solve the PDE generated by the ABM process in equation 9.2.

---

[6] A colleague has pointed out to me that Poitras (1998) uses an ABM derivation similar to mine to price spread options.

Let us use the Merton no-arbitrage technique to derive the PDE (see section 4.4.1). I repeat Itô's Lemma as equation 9.6, where V is the derivative value we seek:

$$dV = \frac{\partial V}{\partial S}dS + \frac{\partial V}{\partial t}dt + \frac{1}{2}\frac{\partial^2 V}{\partial S^2}(dS)^2 \qquad (9.6)$$

If $dS = \mu dt + \sigma_A dw$, and $(dw)^2 = dt$, and all higher-order terms are zero, then equation 9.6 yields equation 9.7:

$$dV = \sigma_A \frac{\partial V}{\partial S}dw + \left(\mu\frac{\partial V}{\partial S} + \frac{\partial V}{\partial t} + \frac{1}{2}\sigma_A^2\frac{\partial^2 V}{\partial S^2}\right)dt \qquad (9.7)$$

You can compare equation 9.7 to equation 4.8 (p74) to see the differences due to the arithmetic, as opposed to geometric, process.

Now build a portfolio where you are long one European call option and short Δ units of the stock. Let Π denote the value of this portfolio, then $\Pi = V - S\Delta$; and over a time interval, dt, the change in the value of this portfolio is given by equation 9.8:

$$d\Pi = dV - dS \cdot \Delta, \qquad (9.8)$$

where Δ is held fixed over the time interval dt. Now plug equations 9.2 and 9.7 into equation 9.8:

$$d\Pi = \sigma_A\left(\frac{\partial V}{\partial S} - \Delta\right)dw + \left(\mu\frac{\partial V}{\partial S} + \frac{\partial V}{\partial t} + \frac{1}{2}\sigma_A^2\frac{\partial^2 V}{\partial S^2} - \mu\Delta\right)dt.$$

If we eliminate the stochastic component of the portfolio by choosing $\Delta = \frac{\partial V}{\partial S}$, then the changes in portfolio value must be deterministic:

$$d\Pi = \left(\frac{\partial V}{\partial t} + \frac{1}{2}\sigma_A^2\frac{\partial^2 V}{\partial S^2}\right)dt \qquad (9.9)$$

With no random component, the portfolio must offer the riskless rate of return, or there would be arbitrage opportunities available. Thus, it follows that $d\Pi = r\Pi dt$.

Now plug $\Pi = V - \Delta S$ plus the definition of Δ into $d\Pi = r\Pi dt$ and equate with $d\Pi$ in equation 9.9. This yields the ABM Partial Differential Equation in equation 9.10:

$$\frac{\partial V}{\partial t} + \frac{1}{2}\sigma_A^2\frac{\partial^2 V}{\partial S^2} + rS\frac{\partial V}{\partial S} - rV = 0 \qquad (9.10)$$

Compare the ABM PDE in equation 9.10 to the GBM PDE in equation 4.11 (p75). The only difference is that equation 9.10 has a σ_A^2 as a pre-multiplier in the convexity term, whereas equation 4.11 has $\sigma^2 S^2$. In fact, having σ as volatility of (continuously compounded) returns implies immediately that volatility of price must be close to σS (i.e., $\sigma_A \approx \sigma S$). It follows that the two PDEs (equations 9.10 and 4.11) are very similar.

We seek the solution to equation 9.10 that satisfies the boundary conditions for a European call option on an ABM stock price process. A certain level of

Orwellian "doublethink" is required here for at least two reasons. First, we already know that the ABM process unreasonably admits negative stock prices. Second, as an empirical economist, thinking about calibrating the ABM process to a stock, I have to assume that when S gets near zero, then σ_A gets near zero too (because $\sigma_A \approx \sigma S$). Thus, any ABM solution I have is local only. That is not, however, what the mathematics says, and it is not the problem we are solving. So, what are the boundary conditions?

The GBM boundary condition that says call price is zero when stock price is zero does not make sense for an ABM.[7] In other words, restriction R1 from table 3.3 (p48) does not apply to the ABM call price because the data-generating process in equation 9.2 is too rigid to allow $\sigma_A \approx \sigma S$ to tend to zero as S does. Restriction R1 says that if stock price goes to zero in the GBM case, then it will take infinite time for the stock price to reach the strike, and so the call option is worthless. In the ABM case, stock prices can, however, freely go negative. The appropriate ABM boundary condition is thus that if stock price is infinitely negative, it will take infinite time for the stock price to reach the strike price, and so the call option is worthless (as per the transformed boundary condition, equation 9.19, below).

We shall change the variables in equation 9.10 from $V(S,t)$ to $u(x,\tau)$, apply the chain rule results, equations 7.9–7.11 (p105), and then demonstrate that the reduced PDE so obtained and the transformed boundary conditions that go with it, correspond to a problem that we have already solved.

Begin with the change of variables in equations 9.11–9.13:

$$x = Se^{r(T-t)} \tag{9.11}$$

$$\tau = \frac{1}{2r}[e^{2r(T-t)} - 1] \tag{9.12}$$

$$u(x,\tau) = e^{r(T-t)}V(S,t) \tag{9.13}$$

Equation 9.13 implies $V(S,t) = e^{-r(T-t)}u(x,\tau) = u(x,\tau)/\sqrt{(1+2r\tau)}$, where I used $e^{r(T-t)} = \sqrt{(1+2r\tau)}$. The chain rule results, equations 7.9–7.11, now yield equations 9.14–9.16:

$$\frac{\partial V}{\partial t} = \sqrt{(1+2r\tau)}\left[-\frac{\partial u}{\partial \tau} + \frac{r\left(u - x\frac{\partial u}{\partial x}\right)}{(1+2r\tau)}\right] \tag{9.14}$$

$$\frac{\partial V}{\partial S} = \frac{\partial u}{\partial x} \tag{9.15}$$

$$\frac{\partial^2 V}{\partial S^2} = \sqrt{(1+2r\tau)}\frac{\partial^2 u}{\partial x^2} \tag{9.16}$$

Plugging equations 9.14–9.16 into the ABM PDE equation 9.10, collecting terms, and cancelling yields the reduced PDE equation 9.17:

$$\frac{\partial u}{\partial \tau} = \frac{1}{2}\sigma_A^2 \frac{\partial^2 u}{\partial x^2} \tag{9.17}$$

---

[7]A transformed version of this boundary condition appears in equation 7.17.

Now, if we pause to reconsider the simpler problem where $r = 0$, we see that the transformations $x = S$, $\tau = T - t$, and $V = u(x, \tau)$, when applied to the ABM PDE, equation 9.10, produce exactly the same reduced PDE, equation 9.17. Indeed, these transformations are obtained when you let r tend to zero in equations 9.11–9.13. The boundary conditions equations 9.18 and 9.19, and the initial condition, equation 9.20, are also the same in the two problems (see exercise 2 on page 162):

$$\lim_{x \to +\infty} u(x, \tau) \sim x - X \tag{9.18}$$

$$\lim_{x \to -\infty} u(x, \tau) = 0 \tag{9.19}$$

$$u(x, 0) = \max(0, x - X) \tag{9.20}$$

Thus, the solution to our general problem must take exactly the form of the $r = 0$ case in equation 9.4: $u = \sigma_A \sqrt{\tau}[N'(d) + N(d) \cdot d]$ with $d = (x - X)/(\sigma_A \sqrt{\tau})$. Unwinding equations 9.11–9.13 then yields the final solution as in equations 9.21–9.23:

$$c(t) = e^{-r(T-t)} \sigma_A \sqrt{\frac{e^{2r(T-t)} - 1}{2r}} \left[N'(d) + N(d) \cdot d \right] \tag{9.21}$$

$$= e^{-r(T-t)} \sigma_A \sqrt{\frac{e^{2r(T-t)} - 1}{2r}} \left[\frac{e^{-\frac{1}{2}d^2}}{\sqrt{2\pi}} + N(d) \cdot d \right] \tag{9.22}$$

$$\text{where } d = \frac{S(t)e^{r(T-t)} - X}{\sigma_A \sqrt{\frac{e^{2r(T-t)} - 1}{2r}}}. \tag{9.23}$$

Exercise 1: Substitute $r = 0$ into equation 9.21 to arrive at my less general equation 9.4. **Hint:** You may need to use L'Hôpital's rule with respect to r:

L'Hôpital's rule: Let $\lim_x$ denote some limit (e.g., $x \to 0$ or $x \to +\infty$). Let $g(x)$ and $h(x)$ be the numerator and denominator of a ratio whose limiting behavior we are interested in. If $\lim_x g(x) = 0$ and $\lim_x h(x) = 0$, but $\lim_x \frac{g'(x)}{h'(x)}$ is a finite limit, then $\lim_x \frac{g(x)}{h(x)} = \lim_x \frac{g'(x)}{h'(x)}$.

Exercise 2: Demonstrate that the ABM solution equation 9.4, when transformed using $x = S$, $\tau = T - t$, and $V = u(x, \tau)$, satisfies the reduced PDE, equation 9.17, and the boundary conditions equations 9.18 and 9.19, and the initial condition equation 9.20, and is thus, as claimed, the solution to the reduced problem in the general ABM case. **Hint:** $\lim_{d \to -\infty} N(d) \cdot d = 0$.

The aforementioned similarity between the ABM PDE in equation 9.10 and the GBM PDE in equation 4.11 leads to a similarity between the numerical output of the Black-Scholes formula and of the generalized ABM formula equation 9.21. Replacing σ in the Black-Scholes formula with σ_A/S gives Black-Scholes results very close to equation 9.21, but with some biases related to moneyness. The majority of the biases are removed by replacing σ in the Black-Scholes formula with the ad hoc term $\sigma_A/[(S + X)/2]$ (i.e., using the average of stock price and strike price to scale the volatility); in this case, the two formulae agree quite closely.[8] It follows that although equation 9.21 has a functional form quite different from that of the Black-Scholes formula, it is, in fact, economically and numerically very similar to it.

Exercise: Three ABM option pricing formulae are given in this section: equations 9.3, 9.4, and 9.21. Use put-call parity to deduce the price of the put in each case. Remember that $S = X$ and $r = 0$ in the first case, $r = 0$ in the second case, and there are no restrictions in the third case.

Exercise: Prove that for the two generalized ABM formulae, equations 9.4, and 9.21, $\Delta \equiv \frac{\partial c(t)}{\partial S(t)} = N(d)$, with d given by equations 9.5 and 9.23, respectively. Having done that, ask yourself what is the delta for Bachelier's original ABM option pricing formula, equation 9.3? **Hint:** Equation 9.3 does not vary with S. If we need to estimate σ_A, however, then $\sigma_A \approx \sigma S$, and, at least empirically, $\Delta \equiv \frac{\partial c(t)}{\partial S(t)} \approx \sigma \sqrt{T-t}/\sqrt{2\pi}$, or, alternatively, $\Delta \approx \sigma_A \sqrt{T-t}/[S\sqrt{2\pi}]$.

Exercise: Let $\sigma^\dagger \equiv \sigma \sqrt{\frac{1-e^{-2r(T-t)}}{2r(T-t)}}$, and show that equations 9.21–9.23 may be rewritten as

$$c = \left(S - e^{-r(T-t)}X \right) N(d) + \sigma^\dagger \sqrt{T-t}\, N'(d) \qquad (9.24)$$

$$d = \frac{S - e^{-r(T-t)}X}{\sigma^\dagger \sqrt{T-t}}, \qquad (9.25)$$

where d from equation 9.23 has been rewritten in terms of $\sigma^\dagger$.

Now show, using the same notation, that

$$c = e^{-r(T-t)} \left[E^{**}(S(T)|S(T) > X) - X \right] N(d), \qquad (9.26)$$

where $e^{-r(T-t)}E^{**}(S(T)|S(T) > X) = S + \frac{\sigma^\dagger \sqrt{T-t}\, N'(d)}{N(d)}$, and $E^{**}(\cdot)$ is risk-neutral expectation in the ABM world. Compare equation 9.26 with equation 8.39 (p133) and equation 8.42 (p135).
Hint: You might like to begin by proving that $P^{**}(S(T) > X) = N(d)$.
Note: I thank Andreas Stirnemann for suggesting the results in this exercise.

9.2.2 Power Option I: Crack (1997)

The payoff to the European power call is $\max\left[S^\alpha(t) - X, 0\right]$. Crack (1997) provides a general formula, under Black-Scholes assumptions, when the underlying pays a continuous dividend at rate ρ. It is difficult to imagine this option used for anything

---

[8]Schachermayer and Teichmann (2008) give a detailed comparison of Bachelier pricing and Black-Scholes pricing, but they do not mention my $\sigma_A/[(S+X)/2]$ approximation.

other than speculation. See Crack (2008) for more details, including the strange curvy-kinked payoff plots.

The power options described here and in the next section are exotic because, although they are European calls and puts, their payoffs are non-standard. You could, however, view the power call in this section as a standard European call on $S^\alpha(t)$, but $S(t)$ is the natural asset price, and with respect to that asset price the option is certainly exotic.

$$c(t) = S^\alpha(t)e^{(m-\alpha\rho)(T-t)}N(d_1') - e^{-r(T-t)}XN(d_2'), \text{ and}$$

$$p(t) = e^{-r(T-t)}XN(-d_2') - S^\alpha(t)e^{(m-\alpha\rho)(T-t)}N(-d_1'), \text{ where}$$

$$d_1' = \frac{\ln\left(\frac{S(t)}{K}\right) + \left[r - \rho + (\alpha - \frac{1}{2})\sigma^2\right](T-t)}{\sigma\sqrt{T-t}},$$

$$d_2' = \frac{\ln\left(\frac{S(t)}{K}\right) + (r - \rho - \frac{1}{2}\sigma^2)(T-t)}{\sigma\sqrt{T-t}} = d_1' - \alpha\sigma\sqrt{T-t},$$

$$K \equiv X^{\frac{1}{\alpha}}, \text{ and } m \equiv \left(r + \frac{\alpha}{2}\sigma^2\right)(\alpha - 1).$$

Exercise: Check that plugging in $\alpha = 1$ reduces the power option I formulae to the Merton formulae, and that plugging in both $\alpha = 1$, and $\rho = 0$ yields the standard Black-Scholes formula.

9.2.3 Power Option II: Crack (1997, 2008)

Jarrow and Turnbull (1996, p175) describe a European "powered option" with payoff $[S(T) - X]^\alpha$ if $S(T) \geq X$, and zero otherwise (where $\alpha = 2$). No pricing formula appears. Crack (1997, 2008) gives the general integer-α formula for the no-dividend case under Black-Scholes assumptions (see also Haug [2007, p119]).

$$c(t) = \sum_{j=0}^{\alpha}(-X)^{\alpha-j}\binom{\alpha}{j}S^j(t)e^{\left[(j-1)\left(r+j\frac{\sigma^2}{2}\right)(T-t)\right]}N(d_{2-j}), \text{ where}$$

$$d_l = \frac{\ln\left(\frac{S(t)}{X}\right) + \left(r + \left[\frac{3}{2} - l\right]\sigma^2\right)(T-t)}{\sigma\sqrt{T-t}}, \text{ for } l = 2, 1, \ldots, 2 - \alpha,$$

and $\binom{\alpha}{j} \equiv \frac{\alpha!}{j!(\alpha-j)!}$ is the usual binomial coefficient.

To extend the formula to the case of continuous dividends at rate ρ, replace $S(t)$ by $S(t)e^{-\rho(T-t)}$ throughout to get

$$c(t) = \sum_{j=0}^{\alpha}(-X)^{\alpha-j}\binom{\alpha}{j}S^j(t)e^{\left\{\left[(j-1)\left(r+j\frac{\sigma^2}{2}\right)-\rho j\right](T-t)\right\}}N(d_{2-j}), \text{ where}$$

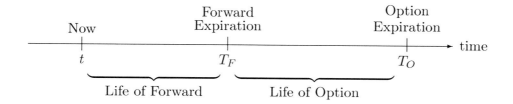

Figure 9.1: Forward on an Option: Timeline

Note: At time T_F, the forward expires and the long position takes delivery of an at-the-money European call option that lives until time T_O.

$$d_l \;=\; \frac{\ln\left(\frac{S(t)}{X}\right) + \left(r - \rho + \left[\frac{3}{2} - l\right]\sigma^2\right)(T - t)}{\sigma\sqrt{T - t}}, \text{ for } l = 2, 1, \ldots, 2 - \alpha.$$

Exercise: Check that plugging in $\alpha = 1$ reduces the power option II formulae to the Merton formulae, and that plugging in both $\alpha = 1$, and $\rho = 0$ yields the standard Black-Scholes formula.

9.2.4 Forward on an At-the-Money Option: Crack-Maines (Crack [1997])

A corporation wanting to hedge exposure to its issue of executive compensation options can hedge with a forward on an option (see figure 9.1). In the case where the underlying pays continuous dividends at rate ρ, the Crack-Maines formula (Crack [1997]) for the forward price of an at-the-money call option is given in equation 9.27:[9]

$$F \;=\; S(t)e^{(r-\rho)(T_F - t)}\left[e^{-\rho(T_O - T_F)}N(d_1) - e^{-r(T_O - T_F)}N(d_2)\right] \quad (9.27)$$

$$\text{for } d_1 \;=\; \frac{(r - \rho + \frac{1}{2}\sigma^2)\sqrt{T_O - T_F}}{\sigma}, \text{ and}$$

$$d_2 \;=\; \frac{(r - \rho - \frac{1}{2}\sigma^2)\sqrt{T_O - T_F}}{\sigma} = d_1 - \sigma\sqrt{T_O - T_F}.$$

Exercise: Check that in the special case where $t = T_F$ (i.e., the forward expires today), equation 9.27 reduces to the Merton formula, and that if $t = T_F$, and $\rho = 0$, then it reduces to the Black-Scholes formula. Confirm also that if $T_O = T_F$ (i.e., the option has no life), then $F = 0$.

---

[9]I thank Stanton R. Maines for suggesting this problem to me in 1997.

9.3 Summary of Option Pricing Methods I: Plain Vanilla versus Exotic Options

Table 9.1: Pricing Methods Summary: Plain Vanilla Options

	European-Style		American-Style	
	Put	Call	Put	Call
No dividends	Black-Scholes put formula	Black-Scholes call formula	No exact formula (use approximation formula, tree, or finite differences)	Black-Scholes call formula (early exercise is never optimal)
Lump sum dividend D	Use $S^*=S-PV(D)$ in Black-Scholes	Use $S^*=S-PV(D)$ in Black-Scholes	No exact formula (use approximation formula, tree, or finite differences)	Roll-Geske-Whaley formula, or Black's pseudo formula
Continuous dividends at rate ρ	Use $S^*=Se^{-\rho(T-t)}$ in Black-Scholes (Merton's formula)	Use $S^*=Se^{-\rho(T-t)}$ in Black-Scholes (Merton's formula)	No exact formula (use approximation formula, tree, or finite differences)	Adjust Roll-Geske-Whaley formula
$S=(\frac{USD}{FX})$	Use $\rho=r_{FX}$ in Merton's formula (Garman-Kohlhagen/Grabbe formula)	Use $\rho=r_{FX}$ in Merton's formula (Garman-Kohlhagen/Grabbe formula)	Use $\rho=r_{FX}$ in the above	Use $\rho=r_{FX}$ in the above
All cases: Numerical	Monte Carlo, lattice, or finite differences		Lattice or finite differences	

Table 9.2: Pricing Methods Summary: Exotic Options

European-Style		American-Style	
Path-Independent	Path-Dependent	Path-Independent	Path-Dependent
Lattice, Monte Carlo, or finite difference	Monte Carlo, finite difference, lattice (difficult)	Lattice or finite differences	Lattice (difficult) or finite differences
... or a formula if you can derive it			

9.4 Other Data-Generating Processes

9.4.1 Jump Risk, Replication, and Risk-Neutral Pricing

Black and Scholes (1973) assume that stock prices are continuous. That is, they assume that you can draw the stock price history without lifting your pencil from the paper. You need only stand on the floor of an exchange, watch a real-time feed, or read the *Wall Street Journal* headlines after an "event," however, to see that prices are not continuous. Most big stock price jumps are in response to the arrival of news in the market, whereas most small stock price jumps are due to the random ebb and flow of non-information-based (i.e., liquidity-motivated) transactions.

A "jump" price process is a price process that has infrequent jumps (i.e., discontinuities) in it. If the jump process is a very simple one, both the Merton no-arbitrage technique and risk-neutral pricing can still be used to hedge and price options on an asset whose price follows the process. If the jump process is more complicated, the no-arbitrage and risk-neutral techniques break down.

A simple jump process example (that is *not* a diffusion) has $\frac{dS}{S} = \mu dt + (J-1)d\pi$ (Cox and Ross [1976, p147]). In this example, $J-1$ is the jump amplitude (where $J \geq 0$), $d\pi$ takes the value $+1$ with probability λdt and 0 with probability[10] $1 - \lambda dt$. The percentage stock price change $\frac{dS}{S}$ can thus jump suddenly to $J-1$ (which may itself be random); such a jump pushes S to SJ.

In the simple jump process example, if J is fixed (i.e., $J-1$ is a non-random jump amplitude), a riskless hedge portfolio *can* be formed, and options on an asset whose price follows this simple jump process *can* be valued using the Merton no-arbitrage technique or risk-neutral pricing.[11] The only real difference between this "pure Poisson process" case and the simple binomial option pricing situation (Sharpe [1978]; Cox, Ross, and Rubinstein [1979]; Rendleman and Bartter [1979]; Cox and Rubinstein [1985]; my chapter 6) is that the arrival time of the jump up or jump down is a random variable. You do not need to know *when* the stock price will jump to hedge the risk in a binomial setting. This pure Poisson process is a special case of the more general jump diffusion process discussed next.

Consider a jump diffusion process (using Merton's notation): $\frac{dS}{S} = (\alpha - \lambda k)dt + \sigma dw + dq$, where $dq = 0$ if the "Poisson event" (i.e., the jump) does not occur, $dq = (Y-1)$ if the jump does occur, $(Y-1)$ is a spike producing a finite jump in stock price from S to SY, α is the instantaneous expected rate of return on the stock, σ^2 is the instantaneous variance or returns assuming no jump occurs, dw is a Wiener process, λ is the number of arrivals that you expect per unit time, $k \equiv E(Y-1)$ where E is the expectation operator over the random variable Y, and dw is assumed independent of the Poisson process dq (see Merton [1992, p313]).

When $\sigma = 0$ and $Y \equiv dq + 1$ is non-random, you get Cox and Ross's simple jump process above, and the no-arbitrage technique can be used to hedge and price options on the jump process. Otherwise, when $\sigma > 0$ and $\text{var}(Y) \geq 0$, it is not possible to form a riskless hedge portfolio or use the no-arbitrage technique (Cox and Ross [1976, p147]; Cox and Rubinstein [1985, pp361–371]; Merton [1992, p316]).

Both the (non-jump) diffusion process and the (non-diffusion) simple jump process are the continuous limits of discrete binomial models. However, the jump-diffusion is not. It is for this reason that a riskless hedge cannot be formed in the jump-diffusion case (Cox and Rubinstein [1985, pp361–371]).

The fundamental reason that the no-arbitrage technique can be used to hedge

---

[10]In this example, π is a continuous time "Poisson process;" λ is the "intensity" of the process.

[11]I thank John Cox for explaining to me why such jump processes can be perfectly hedged (personal communication [February 17, 1994]).

and price options in the standard Black-Scholes world is linearity. In continuous time, the Black-Scholes option price is an instantaneously linear function of the stock price; instantaneous changes in the two are perfectly correlated. Portfolio building is a linear operation, and it follows that payoffs to the option can be perfectly replicated by building and continuously rebalancing a portfolio of the stock and the bond. Linearity breaks down when the jump term has positive variance—the call price becomes a nonlinear function of the stock price and perfect hedging is not possible (Merton [1992, p316]).

Although the no-arbitrage technique fails to price the option on the jump diffusion process, you can price the option using an *equilibrium* argument. An instantaneous CAPM approach may be used—as it was in the original Black and Scholes (1973) paper. The information that causes jumps may be assumed to be firm-specific (i.e., unsystematic and diversifiable).[12] You can hedge out the non-jump part of the option and deduce that the remainder (the jump) must have zero beta and, therefore, a riskless rate of return. This yields a PDE that Merton has solved to give the call option price as an infinite summation:

$$C(S(t), T-t) = \sum_{n=0}^{\infty} \left\{ \frac{\exp[-\lambda(T-t)][\lambda(T-t)]^n}{n!} \times \right.$$
$$\left. E_n\{W[S(t)X_n \exp(-\lambda k(T-t)), (T-t); X, \sigma^2, r]\} \right\}.$$

Here X_n is a random variable with the same distribution as the product of n IID random variables each identically distributed to the random variable Y (recall that $Y-1$ is the random percentage change in stock price when a jump occurs), $X_0 \equiv 1$, E_n is the expectation operator over the distribution of X_n, and $W[S, (T-t); X, \sigma^2, r]$ is the standard Black-Scholes pricing formula (see Merton [1992, pp318–320] for a full discussion of the foregoing and Haug [2007, section 6.9.1] for practical issues).

You cannot perfectly hedge the call when the underlying follows the general jump diffusion $[\sigma > 0, \text{var}(Y) \geq 0]$. However, you can hedge out the continuous parts of the stock and option price movements. This leaves a risky hedge portfolio following a pure jump process (with stochastic jump size). If you follow the Black-Scholes hedge when you are short the option, then most of the time you earn more than the expected rate of return on the risky hedge portfolio. However, if one of those occasional jumps occurs (i.e., news arrives), you suffer a reasonably large loss—as per the op quiz on page 149. In the non-diversifiable jump case, the return to the hedge portfolio when there is a jump balances the return during normal time to some extent, but not well enough to make the equilibrium return on the hedge equal to the riskless rate; as mentioned above, the hedge is risky.

In general, there is no way to adjust the parameters of the hedge technique (σ^2, for example) to get a better hedge (see Merton [1992, pp316–317] for a full discussion

---

[12]Note that in situations where the size of the jump is assumed to be systematic, the risk-neutral pricing technique cannot be used to value options. Hull (2000, p446, footnote 13) directs the reader to Naik and Lee (1990) for a discussion of this point.

of the issues).[13]

If the underlying asset price is modelled as a jump process, the standard Black-Scholes call option formula misprices the option. Both the magnitude and the direction of the mispricing of the Black-Scholes model relative to the jump model vary with the assumed distribution for the size of the jump (Trippi et al. [1992]).

Finally, if you model the underlying stock price path as a trinomial tree, then three possible stock price outcomes and only two assets mean you cannot form a perfect hedge. In this case, there does not exist a unique set of risk-neutral probabilities. No-arbitrage arguments do determine bounds on option price, and the option price must fall between the extremes that are possible given the different risk-neutral probabilities that are admitted by the model. Although different risk-neutral probabilities exist, they must lead to the same solution in the limit as step size tends to zero. Equilibrium pricing methods work; and the equilibrium option price in a trinomial world, in general, depends upon risk-preferences. See the summary in table 9.3.

9.4.2 Stochastic Volatility

If the Black-Scholes assumptions are correct, then the implied volatilities of options should fall on a horizontal line when plotted against strike price. However, what we actually see are smiles and skews depending upon the underlying asset and the time period (Hammer [1989]; Sullivan [1993]; Murphy [1994]; Derman and Kani [1994]; and my sections 8.7.2 and 10.3). Prior to the Crash of 1987, you typically saw symmetrical smiles when you plotted implied volatilities against strike price. Now you are more likely to get non-symmetrical skews, or smirks (see figure 8.5 on page 148).

Option prices are determined by supply and demand, not by theoretical formulae. The traders who determine option prices are implicitly modifying the Black-Scholes assumptions to account for volatility that changes both with time and with stock price level.[14] This is contrary to the Black and Scholes (1973) assumption of constant volatility irrespective of stock price or time period. That is, traders assume $\sigma = \sigma(S(t), t)$, whereas Black and Scholes assume σ is just a constant.

If volatility is changing with both the level of the underlying and time, then the distribution of future stock price is no longer lognormal. Black-Scholes option pricing, however, takes discounted expected payoffs relative to a lognormal distribution. As volatility changes through time, you are likely to get contrasting periods of little activity in the stock followed by periods of intense activity in the stock. These periods produce peakedness and fat tails, respectively (together called "leptokurtosis"), in stock returns distributions. Fat tails are likely to lead to some sort of smile effect,

---

[13]For theoretical and empirical comparisons of the Merton (1976) jump process call option pricing and the standard Black-Scholes pricing, see Ball and Torous (1985).

[14]For example, Black (1976a) notes that $\sigma \uparrow$ as $S \downarrow$, and vice versa. This "leverage effect" is discussed further in section 10.4.1. If you have access to a Bloomberg terminal, run the regression analysis VIX <INDEX> SPX <INDEX> HRA <GO> or VIX <INDEX> IBM <INDEX> HRA <GO> and you should see a clear negative effect.

because they increase the chance of payoffs away-from-the-money. The interaction of skewness and kurtosis of returns gives rise to many different possible smile effects (Hull [2000, chapter 17]; Krause [1998, pp145-148]).

Stochastic volatility models attempt to account for volatility that changes as a function of both time and stock price level (Hull and White [1987]; Scott[1987]; Wiggins [1987]; Hull [2000]). Applications to FX options include Chesney and Scott (1989) and Melino and Turnbull (1990).

The effect of stochastic volatility on option values is similar to the effect of a jump component: both increase the probability that out-of-the-money options will finish in-the-money, and increase the probability that in-the-money options will finish out-of-the-money (Wiggins [1987, pp360–361]). Whether an implied volatility smile is skewed left, is skewed right, or is symmetrical in a stochastic volatility model depends upon the sign of the correlation between changes in volatility and changes in stock price (Hull [2000, chapter 17]; Krause [1998, pp145-148]).

9.5 Summary of Option Pricing Methods II: Discrete versus Continuous Models

Table 9.3: Option Pricing Methods (No-Arbitrage versus Equilibrium) for Different Models of Security Price Behavior

Model	Perfect Hedge?	Risk-Neutral Pricing?	Equilibrium Pricing?
Binomial	Yes	Yes	Yes (Discrete CAPM works)
Trinomial	No	Yes (not unique)	Yes (Need Price of Risk)
$dS = \mu Sdt + (J-1)Sd\pi$ Pure Jump (Cox-Ross)	Yes	Yes	Yes (Limit of Binomial)
$dS = \mu Sdt + \sigma Sdw$ Diffusion (Black-Scholes)	Yes	Yes	Yes (Limit of Binomial)
$dS = \mu Sdt + \sigma Sdw + (J-1)Sd\pi$ Jump-Diffusion (with Diversifiable Jump Risk)	No	No	Yes (Inst. CAPM Works)
$dS = \mu Sdt + \sigma Sdw + (J-1)Sd\pi$ Jump-Diffusion (with Non-Diversifiable Jump Risk)	No	No	Yes (Need to Price Jump Risk)

Chapter 10

Trading

I love trading. I love actively trying to beat the market. It is a game of pure skill in which genuine players cannot sit on the fence; they must put their money where their mouth is, and their success or failure is quantified indisputably in dollars and cents. Actively trading stocks is like playing with fire: It takes skill and discipline to avoid getting burned. Actively trading options is the financial equivalent of throwing gasoline on that fire.

From September 1929 until mid-1932, the broad market in the US dropped 90% (Chernow [1990, p323]); each $1,000 invested fell to be worth only $100. You may think that sounds bad, but table 10.1 indicates that about one-third of CBOE options positions that investors enter fare much worse—losing the full 100%. Not only that, but most options are of maturity eight months or less, so the loss is much more rapid than that following the crash of 1929!

The "Hard" Word: I like the old joke "How do you make a small fortune in the stock market?" The punch line is "Start with a *large* fortune!" Making money in the markets is hard work. There are many books, seminars, and videos that promise easy riches from trading; but the "systems" they offer are for suckers. The best financial advice I have ever heard is: "If it looks too good to be true, then it probably is too good to be true." Or, put in other words, *If it looks like a duck, walks like a duck, and quacks like a duck, then it probably is a duck!* Unless you are good at forecasting stocks and the market, you will not consistently make good money in the markets.

The financial outcomes of persistent ignorance and foolishness are often indistinguishable. At least ignorance can be addressed by education. This chapter is a collection of practical observations and advice. With this advice under your belt, I am hopeful that you will at least keep your head above water while you are trying to find out if you are any good at forecasting the markets. If you are good at forecasting, then you will make much more money with my advice than without it. I recommend strongly that you trade only with "risk capital"; that is, money that you can afford to lose in the blink of an eye.

10.1 Institutional Details

The booklet *Characteristics and Risks of Standardized Options* (CAROSO) is available for free from the CBOE both in hard copy form and online.[1] This section presents similar but less detailed information.

10.1.1 Options Specifications

Listed equity options on the CBOE are American-style. Generally, the option covers one round lot of shares or ADRs.[2] The exercise price and option premium must be multiplied by the number of underlying shares to get the aggregate exercise price and aggregate premium. For example, on July 30, 2003, an Eastman Kodak (EK) August \$20 strike call option was quoted at \$7.90–\$8.00. This call gives the right to buy 100 shares of EK for \$20 per share, or a total exercise price of \$2000 (for a total premium of \$800 if you are going long). EK traded around \$28 per share on that day.

Listed equity options have maturities up to about eight months (except for LEAPS). They trade on one of three expiration cycles: in any given month, there are two near-month expirations, and two far-month expirations (see footnote 18 on p13 for more details). Ignoring exchange holidays, equity options expire on the Saturday following the third Friday of the expiration month.[3] Stock LEAPS options have lives of up to three years and always expire in January. LEAPS usually have ticker symbols that differ from regular equity options—often starting with a "V" or a "Z" or an "L." LEAPS convert to regular equity options (and their ticker symbols change) when their maturity is short enough to join the regular expiration cycle.

US index options usually give the right to buy \$100 times the underlying index, though beware "reduced value" options that use only one-tenth the index as the underlying. Index options may be American style or European style. They are always cash settled. Their maturities are usually less than four months, except for LEAPS. Index LEAPS always expire in December.

If you are short an option, and someone who is long exercises, you may be "assigned the exercise." That is, you are forced to buy the stock at the strike if it is a put, and forced to sell the stock at the strike if it is a call. There are a few business days between a properly tended exercise notice to a broker and subsequent assignment to a randomly chosen option writer.

Note that if you are long a call, a cash dividend is bad news (see the dividends section beginning on page 46). Thus, call holders may try to capture dividends

---

[1]Copies of CAROSO are available from your broker, online at www.cboe.com, by calling 1-888-OPTIONS (in the US), or from The Options Clearing Corporation, One North Wacker Drive, Suite 500, Chicago, Illinois 60606. Google the full title and you will find a free PDF copy online.

[2]An ADR is an American Depository Receipt. It is a USD-denominated stock, trading in the US, but representing ownership in a foreign corporation.

[3]Each month I get this type of message from my broker: "The last day to trade equity option contracts expiring on Saturday, May 17th will be Friday, May 16th. If you do not have sufficient buying power to cover potential exercises or assignments, please deposit funds or close out your position before close of market on Friday."

Table 10.1: How Do People Exit Their CBOE Option Positions?

Close Out	60%
Exercise/Assigned	10%
Expire Worthless	30%

Note: Roughly 60% of CBOE options are exited via offset (sell to close a long, or buy to cover a short). Ten percent of options are exercised; Either you are long and you exercise your right to buy or sell, or you are short and the Options Clearing Corporation (OCC) assigns you the exercise of someone who is long. Thirty percent of options expire worthless (your rate of return is -100%!). Source: Personal communication with CBOE staff, 1997.

by exercising (and call writers are more likely to be assigned exercises) as the ex-dividend date approaches.

Adjustments can be made by the exchange to standardized terms of listed equity options. In general, no adjustment is made for ordinary cash dividends (less than 10% of market value of underlying). A stock split, stock dividend, or stock distribution can lead to an adjustment in the number of underlying shares or the exercise price, or both. For example, you hold a MMM 150 call, and MMM has a 3 for 2 stock split. The option could be adjusted to cover 150 shares with strike $100 (total strike is unchanged at $15,000). As a general rule, if the ratio is a whole number (e.g., as in a 2 for 1 split), the number of underlying shares is not adjusted. Instead, the exercise price is decreased, and the number of outstanding options is increased. For example, you hold an MMM 150 put, and MMM has a 2 for 1 stock split. You end up with two put options, each on 100 shares, with strike $75.[4]

Strike prices are initially set close to the underlying share price. Additional strikes are set at $2\frac{1}{2}$-point intervals (if the strike is less than $25), 5-point intervals (if the strike is between $25 and $200), and 10-point intervals (for strikes over $200).[5] Options with identical terms form a series; e.g., IBM 100 Nov calls are one series. IBM puts are one class; IBM calls are another class. New series are introduced when the underlying trades through the highest or lowest strike price available, or when one series expires.

Open interest is the number of long (or short) contracts alive. When an option is exercised, the open interest drops by one. The number of contracts you can hold on one side of the market (i.e., long calls plus short puts, or long puts plus short calls) or exercise over five consecutive business days is limited to the position limit (or exercise limit). This lies between 4,500 and 99,000 options, depending upon market capitalization of the underlying.

The holder of an option considers the Options Clearing Corporation (OCC),

---

[4]Other corporate actions cause adjustments: if a stock is converted to a debt security, the underlying changes to debt; after a spinoff, the underlying may be two companies' stocks in appropriate proportions; similarly for mergers; but no adjustment is made for tender offers or exchange offers.

[5]One "point" is one dollar.

rather than any particular option writer, to be his or her counterparty. Similarly, option writers are obligated under the OCC system, and are not tied to any particular option holder. Once the OCC identifies matching orders from a buyer and a seller, it cuts any link between the parties and steps in as the counterparty. All premiums and settlement payments are made to and paid by OCC (via your broker and a "clearing member" who clears your broker's trades with the OCC). There has never been a default by the OCC.

10.1.2 Exchanges, Regulatory Bodies, and Securities

When you trade stocks on the NYSE or options on the CBOE, there is a designated market maker who must quote a bid-ask spread and buy from you if you want to sell, and sell to you if you want to buy. Exchange rules limit the size of the spread and the speed with which the market maker can move the spread. This is not so in the futures (and futures options) market. In the futures market, the floor traders can step back and not trade if they do not want to—typically at the very time you severely need liquidity. Thus, futures and futures options carry a liquidity risk not seen with NYSE stocks or CBOE stock options.

Limitations on daily price moves in the futures market mean that daily price limits are likely to be hit more frequently than are aggregate price limits in the stock market. When a price limit move up or down happens, the futures market "locks limit up" or "locks limit down," the exchange halts trade, and that may be the end of trade for that day. The market may lock limit again with the first trade of the next day, and so on. You may find yourself locked into your losing position for several days, and unlike the CBOE where you cannot lose more than 100% of the option premium, you can lose much more than 100% of your initial outlay in futures.[6]

When you are short an option, or a stock for that matter, you are at the mercy of whomever is long. You can be forced to cover a short stock position at any time.[7] A short American-style option can, similarly, be exercised at any time by the person in the long position—optimality be damned! If you do have a short as an integral part of your strategy, and someone just pulled the rug out from under your feet, then you

---

[6] Although option contracts contain leverage, that leverage is only implicit, because when you buy options on the CBOE you must pay for them in full up front. When you buy a stock on the NYSE and you *do not* do so on margin, you similarly pay for the stock in full up front. I think of these as "limited liability" trades, because you cannot be asked for any additional money to support the position. This is analogous to owning fully paid-up shares in a limited liability company, where the directors of the company cannot ask you for any additional money to support your holding. This differs from buying a stock and choosing to do so on margin or buying futures where you have no choice but to do so on margin. In these cases, you have an explicitly levered position in the instrument, and your broker and/or the exchange can ask for more money if the trade goes against you.

[7] D'Avolio (2002) indicates that forced covering is a rare event and is accompanied by unusually high trading volume and volatility. He states that in any given month, on average, only 2% of stocks loaned out are recalled. A long put can substitute for a short stock when the stock is too hot to borrow, but beware unsustainable implied volatilities that can quickly eat your long option profits if they fall.

---

will probably have to close your entire position down. For this reason, and others, the CBOE has recently (mid-2001) introduced European-style options (ticker XEO) on the S&P100 to complement the European-style options (ticker SPX) that already trade on the S&P500.

If you are short stock, you face two costs that long stock holders do not. First, there is the general tendency for stock markets to rise over time. If you are short, you are swimming against that current. Second, when you are short a stock, you pay the dividends on the stock to whomever is in the long position. Dividend yields in the US have fallen to the extent that dividend costs are not, on average, very high nowadays. If you are short a call on a stock or long a put on a stock, then you still face the first "swimming" cost, and with leverage to boot, but you are not liable for dividends, because dividends go to the person who is long the stock, not long an option on the stock.

Federal Reserve Board "Regulation T" ("Reg T" for short) governs how much credit may be extended to clients of broker-dealers. Reg T defines which securities are eligible and establishes initial margin requirements for both long and short positions. For options, it defers to the SEC-approved exchange-imposed margin requirements (Sec 220.12[f]).

You can borrow, at most, 50% of the value of marginable securities from your broker. Not all stocks are marginable: For example, section 220.11 of Reg T says that to be marginable, OTC (i.e., not NYSE or NYSE Alternext) stocks must (among other requirements) be priced over $5, have more than $4 million capital, have over 400,000 shares outstanding, be publicly traded for at least six months, and the issuing entity has to have existed for at least three years. The net result is that small stocks (i.e., low market capitalization stocks) and low-priced stocks might not be marginable.

Reg T Sec 220.12 (c) deals with short sales of eligible equity securities. It states, essentially, that margin money must remain in the margin account to the extent of 150% of the current market value of the security sold short, or 100% of the current market value if there exists a security held in the account that is easily exchangeable into an offsetting position. If a long call is to be used as margin to offset a short sale of the underlying security, then it must be an American-style option issued by a registered clearing corporation and listed or traded on a registered national securities exchange, and must have a strike price at or below the price at which the underlying security was sold short. In other words, you cannot use the short sale proceeds except to post them as margin money or to buy a call on the short security.

In 2001, the NASD modified margin requirements for frequent traders. The essentials are that if you make four or more round-trip equity trades during any five-business-day period, and if this represents more than 6% of your total trading activity during this period, then you are labelled a "pattern day trader." You are then required to have at least $25,000 capital in your margin account. You are also allowed to use up to four times this for intraday trading (i.e., you are allowed to trade on as little as a 25% margin), but you must go home flat or face a margin call for the other 25%. "Going home flat" means that you close out your positions at day's end; i.e., that the plot of your wealth versus the stock price is flat—hence the term.

Regular trading hours (RTH) for stocks in New York are 9:30AM to 4:00PM EST (New York time). RTH for equity options in Chicago are 8:30AM to 3:02PM CST (Chicago time). Note that 9:30AM EST is 8:30AM CST. RTH hours for other option products in Chicago may differ. The exchange Web sites give the trading hours for each product.

Extended trading hours for stocks in New York are 8:00 to 9:15AM and 4:15 to 6:30PM EST Monday to Friday. The extended trading hours sessions use order matching by Electronic Communication Network (ECN). The ECN looks for matching orders, so round lot orders are much more likely to fill. After hours (AH) stock trading often takes place at the NYSE close price, though it need not. I think people trading in the AH market want fills, and are happy to go with the NYSE close to get it done. The fact that a stock's price does not move during AH trade does not therefore tell you anything about the information flow; it does not imply that the stock will not jump tomorrow morning. Spreads and price fluctuations can be large outside of RTH. For example, in the AM session on July 8th, 2003, Eastman Kodak was quoted at $26.77–$27.39 and AT&T was quoted at $19.56–$20.50. During extended trading hours, my broker allows only unrestricted limit orders (no fill-or-kill, all-or-none, etc.), no short sales, no options, no mutual funds, and no bonds.

There are over 10,000 stocks available to trade in the US. They trade on the NYSE, the NYSE Alternext, the NASDAQ, the OTC "Bulletin Board," and the "Pink Sheets." Stocks trading on the Bulletin Board and Pink Sheets are ones that do not satisfy the requirements for trading on the NASDAQ or for listing on the NYSE Alternext or NYSE. There is not much liquidity in or reliable information about these stocks; execution of orders for them may be slow and costly.

Options can be purchased from investment banks rather than organized exchanges. This is an over-the-counter (OTC) market.[8] Financial institutions trade these options with other financial institutions and with corporate clients. Most OTC options are European-style, whereas most exchange-traded options are American-style.

OTC options are more expensive than exchange-traded options. This is because you must pay for an investment bank's expertise in structuring complicated deals, and because the bank must make a profit. Competition between investment banks reduces the cost of common OTC products. However, unique or complicated products may have a large premium attached—perhaps an ROF.[9] It should be pointed out, however, that you are often getting what you pay for; e.g., peace of mind.

When I started investing, you could tell from a stock's ticker symbol whether it

---

[8] Do not confuse the term OTC used for an investment bank with OTC used to refer to the Bulletin Board now, or the NASDAQ in the past; they are distinct in their meaning. Although they both refer to marketplaces with no physical exchange floor, the investment bank provides potentially non-standardized financial instruments whereas the Bulletin Board now (or the NASDAQ of 20 years ago) attempts to be exchange-like.

[9] At least one investment bank is on record as having routinely referred to the "rip-off factor," or ROF, in complicated deals with clients.

traded on the NASDAQ or on the NYSE or the AMEX (now the NYSE Alternext); three or fewer letters meant the NYSE or the AMEX, and four or five letters meant NASDAQ. That is not strictly true any more, but it is often true.

It is relatively easy to find ticker symbols for stocks; many Web sites have "ticker lookup" facilities. If you know the ticker for the stock, you can look up the "option chain" to find the "chain" of options that is attached to the stock (i.e., all the different option series). Some Web sites will, however, just give you the near-the-money options; be sure you know what you are looking at because many other option series may exist that are not listed by default. I have noticed that different data vendors may use slightly different tickers for the same option, so the CBOE's Web site may have a slightly different ticker for an option than you see on your online brokerage screen.

There has been an excellent trend in recent years toward the introduction of exchange-traded funds (ETFs). An ETF is a portfolio that can be bought and sold just like a stock, but which is designed to track very closely a broad market index, a sector index, or some other index or group of stocks. ETFs are useful for hedging stock or options positions. ETFs have numerous advantages over mutual funds: ETFs can be bought and sold (and sold short) at intraday prices, whereas most mutual funds can be traded only at market close prices; there is no uptick rule for most ETFs;[10] ETFs are often very heavily traded and that goes hand-in-hand with very low T-costs (e.g., the NYSE Alternext ETFs DIA and SPY that track the INDU and SPX, respectively, have extremely low spreads). ETFs, unlike mutual funds, do not have to sell their holdings to redeem institutional investors who sell. This means that they are less likely to generate capital gains that could generate a tax bill for those still in the fund. One disadvantage of ETFs over regular mutual funds is that their flexibility may tempt poor market timers into active strategies that lose over the long term.

Finally, roughly half of all individual equity option trading and 90% of all equity index option trading takes place on the CBOE. The CBOE is one of five US exchanges that trade options (source: `www.cboe.com`).

10.1.3 Brokers

There are discount brokers and full-service brokers. Full-service brokers offer advice and assistance in placing trades. They charge you 10–20 times what a discount broker charges you for the same execution. They may get commissions based on your trades, and they may be trying to dump stock that their company owns. The former is an incentive for them to advise you to trade too much; the latter is an incentive for them to advise you to trade the wrong securities. A discount broker may charge you only $5–$20 to place an order. Shop around for a discount broker

---

[10]The uptick rule was introduced by the SEC in 1938 a half-dozen years after the stock market collapse. It says you cannot sell short unless the most recent trade was on an uptick; that is, unless the price just ticked up. The SEC rescinded the rule in July 2007, but I think there is a 50-50 chance that a tick rule will be re-introduced in some form by 2010.

who has been in business for a while and has charges that are low for the type of trading you typically do.

One problem with using a discount broker is that naive investors might accidentally buy the wrong stock (Rashes [2001]). For example, they might buy the stock with ticker symbol FORD thinking it is Ford Motor Company, which actually has ticker symbol F, or they might buy RYN (Ryonier) thinking it is Ryan Air, which actually has ticker symbol RYAAY.

My discount broker executes trades very quickly: typically within five seconds, and usually within one or two seconds if I am trading round lots. The slowest US trade I ever did was shorting the DIA, and that took maybe 15 seconds to fill.

I used to get phone calls from Chicago futures brokers with heavy foreign accents saying something like "...now surely, Dr. Crack, you have seen that sugar prices are at a three-year low..." or "...if you have two thousand dollars that you can afford to lose..." They wanted to run a portion of my money for me (and generate commissions for themselves). You would be better off giving your $2,000 to the American Red Cross; at least the life you save might be your own.

Section 10.1.2 discusses Reg T and margins. For stocks that are marginable, your online broker should have a list online of the maintenance margin requirements for each stock. This should be something like 40%, but with requirements of 50% or 100% for more volatile stocks. Thus, $5,000 in your margin account may give you a buying power of as much as $12,500 of stock.

Equity options can be illiquid. If you hold options in your account, it may be that no one has traded any options from that series in the last few days. Your broker may mark to market using the last trade rather than the most recent bid or ask. This means that the value of your option position reported by your online broker may be extremely stale. It may show a large gain or loss over the last time you checked your balance, when in fact the security is currently quoted very differently. Also, even if the option traded only 10 seconds ago, option spreads mean that you may see your option value reported at the ask (if the last transaction was a customer buy), and this is different from what you can get if you try to sell now at the bid. The bottom line is that illiquidity leads to infrequent trade and wide spreads, so the last transaction in an option does not necessarily reflect relevant information for your next trade. Be sure to check the current bid-ask spread before trading. In similar vein, option illiquidity can lead to non-execution of some order types that are linked to actual trades. See section 10.4.4 for an example.

My broker gives a "liquidation value" for my account that completely ignores any margin borrowing that has to be repaid. As such, it does not represent what I think of as liquidation value. Be sure to understand how your broker reports your positions, and do the arithmetic before trading.

10.1.4   T-Costs

Traders incur transactions costs (T-costs). T-costs are either direct or indirect. Direct T-costs include commissions, spreads, and margin interest. Indirect T-costs include price impact, price slippage and execution risk, price improvement (negatively), payment for order flow, and the consequences of internal crossing. It is arguable whether other costs, like taxes or dividend obligations on a short sale of stock, are T-costs.

Commissions. Most brokers charge at least a fixed dollar sum. For example, $8 for a market order (see section 10.4.4) in shares and $10 for a market order in stock options, in unlimited quantity. There may, however, be a schedule of prices depending upon the number of contracts traded. For example, one well-known discount broker charges a $5 commission for market orders up to 5,000 shares, but an additional one cent per share, retroactive to the first share, for market orders over 5,000 shares. They charge $5 plus $1.50 commission per contract for market orders in listed equity options or index options, with a minimum commission of $15. For limit orders (see section 10.4.4), they have an identical schedule, except that $10 replaces $5. The numbers given here are all for online trades. If you place a broker-assisted trade, they charge an extra $12 for shares and a minimum of $25 for options. Using all these numbers, the least expensive commission is for an online market order in fewer than 5,001 shares ($5); the most expensive is for a broker-assisted limit order in options (at least $25). This discount broker charges a flat commission of $19 for option exercises or assignments. If the option expires unexercised, no commission is charged for its expiration.

As already mentioned, commissions from full-service brokers can be 10–20 times larger than the above-mentioned commissions from discount brokers.

Spreads. We discussed bid-ask spreads in section 1.3.2 (p10), and in many other places throughout this book. Small traders typically buy at the ask and sell at the bid. In theory, the difference is pocketed by the market maker.

In practice, prices can be so volatile that the market maker collects only a portion of the spread, and some markets do not even have market makers. For example, the New Zealand Stock Exchange (NZX), as of 2009, does not have designated market makers. The bid-ask spread on the NZX is determined solely by how tightly spaced the inner limit orders on a stock are in the centralized limit order book. At least five levels of limit orders and depth are freely visible to all traders, with only the occasional hidden order.

The relative spread (i.e., spread divided by option price) on an option can be 10 times the relative spread on the underlying stock. I argue in section 1.3.2 that this is not usurious, but appropriate. Making a market in options is a risky and expensive business, and there is substantial regulatory oversight on the size of spreads in stocks and options in the US.

Margin. Long puts or calls must be paid in full; they cannot be bought on margin. Uncovered (i.e., naked) writers must, however, deposit an initial margin of 100% of the option proceeds plus 20% of the aggregate contract value (current equity price multiplied by $100) minus the amount by which the option is out-of-the-money, if any. Minimum initial margin is 100% of the option proceeds plus 10% of the aggregate contract value. Your broker may require a higher initial margin. So, to be clear, you do not get to use the option proceeds if you sell naked options.[11]

No options margin is required for writing covered calls; i.e., when you own the stock already. This is because the credit risk is zero. However, if the underlying stock is bought on margin, and the option is in-the-money, the extent to which the call is in-the-money is subtracted from the stock price when calculating the investor's equity position (meaning that you may not be able to withdraw margin funds as the stock price rises).

Margin Interest. A stock margin trade is partially funded using money borrowed from your broker. You pay margin interest on the borrowing. The interest rate is usually some quoted prime or base rate with an adjustment depending upon the level of borrowing (i.e., the debit balance). Margin rates are quite competitive. For example, in 2009, one well-known US discount broker charged a base rate of 3.99% but an adjustment of +3.00% for a debit balance of $1–$49,999, +2.00% for $50,000–$249,999, +1.00% for $250,000–$999,999, and no adjustment (equal to the base rate) for $1,000,000 or more.

Price Impact. If you buy stock, you consume part of the depth at the ask, and you create upward pressure on the stock price. A very large market order can consume all the depth at the ask and then walk up the limit order book, thereby pushing prices against the trader. This movement of prices against your favor is called "price impact" or "market impact." Do not be fooled into mistaking this upward move in prices as good for you. Even though you are going long and price rises are good for people in long positions, the temporary order imbalance that forces you to pay higher prices is a genuine cost to you.[12]

The larger the capitalization of the stock, the more liquid it is, and the less likely is price impact. The smaller the trader and the smaller the trade, the less likely is price impact.

You can move the stock price against you without trading in the stock. For example, if you buy a call option on a stock, and the option market maker hedges by buying stock, then the market maker's buying creates upward price pressure on the stock. That is, even though you yourself are not buying stock, your trade can still move the stock price against you. The option market maker has already built this hedging cost into his or her bid and ask quotes.

Price Slippage and Execution Risk. Between your deciding to place an order, placing an order, and having it filled, the price can move. This "price slippage" is a particular concern in fast markets, in illiquid securities, or when you are trying

---

[11]Aside: If you want to create a long-short position in equities, then each $1 you have in your margin account allows you to go long $1 and short $1. Half of your original dollar is the 50% margin for the long side, and the other half, together with the $1 short proceeds, is the 150% margin for the short side.

[12]An exception might be if you are an informed trader known to be informed, and your price impact is a permanent repricing to reflect your perceived information.

to execute different legs of a strategy. For example, I once wanted to trade an index option that did not appear on my online brokerage screen. I called them up, and they did a broker-assisted trade for me. They charged me only the online commission, but the price had moved against me a couple of eighths in the interim.

Price Improvement. One broker used to advertise in the *Wall Street Journal* with a picture of a French Revolution guillotine and the phrase, *The way some brokers handle your trade, it's no wonder they call it an execution!*

The faster your order is executed, the less likely it is that you get a "price improvement" on the quoted bid or ask. I remember standing on the floor of the NYSE in mid-1994 watching a specialist "stop" incoming small orders. A "stopped order" is guaranteed the quoted bid or ask, but given the ability for price improvement should an opposing order appear that can be crossed with it strictly within the spread (Ready [1999]). Price improvement can also come from an off-exchange competing market maker; for example, a regional exchange like the Boston Stock Exchange (BSE).[13]

The opportunity for price improvement means a higher quality execution. It follows that rapid execution by discount brokers may go hand-in-hand with poorer quality execution. There is thus a trade-off between speed of execution and quality of execution.

Payment for Order Flow and Internal Crossing. Your broker does not necessarily send your trade in a NYSE stock to the floor of the NYSE. Other exchanges and market makers exist, and they may pay your broker a penny or two a share to route your order to them. Your broker may even cross the trade internally by matching your order with another customer's order, or by trading from their own inventory, and therefore keep the spread for themselves.

You may still hit the quote that the NYSE specialist broadcasts, but you miss out on any opportunity for price improvement. Again, a rapid execution might not be a high-quality execution. I have even seen brokers advertise $0 commissions; presumably, the quality of execution was exceptionally poor.

Tax. Laws change and different traders have different tax situations, so you must confirm any information here with your tax advisor.

Gains and losses on options are taxed as capital gains and losses. Gains and losses are recognized when an option expires unexercised,[14] or when an option position is closed out with an offsetting trade. Commissions are all tax deductible.

When a call option is exercised, the person in the long position is treated as if he or she purchased the stock at the strike plus the call premium (and this total is

---

[13]The BSE was acquired in 2008 by the NASDAQ. I visited the BSE in the mid-1990s before it moved to its new building. It was all screen-based, not open outcry; so, unlike the NYSE floor, it was nearly silent.

[14]You might let an in-the-money option expire without exercise if the T-costs exceed the intrinsic value. Many brokers automatically exercise your option at expiration if it is sufficiently in-the-money to cover T-costs.

compared to the subsequent sale price of the stock to calculate taxable profits); a call option writer who is assigned an exercise is treated as if he or she sold stock at the strike plus the premium (and this is offset against the price of the stock purchase required to meet the assignment).

When a put option is exercised, the person in the long position is treated as if he or she sold the stock at the strike less the premium (and this is offset against the original stock purchase price); a put option writer who is assigned an exercise is treated as if he or she purchased the stock at the strike less the premium (and this net cost is offset against the subsequent selling price of the stock).

If you think a stock that you lost money on and sold is going to bounce back, and you repurchase the losing stock within 30 calendar days of the date you sold it, you cannot claim a loss for tax purposes—it is a "wash sale." This applies to the 30 days prior to the sale, as well as the 30 days after the sale (i.e., a 61-day period). Selling a stock and buying a call also comes under the wash sale rule because buying a call is tax-equivalent to buying the stock itself.

10.2 Black-Scholes Assumptions and Violations

The assumptions of Black-Scholes option pricing are severe; they have to be to lead to a simple closed-form formula. The real world differs from the assumptions used to derive Black-Scholes pricing in at least the following respects: the volatility σ changes with changing stock price; bid-ask spreads exist and they are necessarily large in options markets; stock and option prices are often restricted, either explicitly by minimum tick sizes[15] or implicitly by market participants, and are thus not continuous variables but discrete ones; there exist many different interest rates r, and they change through time; most exchange-traded options are American style not European style; many OTC options are more complex still; stock prices do not follow a GBM, but a process that is often at least partly predictable; options markets are not open always—you cannot trade in continuous time; commissions exist; price processes for the underlying stock are discontinuous—not just because prices are restricted by tick size, but because significant news moves prices significantly creating "jump discontinuities"; the implied volatility used to price options of different maturity differs and similarly for options of different moneyness, giving rise to a "term structure of implied volatility" and "volatility smiles" or "volatility skews," respectively.

The net result of all this is that the Black-Scholes formula appears, at first blush, to be mis-specified in a dozen different ways if you want to use it to help you trade equity options in the US. From a practical standpoint, however, the formula is quite robust with regard to the majority of these mis-specifications. So, I find the Black-Scholes formula a helpful and accurate guide for my options trading. I do, however,

---

[15]The tick size is the minimum allowable price variation. The tick size in equity options and equity LEAPS on the CBOE is $0.05 for premiums below $3, and $0.10 otherwise.

have to allow for spreads, commissions, and variations in volatility through time, across moneyness, and across maturity. This is described in a spreadsheet setting next.

10.3 The Spreadsheet Tools

Two simple EXCEL spreadsheet tools accompany this book. The first spreadsheet is a learning tool focused on the Greeks; The second spreadsheet is a trading tool into which you feed a view on a stock. The first spreadsheet (and any subsequent revised version) is named bbsGREEKS.xls and can be downloaded from www.BasicBlackScholes.com and opened using the password "marylebone" (in lowercase letters and without the quotes). This spreadsheet is about 100Kb, and uses no VB. The second spreadsheet (and any subsequent revised version) is named bbs.xls and can be downloaded from www.BasicBlackScholes.com using the password "marylebone" (in lowercase letters and without the quotes); be sure to enable macros when you use this one. This spreadsheet is about 140Kb, and uses VB to reset spinner-controlled cells to original values.

Let us return to the speculative call example in section 1.3.3 (p13). Assume that it is Monday, April 21, 2003, that MCD closed most recently at $16, that you think that it will rise to $20 per share within three months and that this will be accompanied by no change in the shape of the volatility skew. Let me assume that you have 90% confidence in your view. Your worst-case scenario is that MCD will fall to $14 per share after three months, but there is little likelihood of that—MCD having recently risen from its roughly 10-year low of just over $12. Your confidence level is high enough that options are viable, but which options position should you choose? Let me restrict the choice to long call options (anything more complicated can be analyzed using the same methods).

MCD is on the March expiration cycle with equity options expiring in May, June, September, and December 2003 (you discover this as soon as you look at the option chain attached to MCD on your brokerage screen or investment Web site). There are also LEAPS that expire in January 2004 and January 2005. If your three-month horizon is quite firm, then the May and June expirations are too soon, and there is no point paying extra for the December expiration or the LEAPS. That leaves just September. Near-the-money strike prices are available from $10 to $22.50 in $2.50 steps. The most recent quotes (i.e., bid and ask prices) for September MCD call options were reported in table 1.3 (p14), and are repeated here in table 10.2.

I mentioned the simple EXCEL spreadsheet trading tool bbs.XLS above. You can feed in my above-mentioned view on MCD (forecast stock price at forecast horizon) and get out the answer to my question: "Which option best capitalizes on my view?" This is a simple and parsimonious tool that I have found very useful in day-to-day trading.

Beyond the instructions, there are four worksheets within the spreadsheet. The content and function of the worksheets are as follows:

I. Source Data. Enter the horizon of your forecast $t = h$, your forecast, your

Table 10.2: September 2003 Call Option Data: MCD, April 17, 2003.

Strike	Ticker	Bid Price	Ask Price	Vol.	Op. Int.
$10.00	MCDIB	$6.00	$6.20	0	573
$12.50	MCDIV	$3.70	$3.90	3	1,547
$15.00	MCDIC	$1.80	$1.90	30	5,119
$17.50	MCDIW	$0.60	$0.65	99	2,115
$20.00	MCDID	$0.15	$0.25	4	524
$22.50	MCDIX	$0.00	$0.10	0	0

Note: These market data are for September 2003 MCD call options. They were available pre-trade on Monday, April 21, 2003, and therefore describe the most recent close of trade on Thursday, April 17. The bid and ask prices for these calls are in dollars per share, and each contract covers 100 shares. Table 1.3 (p14) contains the same data as this table, but with more details. (Data supplied by Thomson Financial, and provided as a courtesy by the Chicago Board Options Exchange, Incorporated.)

worst-case scenario, the term to maturity of the option series you want to use, the bid and ask prices of these options, your budget constraint, and the requested stock-specific and market data. Click on the toggle boxes to indicate whether to use the forecast or worst-case scenario in the rest of the spreadsheet, and whether you are looking at calls or puts. *For my MCD scenario*, I click on the spinners to increase my forecast of stock price at $t = h$ from $16 to $20, and to decrease my worst-case scenario from $16 to $14.

II. Calibrate Volatility, Fit Skew and Spread. By default, the default implied volatility from worksheet I is used to price the options at $t = 0$. Click on the spinners until the indicated pricing error is as small as possible for each option; doing so fits the volatility smile/skew. Below the calibration section are two simple models: The first fits the volatility skew as a function of moneyness; the second fits the bid-ask spreads you implicitly entered in worksheet I as a function of option price and moneyness. Details of the modelling technique appear in the text boxes in the worksheet. As mentioned, the models are simple and parsimonious, yet perform quite well over a wide range of examples and scenarios. You may alter the two moneyness-related inputs to the spread model, if you wish. *For my MCD scenario*, I am able to fit the volatility skew quite well at $t = 0$. The option pricing is within a penny, and the percentage pricing error is below 2.5% in all cases. You should look at figure 8.5 (p148) to see a sample of the range of shapes that smiles/skews can take on.

III. Forecast Ignoring T-Costs. The forecast of stock price together with the model of the volatility skew are imported from worksheets I and II; you have the option to override both without affecting the content of the earlier worksheets. Forecasts of option price at your horizon $t = h$ are calculated assuming the same volatility skew as a function of moneyness. *For my MCD scenario, the fit of the volatility skew at $t = h$ looks reasonable, and I see no reason to override the model. So, I go straight to the final worksheet.*

IV. T-Costs and Option Return. Forecast option prices at $t = h$ (from worksheet III), together with actual prices at $t = 0$ (from worksheet I) are combined with forecast spreads (using the model from worksheet II) to calculate returns on each option. A plot appears that shows the theoretical Black-Scholes return ignoring T-costs[16] and the actual return using your stated budget and T-costs. A third return is calculated using T-costs and assuming investment in exactly one contract. You can override the worksheet I budget constraint here without affecting the content of worksheet I. *For my MCD scenario, the fitted spreads look fine, and I see no reason to override the model.* The two best real-world strategies (strike \$17.50 and \$20), shaded green and blue, respectively, are also the two best strategies in the theoretical Black-Scholes world (but with transposed rankings). The worst real-world strategy (strike \$22.50), however, looks very attractive in the theoretical Black-Scholes world, ranking a close third behind the two leaders. This marked difference illustrates the importance of accounting for T-costs.

Notes on the Spreadsheet Trading Tool

- Source data appear as blue text, and you can edit these at will. You should not, however, alter the contents of cells with red or black text: The former are driven by spinners or toggle boxes, and the latter feed off other cells; changing them alters the function of the spreadsheet.

- Beware stale data when pulling bid and ask prices from the Web. Did the option trade on this day? Is there any open interest? If the option's price/quote looks wrong relative to those of its peers, then it probably is and you should revise it to make it consistent with its peers.

- The spreadsheet tool uses the Merton form of the Black-Scholes formula (equations 8.53 and 8.54 on page 139). This ignores the fact that the traded options are American-style. Fitting the volatility skew accounts for much of the mispricing, but there could be problems if big stock dividends are expected close to the expiration of a call option, or if puts are deep in-the-money. The latter is not really a problem when interest rates are very low.

- The spreadsheet tool deals only with calls and puts. If you create a new spreadsheet for more complicated positions (e.g., option spreads), then to the extent

---

[16]Mathematicians only: If you are up for a challenge, try solving $\frac{\partial [c(\hat{S}(h), X, t=h)/c(S(0), X, t=0)]}{\partial X} = 0$ for X to see the formal theoretical Black-Scholes strike-optimal call option. Be sure to check the SOC to confirm that it is a maximum.

that the options offset, the bid-ask spread of the spread position should be slightly lower than the sum of the bid-ask spreads for the component parts.

- The spreadsheet model of volatility takes into account the volatility smile or skew, but ignores any term structure of volatility. You can adjust the spreadsheet to account for this by sampling a short-dated option (probably best to use one of maturity $T - h$ observed at $t = 0$) and using the relative shapes of the volatility skews as a function of moneyness to forecast the change in the shape of the skew between $t = 0$ and $t = h$.

- The Black-Scholes formulae in all their many forms can never return a negative option value. If you enter the Black-Scholes formula and you get a negative number, then you have made a mistake.

- Forecast option prices in my spreadsheet tool must be a multiple of a one-nickel tick size if below \$3, and a one-dime tick size if above \$3. Forecast spreads must be multiples of these same tick sizes depending upon the location of the spread mid-point relative to the \$3 boundary. You can override forecast spreads, but they must be a multiple of nickels.

- Finally, for the MCD case, using the worst-case scenario indicates substantial losses for the option series under consideration. A longer-dated option, however, has slower time decay, and gives a smaller percentage loss, albeit at a greater up-front cost. If the confidence you hold in your view is low, or if your risk aversion is high, then use a longer-dated option than the expiration that is immediately beyond your horizon. The lower your confidence or the higher your risk aversion, the longer-dated should be the option you use. If your confidence is quite low or your risk aversion quite high, then either trade the stock, or do not trade at all! My threshold for trading the option as opposed to the stock is 80–90% confidence; below that, I use either LEAPS or the stock.

Epilogue. MCD did rise by 25%, but within two months rather than within three as shown in figure 10.1 (p188). My three-month view was still correct, with MCD dropping back to roughly \$20 at the three-month mark before rising again. Table 10.3 shows the prices of the table 10.2 options at the two-month mark. The spreadsheet tool's forecast of option prices and spreads was surprisingly good for such a simple model (e.g., at the three-month mark, the price forecast was within a few percentage points of realized prices, and four of the six spreads were perfectly correct, with the other two quite close). In practice, the volatility skew steepened slightly for the in-the-money options, but my forecast pricing was close because deep in-the-money options are not very sensitive to volatility. The steepening volatility skew may have been a term structure of volatility pattern.

Note that MCD continued to appreciate, reaching almost \$66 per share in August 2008. Unlike BA (see figure 1.1 on page 11), MCD's price was very resilient during the 2007/2008/2009 global credit crisis. MCD is thus a stalwart (Lynch [2000, p112]), whereas BA is a cyclical (Lynch [2000, p119]).

Table 10.3: September 2003 Call Option Data: MCD, June 09, 2003.

Strike	Ticker	Bid Price	Ask Price	Vol.	Op. Int.
$10.00	MCDIB	$11.00	$11.20	0	440
$12.50	MCDIV	$8.50	$8.70	3	1,523
$15.00	MCDIC	$6.10	$6.30	132	5,438
$17.50	MCDIW	$3.90	$4.10	259	4,473
$20.00	MCDID	$2.05	$2.20	1,860	2,951
$22.50	MCDIX	$0.80	$0.90	313	427

Note: These market data are for September 2003 MCD call options. They were available pre-trade on Monday, June 9, 2003, and therefore describe the most recent close of trade on Friday, June 6. MCD closed at 21.06 on this day (rising to 21.12 in after hours trading). The bid and ask prices for these calls are in dollars per share, and each contract covers 100 shares. (Data supplied by Thomson Financial, and provided as a courtesy by Chicago Board Options Exchange, Incorporated.)

10.4 Trading Experiences and Lessons

Eight common sense trading lessons:

1. Naked options are riskier than stocks, and the T-costs can eat you alive if you choose your options poorly. Do not trade options until you understand them. Once you understand them, do not trade them in place of the stock unless your confidence is justifiably high (in my case, 80–90%).

2. Do not blindly follow the advice of others. Before entering a position, conduct your own fundamental and technical analysis of the stock.[17] Remember to analyze your stock relative to others within its industry. Lynch (2000) has much good advice on this.

3. After a stock gets hammered down in price, implied volatility is high and dies down over the next couple of weeks. If you want to buy options on a stock that has just dived, wait a couple of weeks for the commotion to die down. At-the-money options are roughly linearly priced in sigma (see equation 8.51 on page 138), so if you buy call options immediately after a dive, and during a panic, and if implied volatility halves over the coming fortnight, then you lose half your money while the stock is doing nothing. You probably also face a wide spread because the market maker needs to be compensated for

---

[17]Fundamental analysis is almost the oppostive of technical analysis. Fundamental analysis looks at fundamentals like earnings, PE ratios, leverage, cash flow, etc. Technical analysis looks for patterns in stock prices and volumes. Fundamental analysis tends to be long-term oriented whereas technical analysis tends to be short-term oriented.

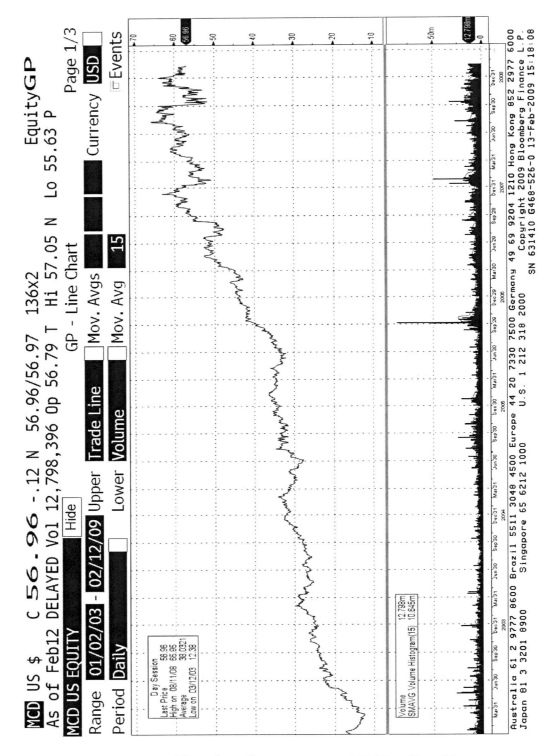

Figure 10.1: Bloomberg Screen: MCD <EQUITY> GP <GO>
Note: This figure shows the stock price of McDonald's (MCD) from January 2003 until February 2009. Note the resilience in price during the global credit crisis.

uncertainty. The high and decaying implied volatility problem is not an issue for the stock except insofar as it implies higher spreads. The relative spread (spread divided by security price) is so much lower for the stock than for the option, however, that this is not really an issue.

4. Take account explicitly of the T-costs for entering and exiting the options position (as in my spreadsheet tool in section 10.3). An attractive strategy that ignores T-costs may be unattractive once T-costs are taken into account.

5. Do not buy cheap, deep out-of-the-money options unless you recognize that they are essentially lottery tickets. Not only is the likelihood of profit low, the T-costs as a portion of price may be over 100%. Conversely, why buy deep in-the-money options when you can buy the stock on margin with lower T-costs?

6. Options positions magnify stock-specific risk. Undiversified option portfolios jump around like the proverbial pig on a pogo stick. Holding options on at least three stocks substantially reduces this risk.

7. Trade actively only with risk capital; that is, money you can afford to lose all of tomorrow.

8. Be unemotional. Sell when it is time to sell and buy when it is time to buy—without hesitation.

10.4.1 Stylized Facts

For options on a given stock, other things being equal, the higher the open interest, volume of trade, and price of the option, the lower the T-costs as a percentage of the premium. Conversely, the higher the degree of leverage, other things being equal, the higher are the T-costs as a percentage of the premium. Historically, there has been more open interest and volume of trade in calls than in puts. Within an option series, open interest and volume of trade are typically highest near the money, but relative T-costs are typically lowest for deep in-the-money options. After significant price moves, however, lagging residual open interest can exist for a time away from the money. Across option series, the near-month or second-month contracts often have the largest open interest. LEAPS can be relatively stock-like in their behavior; and thus, although they may be thinly traded, their premiums may be so high, and their leverage so low, that their relative T-costs can be quite small.

There is a well-known J-shaped pattern in T-costs during the trading day: T-costs fall after the open and rise again later in the day. Late morning is often the cheapest time to place trades. If I want to enter or exit a position, and I do not expect much activity in the stock, I wait until 10AM EST and try to complete the trade before 11AM EST.

CBOE bid-ask spread updates are partly driven by NYSE and NASDAQ transactions and quote revisions. There is, however, a delay of perhaps 5–10 seconds. So, if you are trading in large enough size, and react quickly enough, you can sometimes get a fill before the CBOE market maker's quote is revised. In a rising market, the options market maker may walk the ask up, then pause with a temporarily wider spread, then walk the bid up. The end result is that if you are selling, it can pay to wait a minute; similarly for buying in a falling market.

Fischer Black argued that as stock price rises, other things being equal, volatility of stock returns falls (Black [1976a]). This is called the leverage effect. A balance sheet constructed using market values of debt and equity is less levered after a stock price rise, and so, volatility of returns to equity holders should decline. If you are forecasting volatility and stock price, then this is worth considering, but any change in stock price strong enough to alter the financial leverage of a company probably goes hand-in-hand with a change in market perceptions strong enough to revise the original estimate of volatility of the returns to equity holders.

It has been well known for many years that stocks exhibit both reversals and momentum. These are simple examples of stock price patterns associated with technical analysis. Reversals are short-term changes in direction. For example, a stock that jumped up 4% today is likely to fall 1–2% tomorrow; and a stock that fell 8% today is likely to rise 2–4% tomorrow. Momentum is a longer-term phenomenon: A stock that has consistently risen over the last six months is likely to continue rising in the near future. These (sometimes) unreliable patterns in individual stocks translate into (often) reliable patterns in the broad market. A consequence of this is that, if the stock you are watching is whiplashing to and fro without any trend and you want to enter or exit, you should wait for an up (if selling) or a down (if buying). If not, you may regret it the next day.

I read a biography of Jesse Livermore (Smitten [2001]). Apparently, JL (as he was called) made about USD100m during the crash of 1929. He went from rags to riches several times during his life and ended up shooting himself dead. There is much advice in Smitten's book, and also in JL's own stock trading book, but some of it is out of date now. My opinion is that online trading and increasing automation in the markets has increased the speed with which stocks react (and overreact) to information. I think one-day reversals in the market are now much more frequent than they were in JL's day, and that this provides new opportunities, while simultaneously removing some momentum opportunities that were there.

Suppose you have been watching a stock for a month, and you have had the growing feeling in your gut that it is almost time to trade, and then you get the strong desire to pull the trigger, and then you finally know that you have to do the trade. My experience is that if it is a Friday, then do not wait until Monday to put the trade on. Waiting until Monday gives everyone else the weekend to process the data, and the stock may "gap up" at the open on Monday. An exception is that if you have watched a sudden run-up in price during the week, then waiting to buy until a reversal on Monday or Tuesday is a good idea if you think the run-up is overdone.

I mention several times in this book that markets behave differently around holidays because people behave differently around holidays. If you are actively trading, you need to be aware of exchange holidays and holidays that are not exchange holidays. For example, I was holding two round lots of AT&T (T) and saw a nice run-up in the price of T leading up to the Memorial Day long weekend. I dumped the 200 shares last thing Friday because I assumed that the market would drop like a stone first thing Tuesday on low volume, and that I could buy the shares back more cheaply before the people who took a four-day weekend returned to work and heavy volume continued to lift the price—and that is exactly what happened.

You are often "shadow boxing" with other market participants. It helps if you can forecast how they will behave. For example, I was watching T move during early July 2003 and noticed on several days that the stock price would rise no higher than $19.99 during the trading day. This resistance level was clearly due to limit orders to sell placed at $19.99. Some market participants had placed limit sells at $19.99 because they thought that still other participants had placed limit sells at $20, and the $19.99 traders wanted to capture the price rise without having to compete for execution with the $20 traders. The selling pressure at $19.99 was sufficient to eat up all demand and stop the stock going any higher. Thus, the orders to sell at $19.99 were filled, or partially filled, but no limit orders to sell at $20 were executed. Similarly, watching Eastman Kodak (EK) during mid-July 2003, it fell to $26.01 then rebounded strongly due to limit orders to buy placed just above $26. Noone with a limit order to buy EK at $26 got filled. Similarly, I watched Ford (F) stock trade down to $1.01 in late November, 2008, without ever hitting $1 (see figure 10.2); Noone with a limit order to buy F at $1 got filled. Within a few weeks, F had rebounded strongly back to $3.55. Placing a limit order at a round dollar figure may lead to non-execution. Rather, you must shadow box with your opponents and give up a few pennies to make it more likely that you get the fill.

There are patterns in volume, too. For example, on July 2, 2003, AH volume on T was 1,012,000 shares compared to 5,657,700 shares during the day and 2,728,300 shares the next day. This extraordinary AH volume was because the NYSE closed at 1:00PM on July 3 for the July 4 long weekend, and many people wanted to get their trades off ahead of time to take the extra half-day holiday.

Mondays and Fridays differ from other weekdays. Many academic papers explore "day-of-the-week anomalies." They try to explain how and why the first and last day of the trading week, or days on or around holidays (e.g., Easter, Passover, Rosh Hashanah, Yom Kippur, MLK Day, Presidents' Day, etc.), differ from other "normal" trading days.[18] Many academics seem to think that all trading days should be the same. I used to think so myself until I started trading actively. Now I think the academics have their heads in the sand and need a swift kick in the rump. Of course, Mondays and Fridays and days following holidays are different. People behave differently on these days! They have had time to think at the beginning of the week, and they want to close out positions and go home flat at the end of the week—so that they can have more time to think. When do you get the most liquidity on the NYSE? Probably 10:30AM on a Tuesday if Monday was not a holiday. Why?

---

[18]Of course, some anomalies are bogus and are caused by data snooping. See, for example, my lunar phase anomaly paper (Crack [1999]).

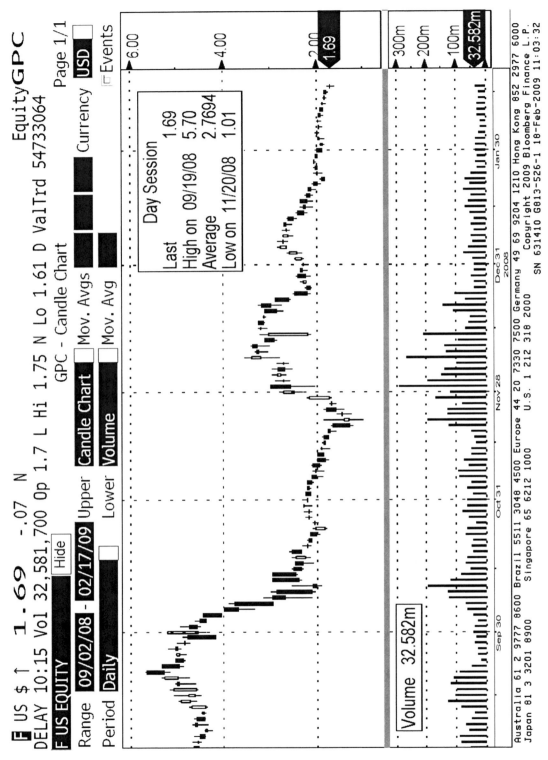

Figure 10.2: Bloomberg Screen: F <EQUITY> GPC <GO>

Note: The intraday low of $1.01 attained on November 20, 2008 means that no limit order to buy at $1.00 was filled. You must shadow box with your opponents and give up a few pennies on a limit order to get the execution.

...because people had the weekend to think about what they were going to trade; they watched the market on Monday to confirm that everything was in order; they got their trades ready and did some checking on Tuesday morning; and they wanted to get their trades in before lunch.

10.4.2 Information Sources

The World Wide Web is an excellent information source. For example, if you want to know the trading hours of the major exchanges, when exchange holidays are, or the detailed contract specifications of a LEAP, you will find them on the official home page of the relevant exchange.

Market data are freely available from your online brokerage company or from Web sites like `www.bigcharts.com` or `www.bloomberg.com`. Up-to-date accounting data (the most recent quarterly and annual statements) are free from sites like `www.marketwatch.com`. You also find legal insider trading reports there. You can download 10-Qs, 10-Ks and the like from the EDGAR section of `www.sec.gov`. If you are a professional, then you have Bloomberg or Reuters machines close by and ready access to data sources like DataStream, IBES, WorldScope, FactSet, or Compustat.

Corporate Web sites' investor relations sections often give a calendar of events (e.g., earnings announcements), but their financial data are typically stale. Earnings announcement dates can help you understand when to expect price moves. For example, one mid-July I knew that Eastman Kodak (EK) was to announce second-quarter performance and, almost certainly, a recovery strategy on July 23. The stock was down and heading down going into the announcement. I expected good news and plans for further recovery, so I bought options on 2,000 shares. EK jumped 10% as soon as the news arrived, and I made a healthy profit.

If you like graphical presentations to help you trade, you are in trouble when it comes to options. You cannot easily look at plots of time series of prices for options because, unlike stocks, the liquidity is so low that a time series of prices is distorted. So, I look to the time series of stock prices to gain technical information.

Some Web sites provide free tools. For example, `www.bloomberg.com` lets you rank all members of the SPX (S&P500) or INDU (Dow Jones Industrial Average) by dollar price change or rate of return. This tells you how your stock has done relative to other members of the index it belongs to. My online broker now offers free tools for calculating all the Greeks.

I have found that formal training in financial statement analysis is very valuable. You do not necessarily have to take a class, but you should get some books and do some studying. You need to be able to at least read a balance sheet, income statement, and statement of cash flows, and understand how they are intimately linked. Knowing a half-dozen key accounting ratios is also important. I think an elementary understanding of financial statement analysis is a prerequisite to reading Lynch (2000). My personal favorites are Brigham and Gapenski (1985, but not the later editions) and Anthony (1999); the latter is easier to find.

10.4.3 Other Trading Tips and Tools

If you have never traded options or stocks before, I recommend that you spend six months "paper trading." Paper trading means that you record trades in real time in a book or spreadsheet and track their performance. You take account of T-costs, and you learn lessons without losing money. Paper trading helps you identify your strengths and weaknesses as a trader.

Once you know your strengths and weaknesses, you can fight them actively. For example, one weakness of mine is that I trade too much. Another is that, although I am good at picking lows both in individual stocks and in the broad market, I am usually one or two days early. I am less talented at picking short-term highs, and often want to exit a position 10 days too soon. To counter these weaknesses, I now like to place an exploratory trade, which I then expand upon within a week. A position entered into five or 10 contracts at a time can be exited five or 10 contracts at a time. This helps me smooth out my tendency to both buy too soon and sell too soon, and also meets my basic (irrational?) desire to trade too much. The moral of the story is that weaknesses, once identified, can be addressed actively.

Nine times out of 10 I trade in Dow 30 stocks. That is, members of the Dow Jones Industrial Average. There are four reasons for this. First, liquidity is very high in these stocks, and that goes hand-in-hand with low T-costs. Second, there is a lot of information about these stocks readily available in the public arena. Third, so many people follow these stocks, that they often get hammered down in price when bad news arrives—creating a buying opportunity. Fourth, I have limited time to trade. I can therefore follow only a limited group of stocks.

Choose the group of stocks you are most interested in and follow them every day. Do not look only at closing price, but at intraday prices for today and for the last 10 days and daily prices for the last six months and the last year or two. After doing this for the stocks that interest you, focus more seriously on those that pass some sort of filter that is meaningful to you (price has moved more than x percent in the last n days, P/E ratio is below a certain level, etc.). My online brokerage site has free filter tools.

Be aware of exchange holidays, holidays that are not exchange holidays, regulatory meetings (e.g., FOMC meetings), and important days in the lives of the stocks that interest you (e.g., preliminary earnings announcements, dividend payments, etc.). Also, be aware of what price level represents a breakeven, given spreads and commissions, on your existing positions.

When you do settle on a stock, and want to choose an option, use some sort of tool to help you (like my spreadsheet trading tool discussed in section 10.3). Be sure to build a buffer zone into the horizon of your options in case your view is correct, but not realized until a month after your expectation. There is nothing worse that having your options expire worthless two weeks before a massive price spike that would have been in your favor.

Efficient markets be damned! I often watch the markets during the trading day. When a piece of good news arrives about a stock, there is often an almost immediate pop upwards in price as those folks watching the market adjust for it.

However, lots of people get their market news from PBS's *Nightly Business Review*, or the *Wall Street Journal*, or *Morning Business Report*, or some Web site that is updated overnight. So, sure enough, that stock rises the next day when the "second crowd" want to buy. This one-day lag in the reaction to news is something I see over and over again. What should you do about it? Well, if the second crowd cause the stock to open higher the next day, you already missed both the first reaction and the jump at the open, so you may want to find something else to trade. There is, however, often a slower movement as the second crowd trickle their trades in during the course of the day. It pays to watch stocks during the day and get trades off well before the close.

I am almost always on the long side only; that is where my strengths lie. It also means that I am not swimming against the current, and I have no obligation to repay dividends—as short sellers must do. Perhaps it is because the market's reactions are so rapid on the short side that it is easier to trade the long side. This may also explain why people are so much more likely to be long than short, even when the market is diving. Do I risk the broad market swamping my individual stock view? Yes, but as time passes I have realized that my individual stock views are almost always tied into my broad market view. So, I do not place an unhedged bullish trade on an individual stock if I think the broad market is going to sink during my holding period. Two related and overlapping points: First, if you are in the market all the time, then a market-neutral stance can make sense, because you are riding with the ups and downs of the broad market; second, most of my trades are closed out well within 30 days. If you are forecasting big moves for individual stocks at very short horizons, then a market-neutral approach is not necessary. This is, of course, exactly the situation that speculative options are designed for.

For every 10 trades I put on, seven are profitable, one breaks even, one is un-profitable, and the remaining one is like watching a submarine movie: For example, I am long, and the captain of the boat gives the order "Crash Dive! Dive! Dive! Dive!"; my position sinks like a stone and I liquidate immediately. My failure is usually because news arrives in the public arena that damns the stock to hell and back. Knowing the release date for important information (e.g., preliminary earnings) gives me an opportunity to protect myself from news whose timing is known in advance, but there is little I can do about surprise announcements.

If you work for a capital markets firm, you are almost certainly subject to compliance restrictions. My British employer required that UK employees obtain explicit permission to trade before entering any position, that they hold stock for 30 days before selling, and that they not trade options without explicit permission from the UK corporate head. In the US office, it was a 60-day holding period. Clearly, this stifles any short-term or options trading strategy.

A final curious observation is that the proximity of Indiana University (IU) to Chicago meant that my IU students often equated "trading" with "options trading" or "futures trading." They seemed to be strangely unaware that securities trading jobs exist outside of options and futures.

Paratrading

Suppose I find a \$30 stock that I think will rise 30% in the next two months. I know that I will be watching the stock closely over this time period. I also know that during this two-month period there will be half-a-dozen days when my close attention reveals to me that the stock is going to fall 50 cents to a dollar over the next 24 hours followed by a slow climb back up (often this fall comes as a next-day reversal after a rapid rise).

T-costs for round-trip options trades are high—often 10 times what you see in the stock. If I buy options to reflect my long-term (i.e., two-month) view that the stock is going up, T-costs mean that it does not pay to sell the options before a fall and buy them back more cheaply afterward. So, rather than just buying call options, I often buy call options and stock simultaneously. When I forecast a sudden stock price drop in the short term, I continue to hold my options, but I sell my stock. I usually buy the stock back within 48 hours for 50 cents to a dollar less than I sold it. I call this "paratrading." I might do this five times during a two-month option-holding period. Of course, if you are no good at short-term trade timing, then this is a useless strategy for you.

At first glance, holding the stock side-by-side with the options offsets the leverage in my options position and undermines the motivation for holding options as opposed to stock in the first place. Closer inspection reveals, however, that what I am actually doing by trading in and out of the stock is leveraging the information flow that my close examination of the stock generates in support of my options position. This allows me to employ my short-term trade timing skills without being eaten alive by the T-costs of the options.

By moving out of the stock before a fall, and back into it at lower levels, I am not holding the stock continuously, and I am not deleveraging my options position. I am, in fact, leveraging up my options position to squeeze more juice out of it over a limited time horizon. The final payoff to my paratrading may be the same as if I had used a more highly levered option to start with, but the intermediate portfolio values when paratrading are much less volatile.

Paratrading achieves several aims: First, while holding a long-term (e.g., a two-month) bullish view reflected in my options positions, my equity trade timing allows me to profit from short-term bearish moves without being eaten alive by options T-costs. Second, the investment of time I make in following the stock on a day-to-day basis really only allows me to pick a good exit point as far as the options are concerned. Using my investment of time to paratrade in and out of the stock avoids wastage of equity intelligence. Third, and not least, short-term trade timing meets my desire to trade frequently.

One variation on paratrading is that if I have a long-term bullish view on a stock, for example, but my confidence is not yet high enough to buy options, then I can enter a 100% equity position and wait until my confidence builds; at which point, I liquidate some or all of the equity position and buy options.[19] This variation on

---

[19]Be sure you understand the wash sale rules before attempting this sort of trade; see page 182.

paratrading has the added benefit that when it comes time to swap out of the stock and into the option, intraday timing is not very important. For example, if the stock just shot up, the stock position you liquidate recoups part of the opportunity cost of having not yet bought the call option. This is particularly useful if you are trading US stocks from outside the US (because it reduces the importance of trade timing across time zones).

10.4.4 Orders and Executions

Educate yourself in the different types of orders. I suggest the glossary page at your online brokerage or a simple financial information Web site. Be aware of the following:

- A market order is executed at whatever price it hits the spread, and may even get a chance for price improvement. There is no assurance, however, that a market order will hit the most recently quoted bid or ask. Sometimes, I use a limit order with limit price equal to current bid or ask, so that I know that I will get the price I want or not get my order filled at all.

- A stop order is supposed to bail you out of a losing position. It is triggered the first time a trade goes off at your stop price. A stop order does not guarantee order execution at or near the stop price. Once activated, your stop order becomes a market order that competes with all market orders. There are stop limit orders, but they are less likely to get filled.

- A stop loss sell order on an option does not necessarily get triggered when the bid drops to or below the stop price. If no one is trading the option, then no trades are happening, and the order will likely not be triggered simply by the moving quote. That is a serious concern in less liquid options.

- If you are shorting stock, be aware that it can take longer to get the fill than going long because of possible uptick rules (see the footnote on page 177).

- Suppose you are long a stock at \$20. Suppose you are happy to sell and take the profit at \$25, but also want to sell and stop your losses at \$15. Ideally, you place a stop order at \$15, and a simultaneous limit sell at \$25. Unfortunately, it does not work that way. If the stock shoots up over \$25 and falls back below \$15, you are oversold. As such, your broker does not let you place these trades simultaneously.

- I like limit orders. They can be slightly more costly to place than market orders, but they take care of trade timing for me at a fixed price (with the risk, of course, that they are not executed). For example, if I see an option whiplashing up and down in price, and I am happy to buy at \$4, then I leave a limit order to buy in place at \$4. I have even had limit orders hit when I was asleep in a different country and would otherwise have missed a one-off intraday price spike.

10.4.5   Market Views and Opinions

Market views come from experience and two forms of intelligence: access to public information that helps you win the battle and your ability to think and reason to process that information. How you form market views is a very personal exercise. It is different for everyone, and most individual investors are wrong most of the time. I can give you advice, but whether it is useful to you depends upon where your strengths lie.

I have two fundamental philosophies for trading US equities and equity options. My first philosophy is that US investors overreact. This means that there are temporary imbalances in supply and demand for equity that lead to stock prices that are unrealistically high or unrealistically low. I think investors overreact more frequently on the downside than on the upside. I also think that stocks that are hammered down too far in price will reliably come back up at a slow pace, but over a short period of time, and that stocks that are overpriced can remain overpriced for extended periods, but will often drop like a rock when they do correct. In my view, the frequency of over-pessimistic price drops and the pace, reliability, and predictability of the following price appreciation make underpriced stocks more suitable for options trading than overpriced stocks.

My second philosophy is that the US market for corporate control is severe and uncompromising. When an otherwise good US company has a poor quarter due to some temporary influence, the price often gets hammered far below where it should be. The management know that shareholders can vote them out, and they have an extremely strong incentive to cut costs, look for new sources of revenue, increase productivity, increase market share, etc.—or lose their jobs. The end result is that I often see companies with good profit margins, a strong core business, a strong brand name, and extremely good prospects whose stock price has fallen 10–50% in a short period of time because of a poor quarter. Within three months, they announce a strategy for recovery and the stock price jumps back to where it was.

10.4.6   The Deathly Slow Crawl

You buy options at the ask and sell them at the bid; so, even if you are right on the direction of the stock, it can take some time before an option position is profitable. For example, suppose the quoted bid-ask spread on a call option is $5.10–$5.30, and you submit a market order to buy one contract. Assume your order actually gets filled at $5.35, either because another order took out the size available at the ask and the quote moved before your order arrived, or because your quotes were stale when you placed the order, or because of price slippage. Ignoring commissions, you have to wait for the bid to move from $5.10 up above $5.35 before you can sell at a profit. Assume you would be happy to sell at $7.50 for a 40% gain.

Suppose good news arrives that drives up the stock price. Well, the news may increase uncertainty also, and the option spreads may widen, so that the spread may move to $5.20–$5.50. You still cannot sell at a profit. The spreads move around a lot during the day, but the next day you might see $5.25–$5.60 and still not be able to sell at a profit. The next day you might see a quote of $5.40–$5.60 that jumps back down to $5.30–$5.50 by day's end. After a week, you might see a high of $7.50–$7.70 that falls back to $6.80–$7.00 by day's end. You wanted to sell at $7.50 and could have done so if you had placed a limit order to sell at $7.50 that was good until cancelled. You place your limit order now, but the next day the quote falls to $6.20–$6.50. It takes another week for the bid to get back up to $7.50 when, unbeknownst to you, your limit order takes you out of your position while you are on the golf course. You check into the market the next morning and are excited to see your option trading at $9.50–$9.80, but then you realize that you already sold for $200 less.

Compared to the stock, this deathly slow crawl of the option spread into profitable territory can take what seems like an eternity. Option spreads are so wide that it is very hard, for example, to buy and sell an option profitably during the day. For a stock, however, it is much easier to do a profitable round-trip trade within the day.

10.5   Trading Tools: Greeks 103

The Greeks (delta, gamma, theta, and vega) are not some academic head-in-the-clouds, ivory-tower concept. They are real measures of your exposure to gain and loss. In addition to using a spreadsheet trading tool to help choose options positions, I always think about delta, gamma, and theta, and less often about vega. I have in my mind figures 3.3 and 3.4 (pp59–60): The slope (delta) tells me what I make per dollar change in the underlying; the curvature (gamma) tells me how delta changes and is typically directly related to the magnitude of time decay (i.e., of theta). You can explore the properties of delta, gamma, and theta using the spreadsheet Greeks tool that accompanies this book; see section 10.3 for details. I am not a volatility trader,[20] so I do not often worry about sensitivity to volatility (vega). The exception is that if a stock has just crashed, for example, and I think it is underpriced, I will wait for volatility to die down before entering a bullish position, especially one that is very sensitive to volatility (like LEAPS). Conversely, if I am in a position that is sensitive to volatility, and volatility has just spiked in my favor, I do not hesitate to liquidate if I think I can lock in a gain and reenter the position after normalcy is resumed.

10.6   Spread Positions and Other Strategies

There exist many option spreads and other positions. A spread position is typically composed of at least one long option and at least one short option. Many other popular strategies exist that are not spreads. The component option positions used to establish the strategy are often referred to as the "legs" of the strategy. The

---

[20]Volatility traders often use delta-neutral (or close to it) positions like straddles or strangles; these positions are of no use to me. Rather, I take directional bets.

organized exchanges give away free booklets/brochures that detail several dozen of the most popular option combinations.[21] The payoff to a "bull spread" is shown in figure 10.3.

Often the same essential payoff structure can be achieved in multiple ways (due to put-call parity): One choice will generate a cash flow up front (typically retained for margin purposes); the other will cost money up front. It follows that if you are are entering one of these positions, your broker may ask if you want to place a specific "net credit" or "net debit" order; i.e., one that generates a specific amount of money up front, or one that costs a specific amount of money up front (analogous to a limit order).

> **Exercise:** How can you construct a bull spread using puts? How does the payoff diagram differ from figure 10.3?

Option values are additive (the value of a portfolio of options is the sum of the value of the component parts, appropriately signed for long or short positions). All of the foregoing analysis of individual option positions carries over directly to combinations. The only exceptions I can think of are that the options market maker will probably charge a slightly smaller spread for an option position than the sum of the spreads for the component parts, especially if the position involves options that offset to some extent or if it is in large volume (several round lots). If you look at quoted spreads on the individual options, then the sum of those is at least a rough upper bound on what you will pay.

The terms "vertical," "horizontal," and "diagonal" as applied to spread positions are a holdover from the days when options were quoted in a grid with different maturities along the horizontal and different strikes down the vertical.

Vertical spreads use different-strike, same-maturity options. For example, bull and bear spreads are the most popular trades for bulls and bears (see figure 10.3). Calendar (or "time" or "horizontal") spreads use same-strike options of different maturities. For example, you might buy a long maturity option and sell a short maturity option (either both calls or both puts). The higher (alternatively lower) the strike, the more bullish (alternatively bearish) is the position. A "reverse calendar spread" buys the short maturity option and sells the long maturity option. Diagonal spreads use options with different strikes and different maturities.

A final note: If you are a novice who is trading option combinations, you may be tempted to try to enter a position that uses put-call parity or one of the restrictions from chapter 3 to lock in a relative mispricing that seems to exist within the quotes from the exchange floor. Any novice trader who tries to lock in some apparent mispricing on the exchange floor is almost certainly doomed. If you think there is a relative mispricing, then either you read the quotes incorrectly, or your quotes are

---

[21]Some booklets/brochures can be downloaded for free from the education/learning section of the exchanges' Web sites (www.cboe.com, www.cme.com, www.cbot.com), or by calling their toll-free number. The information for spread positions in futures options applies equally well to equity options.

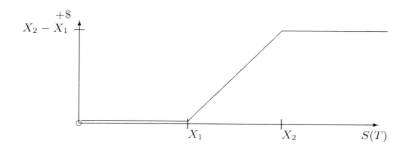

Figure 10.3: Bull Spread (Calls): Terminal Payoff

Note: This plot is of terminal (i.e., time-T) dollar payoffs to a bull spread composed of a long call at strike X_1 plus a short call at strike $X_2 > X_1$. The terminal payoff to this bull spread is nowhere negative—in exchange for the up-front cost of entering the position. Note that $X_2 > X_1$ implies the call with strike X_2 is cheaper than the call with strike X_1 (as per the second row in table 3.2 on page 43). The possible profit is bounded above by $X_2 - X_1$ (as per R5 in table 3.3 on page 48); $X_2 - X_1$ is also the vertical distance covered by the payoff diagram. The general shape of the payoff is upward sloping—hence the name "bull spread." Zero payoffs are drawn here as very slightly different from zero, so that they can be seen.

stale, or the pit traders know that the stock is about to pay a big dividend that you do not know about, or go bankrupt, or something else. The people in the pits are extremely astute. There is no way that you will "take them to the cleaners." Even if there is a mispricing, when you go to place your spread, the market maker will probably quote a price for the spread as a whole, not the individual legs, and his or her spread will not allow for you to exploit a mispricing. On top of that, by the time you get the different legs of the trade done, price slippage means that any mispricing, if it ever existed, will be gone.

Appendix A

HP Source Code

The Hewlett Packard (HP) 17B, 19B, and 12C handheld business calculators provide a convenient level of programming. The HP17B/HP19B Equation Solver is especially user-friendly. This appendix contains option pricing source code for the HP17B, HP19B, and HP12C.

A.1 HP17B/HP19B Black-Scholes

The Black-Scholes European-style call and put option pricing formulae for a stock that pays no dividends are given in equations 8.17 and 8.18 on page 120. In those equations, r is the instantaneous risk-free rate per unit time, σ is the instantaneous annualized standard deviation of continuously compounded returns on the stock, $S(t)$ is the observed stock price at time t, X is the strike price, the call option matures at time T, the time to maturity is $T-t$, and $N(\cdot)$ is the standard normal cdf.

Story: Late one winter's evening at MIT (1994 I think), I was helping Nobel Prize winner Franco Modigliani operate our photocopier. We somehow got onto the topic of the Crash of 1987 and he said "Yes, that is when I made all my money." He said he had been watching the market and, thinking it overvalued, he had bought out-of-the-money index puts (presumably S&P500 index options at that time). He said he made a bundle. He had tried it several times since then without success. At my office doorway another time, he told me that when pronouncing his name I should "drop the 'g'—it's the mark of a true Italian"—and that is how he pronounced it.

Taken from "Heard on The Street: Quantitative Questions from Wall Street Job Interviews," ©2008 Timothy Falcon Crack. See advertisement on last page of this book.

My HP17B call pricing source code appears in table A.1. It uses S, X, R, SIG, and TAU to denote $S(t)$, X, r, σ, and $T-t$, respectively. The terms D1, D2, ND1, and ND2 denote d_1, d_2, $N(d_1)$, and $N(d_2)$, respectively. The "∧" character is obtained by using the regular y^x button on the keypad, or as one of the "other" characters available on the "alpha" menu on the HP17B; the "∼" character is also one of the "other" characters available on the "alpha" menu on the HP17B; there really are blank spaces in "S(ND1) OR S(ND2)" and similarly phrased terms; and each line of the equation follows from the previous one without interruption.

I have adapted a polynomial approximation to the cumulative standard normal from Hull (2000, p252). Hull, in turn, takes the approximation from Abramowitz and Stegun (1972). My version, in equation A.1, is equivalent mathematically to Hull's, but I have reformulated it so that it can be entered into the Equation Solver as a single equation:

$$N(x) = \frac{1}{2} + \text{sgn}(x) \left[\frac{1}{2} - \frac{e^{-\frac{1}{2}x^2}}{\sqrt{2\pi}} \left(t_1 f + t_2 f^2 + t_3 f^3 + t_4 f^4 + t_5 f^5 \right) \right] \quad (A.1)$$

$$\text{sgn}(x) \equiv \begin{cases} 1; & \text{if } x > 0, \\ -1; & \text{if } x < 0, \\ 0; & \text{if } x = 0, \end{cases}$$

$$f \equiv \frac{1}{1 + g \cdot |x|}$$

$$t_1 = 0.319381530,$$
$$t_2 = -0.356563782,$$
$$t_3 = 1.781477937,$$
$$t_4 = -1.821255978,$$
$$t_5 = 1.330274429,$$
$$g = 0.2316419.$$

The order in which variables first appear in the source code determines the order in which they appear on the HP menu. In some places, my source code appears convoluted so as to produce a menu system that is logically ordered.[1]

The call pricing code takes about 20 seconds to verify, but executes quickly.[2] The order of evaluation of terms is important. You must first input S, X, R, SIG, and TAU. You then press the MORE button and press D1, D2, ND1, and ND2 in that order (the order in which they appear on the menu). You cannot, for example, calculate $N(d_1)$ without first calculating d_1. You may then press CALL.[3] You can test my HP17B code with the following example: S=50, X=45, R=0.02, SIG=0.30, and TAU=0.75 imply D1=0.5932, D2=0.3334, ND1=0.7235, ND2=0.6306, and CALL=8.2201.

One advantage of my source code is that, as part of the calculation, the formula gives the values of the option's delta, ND1, and the risk-neutral probability of finishing in-the-money, ND2. One disadvantage of my source code is that you cannot

---

[1]Tony Hutchins has suggested to me a nice trick for avoiding this convolution: Begin the code with something trivial like ...:0×(S+X+R+SIG+TAU)... to set the order of the menu variables (personal communication, August 28, 2003).

[2]If you want to see how they evaluated the Black-Scholes formula many years ago, see the option pricing "nomogram" in Sharpe (1978, pp377–378). It involves the drawing of vertical and horizontal lines and interpolation on a preprinted chart.

[3]My Black-Scholes call pricing source code has been independently verified by many others. If you type it all in, and your HP tells you that the equation is invalid, then check your typing slowly and carefully; do not waste time by deleting it and starting again.

Table A.1: HP17B/HP19B Black-Scholes Call Code

```
BLACK~SCHOLES~CALL:IF(S(D1) OR S(D2):IF(S(D1):(LN(S÷X)
+(R+0.5×(SIG∧2))×(TAU))÷(SIG×SQRT(TAU))-D1:D2-(D1-(SIG×
SQRT(TAU)))):IF(S(ND1) OR S(ND2):IF(S(ND1):ND1-(0.5+SGN(D1
)×(0.5-((1÷SQRT(2×PI))×EXP(-0.5×D1∧2)×(0.319381530×(1÷
(1+0.2316419×ABS(D1)))-0.356563782×(1÷(1+0.2316419×ABS(D
1)))∧2+1.781477937×(1÷(1+0.2316419×ABS(D1)))∧3-1.8212559
78×(1÷(1+0.2316419×ABS(D1)))∧4+1.330274429×(1÷(1+0.2316
419×ABS(D1)))∧5)))):ND2-(0.5+SGN(D2)×(0.5-(1÷SQRT(2×PI))
×EXP(-0.5×D2∧2)×(0.319381530×(1÷(1+0.2316419×ABS(D2)))-
0.356563782×(1÷(1+0.2316419×ABS(D2)))∧2+1.781477937×(1÷
(1+0.2316419×ABS(D2)))∧3-1.821255978×(1÷(1+0.2316419×ABS
(D2)))∧4+1.330274429×(1÷(1+0.2316419×ABS(D2)))∧5)))):CAL
L-(S×ND1-EXP(-R×TAU)×X×ND2)))
```

Note: This code is for the HP17B or HP19B, but also works on the HP17BII, and HP19BII. Hutchins (2003) states that my code also works on the HP200LX. Hutchins (2003) supplies Black-Scholes pricing code for the HP17BII that is shorter and more versatile than my code, but his code uses the newer "G(·)," and "L(·)" functions, and therefore does not run on the original HP17B. Hutchins' code does, however, run on the HP19B which, although not documented in the manual, is the first HP business calculator to recognize the "G(·)," and "L(·)" functions.

solve directly for implied volatility. You can, however, quickly solve for the implied volatility σ indirectly as follows. Let "c" denote the actual call value. Let "$\hat{\sigma}$" be an initial guess of the implied volatility. Calculate $c(\hat{\sigma})$ using your HP. Now update your guess for the implied volatility using the assignment: $\hat{\sigma}' = \hat{\sigma}c/c(\hat{\sigma})$, and repeat this iterative updating until c and $c(\hat{\sigma})$ are as close as you want.

To adjust the European call pricing formula for continuous dividends (either for equity or for FX), we simply replace $S(t)$ by $S(t)e^{-\rho(T-t)}$ throughout the equation, where ρ is the rate of dividends per unit time. This corresponds to replacing S by S×EXP(-RHO×(TAU)) throughout the source code (although some algebraic simplification is possible). You can, alternatively, use the source code as it stands simply by entering the numerical value for $S(t)e^{-\rho(T-t)}$ in place of $S(t)$.

The source code for the European-style put appears in table A.2. Once both the put and call valuation formulae coexist in the Equation Solver, all variables are common to registers in both equations and need not be re-entered. To value the put, you value the call, exit the call valuation equation, enter the put valuation equation, and press the PUT button.[4] This yields 2.5502 as the put price using the numbers

---

[4]To save time, you can use the call equation to value the put. Change the sign of the volatility by pressing RCL, SIG, +/-, and SIG. Then press D1, D2, ND1, ND2, and CALL. The answer is the negative of the put price (Haug [2007, p11]). Alternatively, after calculating d_1 and d_2, press RCL, D1, +/-,

Table A.2: HP17B/HP19B Black-Scholes Put Code

```
BLACK~SCHOLES~PUT:PUT-CALL=-S+X×EXP(-R×TAU)
```

Note: This code is for the HP17B or HP19B, but also works on the HP17BII and HP19BII. It runs side-by-side with the call pricing code in table A.1. The put price is derived from the call price using the put-call parity relationship without dividends.

from the call price calculation.

In the special case where dividends are paid at a continuous rate ρ per unit time, the present value of dividends to be paid prior to the maturity of the option is just $S(t) \times (1 - e^{-\rho(T-t)})$. It follows that the put-call parity relationship with continuous dividends at rate ρ per unit time is $S(t)e^{-\rho(T-t)} + p(t) = c(t) + Xe^{-r(T-t)}$. To adjust the European put pricing source code for continuous dividends, you replace S by S×EXP(-RHO×(TAU)) in both the call and put pricing source code—as mentioned earlier.

A.2 HP12C Black-Scholes

Tony Hutchins has kindly given permission for me to reproduce his HP12C program for calculating Black-Scholes option prices (Hutchins [2003]); it is reproduced here in table A.3. The program is 99 lines. If using the HP12C Platinum, it must be in RPN mode. The program uses the following financial registers: n: $T - t$, i: $r \times 100$, PV: S, PMT: $\sigma \times 100$, and FV: X.

The storage registers R0, R1, and R2 are not used; R3 ends up with $N(d_1)$ (the call delta); R4 ends up with the put value; R5 ends up with the call value; R6 ends up with $PV(X)N(d_2)$. The put delta may be obtained as "RCL 3 1 −" (that is, $-N(-d_1) = N(d_1) - 1$). The final stack registers are as follows: T: 0; Z: d_1; Y: put value; X: call value (you can cycle through the four stack registers using the "R↓" key).

You can test the Black-Scholes HP12C program using the key strokes in table A.4. The input values in table A.4 are the same as those used to test the HP17B/HP19B code in section A.1, but the answers for the option prices differ slightly because different approximations are used here.

Tony Hutchins' approximation for $N(\cdot)$ uses his own clever approximation to the upper-tail probability of a standard normal (UTPN) and is given in equation A.2 (Hutchins [2003]):

$$N(x) = \begin{cases} UTPN(-x) & \text{for } x < 0, \\ 1 - UTPN(x) & \text{for } x \geq 0, \end{cases} \tag{A.2}$$

and D1 to replace d_1 by $-d_1$. Now do the same for d_2, and then press the ND1 and ND2 buttons. Now press the CALL button to get the negative of the put price.

where $\mathrm{UTPN}(x) \equiv e^{-\frac{1}{2}x^2} u(x)[(187 \cdot u(x) - 24) \cdot u(x) + 87] \times 0.002$

and $u(x) \equiv \dfrac{1}{1 + \frac{|x|}{3.006}}$.

Table A.3: HP12C Black-Scholes Call and Put Code

Key Strokes		Display	Comments
f	P/R	00-	start with line 00 showing
RCL	n	01- 45 11	get $(T-t)$ (only the once)
RCL	i	02- 45 12	get $r\%$ (only the once)
%		03- 25	$r \cdot (T-t)$
CHS		04- 16	
g	e^x	05- 43 22	
RCL	FV	06- 45 15	get X (only the once)
$\times$		07- 20	
STO	4	08- 44 4	R4 $= PV(X)$
$x \lessgtr y$		09- 34	$T-t$ again
g	SQRT	10- 43 21	
RCL	PMT	11- 45 14	get $\sigma\%$ (only the once)
%		12- 25	$\sigma\sqrt{T-t}$
STO	3	13- 44 3	temporary until line 26
RCL	PV	14- 45 13	get S (again at line 91)
RCL	4	15 45 4	
$\div$		16- 10	
g	LN	17- 43 23	$\ln[S/PV(X)]$
$x \lessgtr y$		18- 34	$\sigma\sqrt{T-t}$
$\div$		19- 10	$\ln[S/PV(X)]/[\sigma\sqrt{T-t}]$
g	LSTX	20- 43 36	$\sigma\sqrt{T-t}$ again
2		21- 2	
STO	5	22- 44 5	R5 $= 2$, just has to be nonzero
$\div$		23- 10	to flag the first pass
+		24- 40	$d_1 = \ln[S/PV(X)]/[\sigma\sqrt{T-t}] + [\sigma\sqrt{T-t}]/2$
STO	6	25- 44 6	R6 $= d_1$
RCL	3	26 45 3	
$-$		27- 30	$d_2 = d_1 - \sigma\sqrt{T-t}$
STO	3	28- 44 3	Store $x = d_j$ on $(3-j)^{th}$ pass, for reuse at line 65
ENTER		29- 36	
$\times$		30- 20	d_j^2
g	SQRT	31- 43 21	abs(d_j)
g	LSTX	32- 43 36	d_j^2 NB: stack is enabled
2		33- 2	
$\div$		34- 10	
CHS		35- 16	
g	e^x	36- 43 22	$\exp[(-d_j^2)/2]$
$x \lessgtr y$		37- 34	abs(d_j) NB: stack is enabled
3		38- 3	Next 10 lines construct:
.		39- 48	u (defined below)
0		40- 0	
0		41- 0	
6		42- 6	
$\div$		43- 10	
1		44- 1	

Table A.3: continued...

Key Strokes		Display	Comments
+		45- 40	
$1/x$		46- 22	$u = 1/(1 + \text{abs}(d_j)/3.006)$
$\times$		47- 20	$\exp(-d_j^2/2) \cdot u$
g	LSTX	48- 43 36	Place 2 copies of u back in
g	LSTX	49- 43 36	an enabled stack
1		50- 1	Next 15 lines construct:
8		51- 8	$\exp(-d_j^2/2) \cdot u \cdot [(187u - 24) \cdot u + 87] \times 0.002$
7		52- 7	
$\times$		53- 20	
2		54- 2	
4		55- 4	
$-$		56- 30	
$\times$		57- 20	
8		58- 8	
7		59- 7	
+		60- 40	
$\times$		61- 20	
.		62- 48	This multiplies by 0.002 and
2		63- 2	completes the calculation of
%		64- 25	UTPN[abs(d_j)]
RCL	3	65- 45 3	Bring back d_j
$x \lessgtr y$		66- 34	
STO	3	67- 44 3	Store the UTPN[abs(d_j)]
CLX		68- 35	If $d_2 \leq 0$ we have $N(d_j)$
$x \lessgtr y$		69- 34	already,
g	$x \leq y$	70- 43 34	and we jump to the last
g	GTO 77	71- 43,33 77	section
1		72- 1	otherwise, $N(d_j) = 1 - \text{UTPN}(d_j)$
STO	$-$ 3	73- 44 30 3	
CHS		74- 16	
STO	$\times$ 3	75- 44 20 3	R3= alternate $N(d_j)$
$x \lessgtr y$		76- 34	preserves d_1 in stack at end
RCL	5	77- 45 5	Loop 'flag'
g	$x = 0$	78- 43 35	
g	GTO 89	79- 43,33 89	Second pass goes to 89
RCL	6	80- 45 6	Recall d_1 (R6 gets re-used)
RCL	3	81- 45 3	First pass now processes $N(d_2)$
RCL	4	82- 45 4	Recall $PV(X)$ from 1st section
$\times$		83- 20	
STO	6	84- 44 6	R6=$PV(X)N(d_2)$
CLX		85- 35	a zero in R5
STO	5	86- 44 5	signifies second pass.
$x \lessgtr y$		87- 34	Bring back d_1 and off we go ...
g	GTO 28	88- 43,33 28	back to line 28, then back here
$x \lessgtr y$		89- 34	ensures d_1 in the 'Z' register at end
RCL	3	90- 45 3	Processing of $N(d_1)$ etc.
RCL	PV	91- 45 13	second recall of S
STO	$-$ 4	92- 44 30 4	R4= $PV(X) - S$
$\times$		93- 20	$S \cdot N(d_1)$
RCL	6	94- 45 6	$PV(X) \cdot N(d_2)$
$-$		95- 30	This is the Call Value

Table A.3: continued...

Key Strokes		Display	Comments
STO	+ 4	96- 44 40 4	R4 = Put value
RCL	4	97- 45 4	Put Value to stack
$x \lessgtr y$		98- 34	Leave Call Value displayed
STO	5	99- 44 5	R5= Call value (backup)
f	P/R		done

Note: This 99-line program for the HP12C allows you to calculate Black-Scholes call and put prices without dividends. The approximation is quite accurate. The code uses "$r\%$" and "$\sigma\%$," so, for example, $r = 0.02$ implies that $r\% = 2$, and $\sigma = 0.30$ implies $\sigma\% = 30$. If you have an HP12C Platinum, note that at lines 71, 79, and 88 you need to precede the line number with a zero (e.g., line 71 becomes: g GTO 077) because the Platinum uses three digits for line numbers. Also note that the "Display" differs slightly on the 12C Platinum and that you have to have the machine in RPN, not ALG, before entering the code. Source: Hutchins (2003), with permission and slight amendment.

Table A.4: HP12C Black-Scholes Call and Put Code: Example

Key Strokes		Display	Comments
f	4	not blank	sets 'FIX 4' display
0.75	n	0.7500	n=0.75 ($=T-t$)
2	i	2.0000	i=2 ($=r \times 100$)
50	PV	50.0000	PV=50 ($=S$)
30	PMT	30.0000	PMT=30 ($= \sigma \times 100$)
45	FV	45.0000	FV=45 ($=X$)
R/S		running	wait 12 seconds
		8.2199	call value
$x \lessgtr y$		2.5500	put value

Note: After entering the Black-Scholes program in table A.3, you can use these key strokes to confirm that you have it correct. Source: Hutchins (2003), with considerable amendment.

A.3 HP17B/HP19B Binomial Pricing

The binomial option pricing model of chapter 6 (p89) can be evaluated on the HP17B and HP19B handheld calculators. This makes sense, however, only for pedagogical examples where the binomial tree has few time steps; beyond that, the repetitive nature of the pricing method makes practical implementation on the HP17B or HP19B pointless.

Binomial pricing relies on replication. If you are to replicate the payoffs to the option by trading in the stock and the bond, you need to buy Δ units of stock and lend B dollars (with Δ and B given by equations 6.1 and 6.2, respectively). This leads to equations 6.5 and 6.6 that give the current option price V as a function of

Table A.5: HP17B/HP19B Lattice/Binomial Code

```
    V   =  ((VU-VD)  ×  R+U×VD-D×VU)÷(R×(U-D))
DELTA   =  (VU-VD)÷((U-D)×S)
    B   =  (-(VU-VD)+((U-1)×VD)-((D-1)×VU))÷(R×(U-D))
```

Note: This code is for the HP17B or HP19B, but also works on the HP17BII and HP19BII. The three equations correspond to equations 6.5, 6.1, and 6.2, respectively. Note that $R= e^{-r(\Delta t)}$. Judicious use of the HP memories allows the user to work backwards very swiftly through a small multi-period tree to find the initial value.

u, d, V_u, V_d, r, and Δt, where u and d are multiplicative stock price growth factors; V_u is the value of the option next period if the stock price increases from S to $S \times u$; V_d is the value of the option next period if the stock price decreases from S to $S \times d$; r is the continuously compounded risk-free interest rate; and Δt is the length of the time step.

Equations for V, Δ, and B appear in table A.5. The variables are self-explanatory, except for R, which is given by $R= e^{-r(\Delta t)}$. The source code is convoluted so as to produce a logical ordering of variables in the HP menu.

A.4   An HP17B/HP19B Warning

I left my HP17B in my desk for a month, and the batteries died. Even with new batteries, I was unable to get any response whatsoever using either of the two reset commands (CLR+THIRD MENU KEY, or CLR+FIRST MENU KEY+SIXTH MENU KEY). Touching the battery contacts simultaneously with a coin produced some signs of life, but only in the form of meaningless characters. The first reset command above, tried again, produced no change. The second reset command above, tried again, brought my HP17B back to life at the cost of losing continuous memory. Dropping your HP can also reset the memory. If you let your batteries die, these steps may save your repair costs.

References

Abramowitz, Milton and Irene A. Stegun, (editors), 1972, *Handbook of Mathematical Functions and Formulas, Graphs and Mathematical Tables*, United States Department of Commerce, National Bureau of Standards, Applied Mathematics Series, 55 (December) Tenth Printing since 1964.

Arnold, Tom and Timothy Falcon Crack, 2003, "Option Pricing in the Real World: A Generalized Binomial Model With Applications to Real Options," Working Paper, Available at SSRN: http://ssrn.com/abstract=240554, (April 15), 56pp.

Arnold, Tom, Timothy Falcon Crack, and Adam Schwartz, 2008, "Inferring Risk-Averse Probability Distributions From Option Prices using Implied Binomial Trees," Working Paper, Available at SSRN: http://ssrn.com/abstract=749904, (February 12), 81pp.

Anthony, Robert H., 1999, *Essentials of Accounting*, Sixth Edition, Addison-Wesley: Reading, Mass.

Bachelier, Louis, 1900, "Théorie de la Spéculation," *Annales de l'Ecole Normale Supéieure*, Series 3, XVII, pp21–86, Gauthier-Villars: Paris. Note that an English translation by A. James Boness appears in Cootner (1964).

Ball, Clifford A. and Walter N. Torous, 1985, "On Jumps in Common Stock Prices and Their Impact on Call Option Pricing," *The Journal of Finance*, Vol 40 No 1, (March), pp155–173.

Barone-Adesi, G. and Robert Whaley, 1987, "Efficient Analytic Approximation of American Option Values," *The Journal of Finance*, Vol 42 No 2, (June), pp301–320.

Baxter, Martin and Andrew Rennie, 1996, *Financial Calculus*, Cambridge University Press: Cambridge, England.

Biger, Nahum and John Hull, 1983, "The Valuation of Currency Options," *Financial Management*, Vol 12 No 1, (Spring), pp24–28.

Black, Fischer, 1975, "Fact and Fantasy in the Use of Options," *The Financial Analysts Journal*, Vol 31 No 4, (July/August), pp36–41, 61–72.

Black, Fischer, 1976a, "Studies of Stock Price Volatility Changes," *Proceedings of the 1976 Business Meeting of the Business and Economic Statistics section of the American Statistical Association*, pp177–181.

Black, Fischer, 1976b, "The Pricing of Commodity Contracts," *The Journal of Financial Economics*, Vol 3 No 1/2, (January/March), pp167–179.

Black, Fischer, 1989, "How We Came Up with the Option Formula," *The Journal of Portfolio Management*, Vol 15 No 2, (Winter), pp4–8.

Black, Fischer and Myron S. Scholes, 1972, "The Valuation of Option Contracts and a Test of Market Efficiency," *The Journal of Finance*, Vol 27 No 2, (May), pp399–417.

Black, Fischer and Myron S. Scholes, 1973, "The Pricing of Options and Corporate Liabilities," *Journal of Political Economy*, Vol 81 No 3, (May/June), pp637–659.

Boyle, Phelim P., 1977, "Options: A Monte Carlo Approach," *The Journal of Financial Economics*, Vol 4 No 3, (May), pp323–338.

Brennan, M. J., and E. S. Schwartz, 1978, "Finite Difference Methods and Jump Processes Arising in the Pricing of Contingent Claims: A Synthesis," *The Journal of Financial and Quantitative Analysis*, Vol 13 No 3, (September), pp461–474.

Brigham, Eugene F., and Louis C. Gapenski, 1985, *Financial Management: Theory and Practice*, Fourth Edition, Dryden Press: Chicago, Ill.

Brown, Robert, 1828, "A Brief Account of Microscopical Observations Made in the Months of June, July, and August, 1827, on the Particles Contained in the Pollen of Plants; and on the General Existence of Active Molecules in Organic and Inorganic Bodies," *The London and Edinburgh Philosophical Magazine and Annals of Philosophy*, Vol 4 No 21, pp161–173.

Chance, Don M., 1994, "Translating the Greek: The Real Meaning of Call Option Derivatives," *The Financial Analysts Journal*, Vol 50 No 4, (July/August), pp43–49.

Chernow, Ron, 1990, *The House of Morgan: An American Banking Dynasty and the Rise of Modern Finance*, Simon and Schuster: New York, N.Y.

Chesney, Marc and Louis Scott, 1989, "Pricing European Currency Options: A Comparison of the Modified Black-Scholes Model and a Random Variance Model," *The Journal of Financial and Quantitative Analysis*, Vol 24 No 3, (September), pp267–284.

Cootner, Paul H., ed., 1964, *The Random Character of Stock Market Prices*, MIT Press: Cambridge, Mass.

Cox, J. C. and S. Ross, 1976, "The Valuation of Options for Alternative Stochastic Processes," *The Journal of Financial Economics*, Vol 3 No 1/2, (January/March), pp145–166.

Cox, J. C., S. Ross, and M. Rubinstein, 1979, "Option Pricing: A Simplified Approach," *The Journal of Financial Economics*, Vol 7 No 3, (September), pp229–263.

Cox, J. C. and Mark Rubinstein, 1985, *Options Markets*, Prentice-Hall: Englewood Cliffs, NJ.

Crack, Timothy Falcon, 1997, *Derivatives Securities Pricing*, Course Notes, Indiana University.

Crack, Timothy Falcon, 1999, "A Classic Case of Data Snooping for Classroom Discussion," *The Journal of Financial Education*, Vol 25 (Fall), pp92–97.

Crack, Timothy Falcon, 2008, *Heard on The Street: Quantitative Questions from Wall Street Job Interviews*, 11th Edition. See www.InvestmentBankingJobInterviews.com and the advertisement on the last page of this book, for details.

D'Avolio, Gene, 2002, "The Market for Borrowing Stock," *The Journal of Financial Economics*, Vol 66 No 2–3, (November), pp271–306.

Derman, Emanuel and Iraj Kani, 1994, "The Volatility Smile and its Implied Tree," *Goldman Sachs Quantitative Strategies Research Notes*, Goldman, Sachs (January).

Detemple, Jerome B., 2001, "American Options: Symmetry Properties," in J. Cvitanic, E. Jouini, M. Musiela (editors). *Handbook in Mathematical Finance: Topics in Option Pricing, Interest Rates and Risk Management*, Cambridge University Press: Cambridge, U.K., pp67–104. Note that a CERANO working paper version appears in 1999.

Einstein, A., 1905, "Über die von der molekularkinetischen Theorie der Wärme geforderte Bewegung von in ruhenden Flüssigkeiten suspendierten Teilchen" (On the Molecular Kinetic Theory of the Heat-Generated Motion of Particles Suspended in Fluid), *Annalen der Physik*, Series 4, Vol 17, pp549–560.

Evans, Merran, Nicholas Hastings, and Brian Peacock, 1993, *Statistical Distributions*, Second Edition, John Wiley and Sons: New York, N.Y.

Farlow, Stanley J., 1993, *Partial Differential Equations for Scientists and Engineers*, Dover: New York, N.Y.

Fisher, George C., 2001, *All about DRIPs and DSPs*, McGraw-Hill: New York, N.Y.

Garman, Mark, 1989, "Semper tempus fugit," *RISK Magazine*, (May).

Garman, Mark B. and Steven W. Kohlhagen, 1983, "Foreign Currency Option Values," *Journal of International Money and Finance*, Vol 2 No 3, (December), 231–237.

Geske, Robert, 1979, "A Note on an Analytic Valuation Formula for Unprotected American Call Options on Stocks with Known Dividends," *Journal of Financial Economics*, Vol 7 No 4, (December), pp375–380.

Girsanov, I.V., 1960, "On Transforming a Certain Class of Stochastic Processes by Absolutely Continuous Substitution Measures," *Theory of Probability and its Applications*, Vol 5, pp285–301.

Gordon, Myron J., and Eli Shapiro, 1956, "Capital Equipment Analysis: The Required Rate of Profit," *Management Science*, Vol 3 No 1, (October), pp102–110.

Grabbe, J. Orlin, 1983, "The Pricing of Put and Call Options on Foreign Exchange," *Journal of International Money and Finance*, Vol 2 No 3, (December), 239–253.

Hammer, Jerry A., 1989, "On Biases Reported in Studies of the Black-Scholes Option Pricing Model," *Journal of Economics and Business*, Vol 41 No 2, (May), pp153–169.

Harrison, J. Michael, 1985, *Brownian Motion and Stochastic Flow Systems*, John Wiley and Sons: New York, N.Y.

Harrison, J. Michael and David M. Kreps, 1979, "Martingales and Arbitrage in Multiperiod Securities Markets," *The Journal of Economic Theory*, Vol 20 No 2, (July), pp381–408.

Harrison, J. M. and S.R. Pliska, 1981, "Martingales and Stochastic Integrals in the Theory of Continuous Trading," *Stochastic Processes and Their Applications*, Vol 11, pp215–260.

Haug, Espen Gaarder, 2007, *The Complete Guide to Option Pricing Formulas*, Second Edition, McGraw-Hill: New York, N.Y.

Hull, John C., 2000, *Options, Futures, and Other Derivatives*, Fourth Edition, Prentice-Hall: Englewood Cliffs, N.J.

Hull, John and Alan White, 1987, "The Pricing of Options on Assets with Stochastic Volatilities," *The Journal of Finance*, Vol 42 No 2, (June), pp281–300.

Hull, John and Alan White, 1993, "Efficient Procedures for Valuing European and American Path-Dependent Options," *The Journal of Derivatives*, Vol 1 No 1, (Fall), pp21–31.

Hunter, William C. and David W. Stowe, 1992, "Path-Dependent Options: Valuation and Applications," *Economic Review (Federal Reserve Bank of Atlanta)*, Vol 77 No 4, (July/August), pp30–43.

Hutchins, Tony, 2003, "Black-Scholes takes over the HP12C," *Handheld and Portable Computer Club DataFile*, Vol 22 No 3 (June/July), pp13–21. [Tony may be contacted at th@compuserve.com; the HPCC's Web site is www.hpcc.org.]

Jarrow, Robert and Andrew Rudd, 1983, "Approximate Option Valuation for Arbitrary Stochastic Processes," *Journal of Financial Economics*, Vol 10 No 3, (November), pp347–369.

Jarrow, Robert and Stuart Turnbull, 1996, *Derivative Securities*, South-Western College Publishing: Cincinnati, Ohio.

Karatzas, Ioannis and Steven E. Shreve, 1997, *Brownian Motion and Stochastic Calculus*, Second Edition, Springer: New York, N.Y.

Kotz, Samuel and Norman L. Johnson (editors-in-chief), and Campbell B. Read (associate editor), 1982, *Encyclopedia of Statistical Sciences*, Vol 6, John Wiley and Sons: New York, N.Y.

Krause, Robert (editor), 1998, *Global Equity and Derivative Market Risk*, Morgan Stanley Dean Witter Quantitative Strategies Group, Morgan Stanley and Co.: New York, N.Y.

Lewis, William Dodge, Henry Seidel Canby, and Thomas Kite Brown (editors), 1942, *The Winston Dictionary*, The John C. Winston Company: Philadelphia, Pa.

Lintner, John, 1956, "Distribution of Incomes of Corporations among Dividends, Retained Earnings, and Taxes," *The American Economic Review*, Vol 46 No 2, (May), pp97–113.

Lo, Andrew W. and A. Craig MacKinlay, 1988, "Stock Market Prices Do Not Follow Random Walks: Evidence from a Simple Specification Test," *The Review of Financial Studies*, Vol 1 No 1, (Spring), pp41–66.

Lynch, Peter, with John Rothchild, 2000, *One Up on Wall Street*, Simon and Schuster: New York, N.Y.

MacMillan, L. W., 1986, "Analytic Approximation for the American Put Option," *Advances in Futures and Options Research*, Vol 1 Part A, pp119–139.

Melino, Angelo and Stuart Turnbull, 1990, "Pricing Foreign Currency Options with Stochastic Volatility," *The Journal of Econometrics*, Vol 45 No 1/2, (July/August), pp239–265.

Merton, Robert C., 1973, "Rational Theory of Option Pricing," *Bell Journal of Economics and Management Science*, Vol 4 No 1, (Spring), pp141–183. Note that this appears as chapter 8 in Merton (1992).

Merton, Robert C., 1976, "Option Pricing When Underlying Stock Returns Are Discontinuous," *The Journal of Financial Economics*, Vol 3 No 1, (January/March), pp125–144. Note that this appears as chapter 9 in Merton (1992).

Merton, Robert C., 1992, *Continuous-Time Finance*, Blackwell: Cambridge, Mass.

Métivier, M., 1982, *Semimartingales: A Course on Stochastic Processes*, Walter de Gruyter: Berlin and New York.

Murphy, Gareth, 1994, "When Options Price Theory Meets the Volatility Smile," *Euromoney*, No 299, (March), pp66–74.

Musiela, Marek and Marek Rutkowski, 1997, *Martingale Methods in Financial Modelling*, Springer-Verlag: Berlin.

Naik, Vasanttilak and Moon Lee, 1990, "General Equilibrium Pricing of Options on the Market Portfolio with Discontinuous Returns," *The Review of Financial Studies*, Vol 3 No 4, pp493–521.

Nawalkha, Sanjay K., and Donald R. Chambers, 1995, "The Binomial Model and Risk Neutrality: Some Important Details," *The Financial Review*, vol 30 No 3, (August), pp605–615.

Nawalkha, Sanjaj K., and Natalia A. Beliaeva, 2007, "A Practical Guide to Arbitrage-Free Pricing Using Martingales," Working Paper. Available at SSRN: http://ssrn.com/abstract=1002231, (January), 49pp.

Options Clearing Corporation, 1993, *Understanding Stock Options*, (September), The Options Clearing Corporation, 440 S. LaSalle St., Suite 2400, Chicago, IL 60605.

Parkinson, Michael, 1977, "Option Pricing: The American Put," *The Journal of Business*, Vol 50 No 1, (January), pp21–39.

Poitras, Geoffrey, 1998, "Spread Options, Exchange Options, and Arithmetic Brownian Motion," *Journal of Futures Markets*, Vol 18 No 5, (August), pp487–517.

Rashes, Michael S., 2001, "Massively Confused Investors Making Conspicuously Ignorant Choices (MCI-MCIC)," *The Journal of Finance*, Vol 56 No 5 (October), pp1911–1927.

Ready, Mark J., 1999, "The Specialist's Discretion: Stopped Orders and Price Improvement," *The Review of Financial Studies*, Vol 12 No 5, pp1075–1112.

Rendleman, Richard J., Jr., and Brit J. Bartter, 1979, "Two-State Option Pricing," *The Journal of Finance*, Vol 34 No 5, (December), pp1093–1110.

Roll, R., 1977, "An Analytical Formula for Unprotected American Call Options on Stocks with Known Dividends," *The Journal of Financial Economics*, Vol 5 No 2, (November), pp251–258.

Scott, Louis O., 1987, "Option Pricing when the Variance Changes Randomly: Theory, Estimation, and an Application," *The Journal of Financial and Quantitative Analysis*, Vol 22 No 4, (December), pp419–438.

Sharpe, William F., 1978, *Investments*, Prentice-Hall: Englewood Cliffs, N.J.

Smith, Clifford W., Jr., 1976, "Option Pricing: A Review," *The Journal of Financial Economics*, Vol 3 No 1/2, (January/March), pp3–51.

Smitten, Richard, 2001, *Jesse Livermore: The World's Greatest Stock Trader*, John Wiley and Sons: New York, N.Y.

Sprenkle, Case M., 1961, "Warrant Prices as Indicators of Expectations and Preferences," *Yale Economic Essays*, Vol 1 No 2, (Fall), pp178–231. Note that this paper appears in Cootner (1964).

Stoll, Hans R., 1969, "The Relationship Between Put and Call Option Prices," *The Journal of Finance*, Vol 24 No 5, (December), pp801–824.

Sullivan, Sara, 1993, "Risk reversals," *Euromoney Treasury Manager*, (December 3), p15.

Schachermayer, Walter and Josef Teichmann, 2008, "How Close are the Option Pricing Formulas of Bachelier and Black-Merton-Scholes?," *Mathematical Finance*, Vol 18 No 1, (January), pp155–170.

Tian, Yisong, 1993, "A Modified Lattice Approach to Option Pricing," *The Journal of Futures Markets*, Vol 13 No 5, (August), pp563–577.

Trippi, Robert R., Edward A. Brill, and Richard B. Harriff, 1992, "Pricing Options on an Asset with Bernoulli Jump-Diffusion Returns," *The Financial Review*, Vol 27 No 1, (February), pp59–79.

Whaley, Robert, 1981, "On the Valuation of American Call Options on Stocks with Known Dividends," *The Journal of Financial Economics*, Vol 9 No 2, (June), pp207–211.

Wiggins, James B., 1987, "Option Values under Stochastic Volatility," *The Journal of Financial Economics*, Vol 19 No 2, (December), pp351–372.

Wilmott, Paul, 1998, *Derivatives: The Theory and Practice of Financial Engineering*, John Wiley and Sons: New York, NY.

Wilmott, Paul, Jeff Dewynne, and Sam Howison, 1993, *Option Pricing: Mathematical Models and Computation*, Oxford Financial Press: Oxford, England.

Wilmott, Paul, Sam Howison, and Jeff Dewynne, 1997, *The Mathematics of Financial Derivatives: A Student Introduction*, Cambridge University Press: Cambridge, England.

Zimmerman, Heinz and Wolfgang Hafner, 2007, "Amazing Discovery: Vincenz Bronzin's Option Pricing Models," The Journal of Banking and Finance, Vol 31, pp532–546.

Abbreviations, Acronyms, and Symbols

Alphabets and Numerical Equivalences

Greek[a]				NATO Phonetic		Roman (Latin)[a]	
α	A	Alpha	1	A	Alpha	A	50; 500
β	B	Beta	2	B	Bravo	B	300
γ	Γ	Gamma	3	C	Charlie	C	100
δ	Δ	Delta	4	D	Delta	D	500
ϵ	E	Epsilon	5	E	Echo	E	250
ζ	Z	Zeta	7	F	Foxtrot	F	40
η	H	Eta	8	G	Golf	G	400
θ	Θ	Theta	0	H	Hotel	H	200
ι	I	Iota	10	I	India	I	1
κ	K	Kappa	20	J	Juliett	J	_[b]
λ	Λ	Lambda	30	K	Kilo	K	250
μ	M	Mu	40	L	Lima	L	50
ν	N	Nu	50	M	Mike	M	1,000
ξ	Ξ	Xi	60	N	November	N	90
o	O	Omicron	70	O	Oscar	O	11
π	Π	Pi	80	P	Papa	P	400
ρ	R	Rho	100	Q	Quebec	Q	90; 500
σ	Σ	Sigma	200	R	Romeo	R	80
τ	T	Tau	300	S	Sierra	S	7;70
υ	Υ	Upsilon	400	T	Tango	T	160
ϕ	Φ[c]	Phi	500	U	Uniform	U	_[d]
χ	X[c]	Chi	700	V	Victor	V	5
ψ	Ψ[c]	Psi	700	W	Whiskey	W	_[e]
ω	Ω	Omega	800	X	X-Ray	X	10
				Y	Yankee	Y	150
				Z	Zulu	Z	2,000

[a]Some information from Lewis et al. (1942, p1161). The book is out of print and the publisher defunct.

[b]Originally the same as I.

[c]The Greek letters Φ, X, and Ψ were not needed in the medieval Latin alphabet. However, the Romans used them as numerical symbols, writing D (or M), X, and L, respectively.

[d]Originally the same as V.

[e]Not used in medieval Latin.

Index

Heard on The Street: Quantitative Questions from Wall Street Job Interviews

Timothy Falcon Crack

BSc (HONS 1st Class), PGDipCom, MCom, PhD (MIT), IMC

A must read! Over 170 quantitative questions collected from **actual job interviews** in investment banking, investment management, and options trading. The interviewers use the **same questions year-after-year**, and here they are—with solutions! These questions come from all types of interviews (corporate finance, sales and trading, quant research, etc.), but they are especially likely in quantitative capital markets job interviews. The questions come from all levels of interviews (undergraduate, MS, MBA, PhD), but they are especially likely if you have, or almost have, an MS or MBA. The latest edition includes about 125 non-quantitative actual interview questions, and a **new section on interview technique**—based on Dr. Crack's experiences interviewing candidates for the world's largest institutional asset manager.

The latest edition is available at all reputable online booksellers.

http://www.InvestmentBankingJobInterviews.com/
timcrack@alum.mit.edu

CPSIA information can be obtained at www.ICGtesting.com
Printed in the USA
BVOW051712230912

301126BV00001B/9/P